GRAFFITI GRRLZ

Graffiti Grrlz

Performing Feminism in the Hip Hop Diaspora

Jessica Nydia Pabón-Colón

NEW YORK UNIVERSITY PRESS

New York

NEW YORK UNIVERSITY PRESS
New York
www.nyupress.org

References to Internet websites (URLs) were accurate at the time of writing. Neither the author nor New York University Press is responsible for URLs that may have expired or changed since the manuscript was prepared.

ISBN: 978-1-4798-0615-7 (hardback)
ISBN: 978-1-4798-9593-9 (paperback)

For Library of Congress Cataloging-in-Publication data, please contact the Library of Congress.

New York University Press books are printed on acid-free paper, and their binding materials are chosen for strength and durability. We strive to use environmentally responsible suppliers and materials to the greatest extent possible in publishing our books.

Manufactured in the United States of America

10 9 8 7 6 5 4 3 2 1
Also available as an ebook

For all the grrlz who never wanted to be princesses,
and all the princesses who are KINGS!

CONTENTS

Timeline of Crews, Events, and Media   ix

Foreword   xi
  Miss17

Introduction: "The Art of Getting Ovaries"   1

1. Performing Feminist Masculinity in a Postfeminist Era   41

2. Doing Feminist Community without "Feminist" Identity   73

3. Cultivating Affective Digital Networks   108

4. Re-Membering Herstory and the Transephemeral
   Performative   137

5. Transforming Precarity at International All-Grrl Jams   159

   Conclusion: Connecting One Graffiti Grrl to Another   185

   Acknowledgments   197

   Appendix: Blackbook   201

   Notes   213

   Bibliography   239

   Index   257

   About the Author   263

TIMELINE OF CREWS, EVENTS, AND MEDIA

1980: Ladies of the Arts (USA)

1989: PMS (USA)

1997: Altona Female Crew (Germany)

1999: Bandit Queenz (Australia)

2000: Crazis Crew (Chile)

2000: Girls on Top (England)

2003: Bitches in Control (Netherlands)

2003: Stick Up Girlz Crew (Aotearoa/New Zealand, Spain, Portugal, Japan, and Australia)

2004: Transgressão Para Mulheres (Brazil)

2005: *Catfight* magazine (Netherlands)

2005: GraffGirlz.com

2005: GraffiterasBR Yahoo Group

2006: Puff Crew (Germany and Czech Republic)

2006: Turronas Crew (Chile)

2006: Ladysgraff.blogspot.com

2008: Ladie Killerz Paint Jam, Australia (first annual; still running)

2008: Helen Keller Crew (Australia)

2008: *Chicks on Powertrips* magazine (Australia)

2009: Maripussy Crew (Peru and USA)

2010: Ladies Destroying Crew (Nicaragua and Peru)

2010: Rede Nami (Brazil)

2011: Few and Far (USA)

2011: "Female International Graffiti" Facebook page

2011: "Gurls Love Vandal" Tumblr page

2012: Female Soul (Mexico)

2012: "FEMALE CAPS" Tumblr page

2014: Tits 'n' Tampons (UK)

2014: Femme Fierce Paint Jam (UK)

2016: *Girl Power* documentary (Czech Republic)

2016: "@GraffitiHerstory" Instagram

FOREWORD

MISS17

Ah, to travel back in time to 2001, when I was young and enamored by my newfound love: graffiti. With only a few years under my belt, I was still all the things that a writer should be: obsessed, keen, wary, guarded, insatiable. I saw a post on ArtCrimes.org written by a girl, Jess, who wanted to hear the voices of the women who were writing. Though I was totally unsure about her, I, too, wondered where all the women were. I had not really given it much thought up until that point. What a good question! Why are there not more women writing graffiti? I sent what I am sure was a very vague email to a supremely excited young feminist. At that time, I thought "feminism" was a dirty word; for me, the word carried the negative connotation of "man hater." This is right around the time that I started hanging out with Claw. Little did I know that these two women would open my eyes to what it means to be a strong woman. There are no arguments—you cannot be a strong woman and not be a feminist! Just by the nature of the way I live, I am a feminist and these two women taught me how to embrace that; they taught me that feminism was not a dirty word. Whilst I was busy getting an education in feminism, Jess was getting schooled in graffiti. It is always a challenge to educate and inform someone who is outside of a subculture—there are certain things an outsider can never truly know—but Jess stepped up to the plate and became a zealous student, devouring all the information given to her. Fast-forward fifteen years and Dr. Pabón-Colón is one of the leading scholars on the subject of women writers; her reach and network tentacle the globe. She has traveled through several continents and met up with countless women to hear their stories.

To me, the graffiti is the story. The tag name tells the tale and it is either up (seen in the streets) or it is a nonentity. Though I know she disagrees with this point, for me one of the beautiful things about graffiti is its purity. Graffiti writing itself is not sexist, racist, or classist. Graffiti is a game that anyone can play. Take a name, see what you can do with it—those are the rules. There are no "likes." No one counts the views or the balance of your bank account. Your bedfellows, skin tone, gender—none of these are important. Graffiti writers are lucky in that they can choose to be as enigmatic as they want—if they can stay incognito and active, all anyone will know about or talk about will be the work they have put in. Writers can choose how little or how much to let the world know about them. They can be completely private, mysterious, and secretive (PMS), or they can pose for magazines and do interviews. If a writer stays anonymous, they will be judged on the body of work they create, not on the body they inhabit; the evidence they leave behind is their trail and not just on their tail.

However, graffiti subculture exists within the larger culture in which these "isms" continue to be pervasive. Sadly, the purity of graffiti does not necessarily extend to those who participate in it. Once a woman is vocal about who she is, it is possible and even likely that she will be looked at differently. The machismo undercurrents that plague modern culture are ubiquitous within the graffiti community as well, and many females participating in this male-dominated subculture will find themselves the subject of vicious rumors and speculations that are more concerned with their activities in the sheets than their nights in the streets. The "isms" certainly inform the scholarship and study of graffiti. Lucky for the ladies putting in the work that Dr. Pabón-Colón has spent a decade and a half dedicated to carving a place for these women claiming space.

New York City
May 2017

Introduction

"The Art of Getting Ovaries"

I'm slowly realizing I should claim my history more than I
have in the past.
—AbbyTC5 (USA)

On October 18, 2012, I interviewed AbbyTC5 (aka Abby106) and Abi-
Roc about Hip Hop graffiti subculture in front of a small and engaged
audience of faculty, staff, and students at Davidson College in North
Carolina.[1] Hailing from Queens in New York City, Abby is an African American heterosexual ciswoman who started painting graffiti in
1982—making her one of New York City's founding writers.[2] Abby has
been a member of various "old school" graffiti crews, including TPA,
ROCSTARS, TC5, KAOS, TM7, and YNN. She took to the wall about
fifteen years after working-class youth in Philadelphia and New York
City pioneered the form during a time of great economic despair, social
unrest, and civil rights activism.[3]

Though there is controversy about the timeline and birthplace of
graffiti beyond the tag, the culture became what it is alongside Hip
Hop's other forms in New York City. Along with b-boying (breakdancing), deejaying, beatboxing, and emceeing/rapping, writers (another
name for graffiti artists, short for graffiti writers) contributed their own
form of creative expression as part of a collective effort to resist social
convention, economic marginalization, and political invisibility.[4] Af-
fectionately referred to as the "art of getting over," Hip Hop graffiti art
(aka aerosol art, spray-can art) is distinct from other forms of street
art because it centers around the repetitive production of a tag name
within a subculture grounded in Afro-Caribbean diasporic aesthetics:
the construction of a vernacular different from the colonizer's language
produced visually and linguistically (e.g., writers "bomb the system,"
sometimes in a "wildstyle" illegible to nonwriters); collective creativity

Figure I.1. Jessica Pabón-Colón and AbbyTC5, Davidson College, NC, 2012.

(writing with a crew and representing those affiliations on the wall or in your tag name, such as Abby*TC5*); the practice of a visual call and response (a competitive assertion of self that prompts other writers to get up); self-naming and praising via the tag name (an alter ego, sometimes given to you by an "elder" or peer), and polyrhythmic composition (where the rhythm is visual instead of sonic).[5] One's tag name is represented in varying forms: the tag (executed in a few seconds, one color, maybe one line); the throw-up (two or three colors, executed in a minute or two, often appearing in legible bubble letters); the piece (a multicolored tag name with a background and a fill-in, with attention to depth, texture, and clean lines); and the production (a graffiti mural often completed with other writers). The tag is what distinguishes Hip Hop graffiti art from other forms of street art. Hip Hop graffiti art is a kind of street art, but one that prioritizes the name.[6] The tag establishes the writer's identity, and writers perform this identity—ideally distinct from their government-issued identification card—repetitively in order to proclaim their presence: I am here.

Like her peers, Abby was drawn to graffiti art aesthetics at a young age. When she was a child, subway trains thundered through the five boroughs covered in letters painted from top to bottom and flanked by satirical characters from end to end.[7] She was fascinated by the graffiti-covered handball courts and parks in Queens, and mesmerized by the riot of colors and shapes on the F trains that rolled by her aunt's Brooklyn window. On the bus ride to and from the High School of Art and Design in Manhattan, Abby would pay close attention to her friend Dume as he explained the mechanics and methods of painting graffiti illegally—what writers call "bombing science." Soon thereafter, she started her own "science" experiments: "I started piecing by doing tags with a force-field around [them] and a 3d around the force field. Then I tried characters. Then bubble letters and throwies. Then I translated all those to spray paint. First in my closet in my bedroom, then on public bathroom walls, then motion bombing on buses and trains, then on walls, larger, then finally on trains." After experimenting with the tag names Bitch106 (given to her by Web), 2 Toke, and Phoenix 319, she settled on Abby to build her career as one of the earliest graffiti grrlz active in New York City.

I use the term "graffiti grrlz" to refer to girls and women who write graffiti even though the writers in this book are now adults mostly in their thirties and older, like Abby; following the lead of Spanish-speaking grrlz, I also use the term "graffitera" when appropriate. Despite the usage of several less popular variations on Instagram, the typical way grrlz refer to themselves and their peers on social media is through the hashtag #graffitigirls (23,720; #graffitigirl has 22,850). The popularity of "girls" over "women" (#graffitiwomen has 5,422) suggests that writers are attendant to the fact that graffiti is and has been a primarily youth-led subculture. Further, graffiti subculture celebrates social deviance and encourages participants to resist conventional ideas about "growing up," which, of course, has particular meaning for girls (more on this in chapter 1).[8] To emphasize that these writers exceed social expectations for "girls," I call upon and contribute to a lineage of feminist spelling revisions that defy "Proper English" (e.g., wom*y*n, *her*story, *she*roes) by swapping the "i" for an extra "r"—a move that also situates Hip Hop graffiti subculture squarely in conversation with the Riot Grrrl punk-music subculture.[9] Articulating graffiti g*rr*lz, with a "z," also has a sonic and visual quality that marks the "edge" and references the "hard" of Hip Hop that writers like Abby embody.

Abby has long since settled into her art practice after more than thirty years of painting, illegally and legally. While it is true that most writers sketch something out on paper before they "hit" (paint) a wall, her process differs in the level of control and intention devoted to each line of the "sketch"; she likes to have a structure to follow that will create balanced "traditional letters," with "attitude" conveyed through "slants, over-emphasis . . . and/or arrows." Abby's "respect for big letters" and attention to balance in the overall composition can be partially attributed to years of watching her father, a skilled sign painter, work in his basement workshop, which she remembers fondly as a "built-in spray-paint supply." Abby used that built-in supply on the train lines mostly near her home—a geographic limitation she described as a "tragedy" that felt personal, but was rooted in common gendered parenting practices that lead "parents to cloister girls."[10] She was not able to bomb as many train lines as she would have liked because her parents were strict about her curfew and kept her close to home. Consider this in contrast to one of Abby's peers, such as Skeme, a writer interviewed in the 1984 film *Style Wars*, whose mother is fully aware of his exploits and chalks it up to the idea that "boys will be boys."[11]

Abby did her best to keep her graffiti exploits secret from her conservative middle-class family, but her parents found out: "it kind of destroyed them, because I wasn't even supposed to be having thoughts like that, much less behaving . . . so unfeminine and outside of the social norm." Rebelling against familial expectations that were guided by racialized and gendered social norms was risky—there would be repercussions if she was caught. But Abby felt she had the right to assert herself, a sensibility she gained through role models on TV, in politics, and at home. She was "surrounded by images of strong women like politicians Shirley Chisholm, Bella Abzug, Gloria Steinem. Entertainment figures like Foxy Brown, Wonder Woman—even Mrs. Partridge was raising five kids with no father *and* running a band. We even had feminist cartoons like Josie and the Pussycats who were sexy crime-fighting musicians. I had strong women in my family to look up to. My grandmother was a fantastic businesswoman, my aunt was a lawyer. I took them for granted until I was slapped with limits in my personal life that I pushed back against." Not one to be confined by gender conventions or a politics of respectability, Abby managed her parental restraints by ditching school and painting in other boroughs during the day. She had regular weekend "sleepovers" with another writer named 2Cute who lived on the A/C line in Far Rockaway—2Cute's parents were more lenient, imposing just one "restriction": "don't stay out late, girls."

Abby was exposed daily to the tags of a fellow student and graff grrl at the High School of Art and Design: Lady Heart. Heart's "exploits were legendary." She had graduated by the time Abby took an interest in meeting her, but she was not the only graff grrl around—she had a younger painting partner still attending the school who had begun writing in 1979 and was by that time already known as the "godmother" or "first lady" of graffiti, Lady Pink (www.ladypinknyc.com). Even though Abby expressed to her writer friends that she would like to paint with Pink and perhaps be mentored by Heart, they would not introduce her; instead, they made her a part of their own crew, TPA. Happy to be part of TPA, but still wanting to meet Pink and perhaps be down with her crew, Abby persisted. She was told "you had to be down with Ladies of the Arts [Pink's crew] to get close to them, but the L.O.T.A. Crew was closed." Ultimately Abby was not mentored by Heart or Pink, but she found other writers to learn from. "There was plenty of inspiration at Art and Design among the writers that were there [including] Web, Mare139, Fabel, Seen, and Doze, Erni 'Paze' Vales, Marcus 'Ense'/'Ence' Suarez." Even though her mentors were all men, Abby made a point of telling me that they did not treat her differently because of her gender: "I never thought of myself as a female writer. I was just hanging with my friends doing what I liked to do and it never occurred to me that I was a 'female' writer, or that there was a line here that I was crossing because I was a female." Abby provides a different version of an old story about the early days of Hip Hop culture from the perspective of a woman who is not the token representative.

In a panel discussion on gender, race, and graffiti culture at the A/P/A Institute at New York University in November 2009, Lady Pink discussed the dynamics of her tokenization as the only woman included alongside New York City graffiti's founding fathers (e.g., Taki183, Dondi, Lee, Seen, Blade, Iz the Wiz).[12] Though Pink has focused on her fine art/gallery career for decades, she is still regularly called upon to represent all women who write graffiti because she was a groundbreaker. Abby witnessed that ground being broken, and in some ways she reaped the benefits of not being in the proverbial spotlight. "It was kind of heartbreaking because I watched Lady Pink go through a lot of ridicule, very unfairly. I remember as I grew up people would always ask, 'Aren't you jealous of her? Don't you want to be where she is?' I never wanted to be where she was, in the spotlight. She was the first and the light shined brightest on her. She had the most to prove and she was the one that had to go first and she hit all the bumps and they were nasty. They were really, really nasty." On the topic of being female in a male-dominated field, more often than not, Pink describes that nastiness: "It's a lot harder for girls to get into graffiti to begin with. The men are not very supportive. It's hard to get men to say nice things about women in graff. That's the way it's always been and I started painting back in 1979. . . . It really hasn't gotten any easier being a girl, trying to enter the 'boys club of graffiti.' You have to prove yourself and work even harder than the men work."[13] Abby's early experiences differ from Pink's; the combination of the two perspectives provides a more nuanced understanding of the gender politics of graffiti subculture during the late 1970s to early '80s. Having access to both stories also shifts the persistent notion—generated in no small part by the Hip Hop cult film *Wild Style* (1983)—that Lady Pink was the only graff grrl of note painting during that time. For Abby, the "line" of gender difference she crossed with her graffiti art practice was felt at home with her parents, not necessarily on the street with her peers. She did not feel the effects of difference *at the time*, but rather *over* time as books were published, circulated, and canonized—as the history of Hip Hop graffiti art was written without her.

Despite the fact that Abby "didn't save anything," she relates her memories with incredible detail—each description is thick with dates, names, emotion, colors, shapes, narrative arc, context, and connections. Like other original "Hip Hop heads," she did not save because she did not realize she was creating a culture, a way of living that would one day influence the lives of millions all over the world. When I asked her to recount the early "style masters" (graffiti innovators), she did so with the same attention to detail that she paints. She went on for over fifteen minutes without taking a breath while explaining Dondi's ability to scale up (from a sketch to a train), Pink's whole-car train as an incredible feat because of her height, Phase II's innovation of connecting letters, and Kase2's creation of wildstyle (never limited by having just one arm). Abby remembers. She knows what the subway system looked like before the antigraffiti taskforce decided graffiti was a "quality of life" issue and declared war on urban artists, buffing each and every train before it left the yard.[14] She was there when graffiti moved from trains back to walls, then to billboards and street signs; she participated in the refusal to be silenced by urban policing based on conservative ideologies equating the regulation of aesthetics with crime prevention—the notion that clean trains equal safe trains.[15] And she watched from afar, more cautious than most, as writers developed digital personas to broadcast their graffiti adventures in cyberspace. Her memories are part of Hip Hop's oral history—slowly disappearing as often-unnamed originators pass away. She is a living archive and yet up until the morning that I spoke with her at Davidson College, despite a handful of images circulating in various publications, Abby's story had never been publicized.[16] And up until that morning, Abby did not fully recognize her significance as a pioneering member of a now-transnational subculture. The live interview platform allowed her to "claim" her story, to claim ownership of her place in Hip Hop graffiti subculture—a reclamation necessitated by the structural erasure of her historical presence and facilitated by having an opportunity to offer her testimony in front of an audience.

Since *The Faith of Graffiti*, the journalist Norman Mailer's 1974 inaugural text, the journalists, criminologists, sociologists, documentarians, and art historians interested in graffiti art have ignored the politics of difference within the subculture. The well-documented tendency of subcultural research to center the activities of boys and men (a precedent set in no small part by the Birmingham School of Cultural Studies) is reproduced throughout the graffiti studies canon. Authors have examined the subculture's relationship to gangs, crime and urban decay, and fine art.[17] They have examined its Afro-Caribbean diasporic aesthetics; its lost potential as an urban art form; its significance as a major youth culture and harbinger of popular cultural trends; its potential use in curriculum development and education; its history, artistic methodologies, and innovative use of mediums; its utility as a means for making male masculinity; and its role as a training ground for design careers.[18] The fundamental impetus of "getting up" (on as many of the most visible and perilous surfaces as possible) and "getting over" (on the authorities governing citizens and public space), combined with the anonymity provided by tag names, has encouraged scholars (and graffiti writers) to repetitively bolster a rather romantic notion about the subculture's social dynamics.

> Here is where formal art training, class, race, and gender all diminish in importance in the eyes of the innovators, and the ability to tear apart and rebuild the structure of a Roman letter is paramount.[19]

> The graffiti subculture may be the only art form that truly transcends social boundaries. In the world of the graffiti writer, the only thing that one is judged by is artistic skill and attitude. Race, gender, social class, and age of a writer aren't considered.[20]

> For me graffiti represents a way to instantly transcend governmental oppression (and its ignorance), social and racial barriers, and material possessions. It is also a way to take part of a movement which connects people from all over the world, regardless of personal differences, in a way nothing else can.[21]

According to this narrative, the focus on the graffiti art, rather than the graffiti art maker, enables the subculture to transcend the oppressive and unjust function of difference. The idea is that gender, race, ethnicity, class, and sexuality simply do not matter because they do not affect one's ability to "get up" or "get over"; all that matters is proliferation and stylistic innovation. If Kase2 could get up on trains with one arm, and if Lady Pink could paint whole trains alone, and if Iz the Wiz could become one of the most respected all-city "kings"—the highest subcultural status marker—even though he was white, then obviously differences such as physical ability, gender, and race do not really matter.

In "Girls and Subcultures," Angela McRobbie and Jenny Garber ask, "Are girls really not present in youth subcultures? Or is it something in the way this kind of research is carried out that renders them invisible?"[22] They assert that girls' involvement in "subcultures may have become invisible because the very term 'subculture' has acquired such strong masculine overtones," and they conclude by arguing that researchers are not looking in the "right" kinds of places for girls' subcultural activities.[23] Graff grrlz are not absent from graffiti studies simply because there are "not as many women writers"—the standard rationale—but because the lens, or the conventional way of seeing, renders them and their contributions illegible, invisible. Their erasure is and has been taken for granted, naturalized as common sense—a circular and self-fulfilling rationalization: there are no graff grrlz on the walls, at the events, or in the books (beyond the token representatives) because, well, there are/were no active grrlz (worth mentioning).

To his credit, in the first ethnographic account of the subculture, Craig Castleman mentioned writers like Charmin 65, Barbara 62, and Eva 62; however, the significance of their inclusion is undone in instances such as when he asks Candy how much "getting up" a writer needs to complete in order to attain fame. She answers about 200, and the next sentence reads: "Most writers set the figure much higher."[24] The implication here, whether purposeful or not, is that as a graff grrl, her standards are set lower, her opinion not quite accurate, and her place in the subculture not quite important. Janice Rahn includes the graff grrlz Singe, Shana, Swep, and Brain, but she fails to engage them with the same rigor or depth as she does the male writers in her study; inequitable treatment here again implies differing importance. In *Subway Art*, Martha Cooper and Henry Chalfant make a point to mention that "there have always been girls who write," citing Barbara 62 and Eva 62, Lady Pink, Lady Heart, and Lizzie; ultimately though, without contextualization, the names and the handful of images recede in importance and impact.[25] In *The Art of Getting Over*, Stephen Powers mentions a handful of grrlz but only through their relationships with and proximity to men (e.g., lover, sister, or ex-girlfriend): "He [Razz] got immersed into the culture, writing with his sister (she wrote Sass), then after meeting 'a lot of perpetrators,' he met real writers and the days of the brother-sister bombing team were pretty much over."[26] These are just a few of the ways that graffiti grrlz' presence has been reduced, negated, or neglected. Because difference was not interrogated or deemed important, more than forty years of research have been conducted with neither a substantial or adequate consideration of gender difference nor a sustained engagement with graffiti grrlz. It is time to trouble this elision.

In December 2012, two months after interviewing Abby at David-son, I gave a talk about how graff grrlz thrive in "the space between" at the second annual TEDxWomen conference in Washington, DC, to an immediate audience of 300 and a global audience of more than 15,000 people via a live stream.[27] I shared that I began my research as a wom-en's studies graduate student at the University of Arizona in Harmony Hammond's "Lesbian Art in America" course in 2002. I explained that despite growing up in Boston, Massachusetts, among writer friends—in the Universal Will to Become (UWTB) crew—I was mostly indifferent to graffiti writing until I began drawing parallels between the "hetero/sexism" in the fine art and graffiti art worlds. In each sphere, the co-productive and codependent hegemonic tyranny of heterosexism (the institutionally supported ideology that heterosexuality is the norm to be valued above all else) and sexism (the institutionally supported ideology that cisgender males are the norm to be valued above all else) subordi-nate individuals (and communities) based on their deviance from these norms: hence, my usage of "hetero/sexism." After years of riding along, being a lookout, hearing the sounds of shaking cans, and smelling the paint fumes, the graffiti world appeared under a whole new light. My newfound interest led me to ask my friends questions . . . lots of them. The first was about a writer named RenOne.

RenOne's tags incorporated heart-shaped Os and were, at the time, the only indication I had that grrlz (or, at least, a grrl) actually wrote graffiti. When I asked my friends to help me contact her for an inter-view, I was scoffed at and told that she "wasn't a real writer." I was told that her boyfriend got up for her and that she slept around—she was a "jock" (a graffiti groupie who sleeps with writers). At the time I did not know to be more critical of that particular kind of rumor. Under-standing that "in hip-hop, realness is the most valuable form of cultural capital," and trusting my sources because they were my friends, I moved on.[28] Ten years later I was at TEDxWomen, standing onstage, recounting the story and lamenting that I should have known better. On a whim, I took the opportunity to speak directly to her from that stage: "if you're out there RenOne, hit me up! I'd love to talk to you." A few months later, someone did in fact "hit me up" through a Facebook message. He had seen an article in the *Dorchester Reporter* (my hometown newspaper) about my TED talk and claimed he knew RenOne. He wrote, "My friend use to write Ren One [*sic*], but she was from Boston and does not write anymore. This was in the mid to late 90's."[29] About a week later, through the magic of social media and digital communication, I was reminiscing about Boston's graff scene in the '90s with RenOne herself.

Despite having "fallen off the radar of everything having to do with graffiti," she claimed "it still flows in [her] blood."[30] RenOne is in her mid-thirties, Cape Verdean, African American, and white. At the time she was a stay-at-home mother—"the attachment parenting, baby wearing, crafting, breastfeeding until everyone else is uncomfortable with it kind"—who, when asked if she was a feminist, responded,

> How can you not be Female and a Feminist? Yes. . . . As a female I am as relevant as any other male. It means as a female I am able to define my own state of being as a female. I am able to choose to be a mother, or create a child on my own terms and love who I want and it doesn't make me any less powerful to do so. I can choose to have mother be my only title, or I can choose to have a career as my only title, or I can choose both. I respect other women for their choices even if it doesn't agree with my own. You cannot fuck with femininity.

Though we were strangers at the time, her tone was a familiar one—I recognized the same kind of gender "deviant" performance of masculinity in her, what I call feminist masculinity, that I had seen in countless other graff grrlz (discussed in chapter 1). Her interest in writing graffiti sparked when "a light went off like . . . I could be out there just like them [her friends], be 'All CITY.' Fuck a boy putting your name up on a wall for you, or in a piece they painted dedicated to you, do it on your own." She took to the walls in 1997.

By her own admission, RenOne was not the "greatest" graffiti writer—just one of the first, and one of the only grrlz writing graffiti in Boston in the late '90s—but she was prolific with her tagging. After playing with bubble letters and curly cues, she settled into a handstyle she calls "dead letter," a style characterized by letters that are one color, two-dimensional, painted in single lines with no fills, no doodads, no hookups, and a slight lean that does not interlock.[31] She used the tag name RenOne because "it sounded like a classic androgynous and righteous name," a name she had been scribbling in notebooks privately all throughout high school—including the O heart: "I kept the heart because I loved the heart. It remained to me the one nod towards femininity in my tag . . . once I dropped those curly ques. I wanted the heart to represent me. Like I owned it." Her "nod to femininity" was the only way I knew she was a "she"; without that signifying mark her tags would have faded into the realm of total anonymity where most graffiti art revels.

RenOne recounted her writing days with nostalgia; for her, Boston in the late '90s was a "time of buying fat caps from kids out of the trunks of cars"; feeling the adrenaline rush of "near death experiences and a perpetual fear of a certain female [MTA] officer"; of friendships with "other writers showing me how to lift caps from aerosol cans out of hardware stores and make kiwi mops"; and negotiating the subcultural politics of space that manifested in "wars of alley ways and mailboxes and rooftops all along Newbury [Street], Mass. [Ave.], and Copley [Square]." She did not have a steady crew, but she occasionally painted with her boyfriend, Never, and fondly remembered writing with another graff grrl, Dance— "the ONE girl in Boston that I knew, who was serious about getting out

Figure I.2. RenOne, Boston, MA, 1998. Photo courtesy RenOne.

and painting." Dance and RenOne enjoyed painting together as "D.R." despite the rumors that they were enemies. There were other rumors, too, about RenOne's sexual activities. When I told her who, specifically, had shared those rumors with me (although I am not naming him here), she was not surprised.

> I remember being excited because I thought that he was really interested in painting with me, but I learned just as with a few other male writers in Boston, that they weren't all that interested in painting. We went out, some spot I had never been to before, we may have been with a few other people, I think he even threw my tag up at one point and he was giving me some pointers, it may of even been a [his name] plus RenOne type of thing. . . . It was so long ago! I can picture the place being near train tracks. I remember him showing me he had done my name and I was supposed to be all flattered, but I was pissed. . . . I was angry that it was made to seem like we were going to paint, but really was more of a hangout wanna hookup type of "date." I think we got into beef after that, too. I may have been dating Never at that point. I think [he] and I became enemies after. A lot of times in the beginning after boys found out I was a writer, they would want to "hang out" and paint, but it never panned out to be that true. It was always a date disguised as a paint mission. I was forever annoyed and eventually I never took anyone up on that offer and went solo always.

RenOne's version of the story sheds some light on how using a hetero/sexist lens to understand grrlz' relationship to this subculture produces pernicious misconceptions about them and how they get involved in the first place: that they "let" men get up for them because they are unable, or uninterested, in painting themselves; and that they are promiscuous because they go out (on painting missions) with a lot of boys. She makes it clear that the reason she went out with the unnamed writer mentioned above, and later with other male writers, was to paint and maybe get some technical pointers. She went on the "mission" with the understanding that the purpose was painting, but it was actually a cover for a "hookup." He got "pissed" and they "got into beef" because she rejected his disingenuous seduction efforts (painting her name for her). "When he wrote my name it took away the power of proving that I was able to do it myself," she explained. Despite his shadiness, RenOne would ultimately pay the price of their exchange with her subcultural capital because she had less power as a lesser-known writer and as a girl.

Over a Facebook chat in May 2017, RenOne clarified that though she never had a physical altercation with that particular writer, there was another writer from Cambridge "that [she] actually had beef with that could've gone physical."[32] Though, again, there was no actual fight between them, the way the events unfolded shed some light on not only how beef functions in this subculture, but also how it functions when it comes to graffiti grrlz.

> At the time I was living in Somerville, and I would walk to Harvard Square and get up. [The beef] started because of a payphone outside of a convenience store. One day I went and he had crossed me out and called me a toy and then it just escalated from there. There were whole messages to each other on that phone. . . . Anytime I got up in Cambridge, he would cross me out. I'd paint on the train tracks from the commuter rail in Kendall Square and he would always completely diss my piece.

There is nothing out of the ordinary, or unexpected, about two writers sparring over a particular spot—being lined or gone over is a common practice that informs the subculture's characterization as ephemeral (discussed at length in chapter 4). When the battle on the wall becomes personal and is felt as an assault on the writers' masculinity (ownership of public space, pride, dominance), the beef escalates into an actual confrontation. What is less common is how the beef is resolved when the pairing is not between people with the same gender. At first, he did not know RenOne was a girl, but when he found out, the dynamics of the beef shifted. "There was a rumor that he was at a party that I was at and I was all set to go confront him—and he had a girlfriend with him who supposedly was going to fight me—but that never happened. The reality was that I was a girl and he couldn't physically hurt me without getting fucked up himself in the process" (because, presumably, RenOne's guy friends would have stepped in).[33] By sending his girlfriend after a complete stranger simply to defend his masculinity (his graffiti "honor," if you will) he activated one of the most pernicious effects of hetero/sexism on girls and women in the subculture—pinned against one another in a "catfight," they maintain the patriarchal status quo. Abby testified to her experience of this same dynamic:

> It has been my experience that a large percentage of discord between females is seeded and is perpetuated by males. Some men have tried and failed to produce the girl-on-girl mud wrestling battle between female graff writers. I can't tell you how many times people have tried to manipulate me to be an aggressor against a female who I don't even know. The Svengali-type males are the biggest trouble-makers. Luckily, most women in graff see right through this.

While being involved in beef certainly affects one's reputation, the best way to seek revenge in graffiti subculture is to throw doubt on writers' "realness" (question their authenticity or point out their lack of illegal graffiti work), commitment (question their "ups"), and stylistic capability (denigrate the aesthetic value of their work).

Like many grrlz before and after her, RenOne suffered a particularly gendered and sexualized version of that revenge. The rumors meant to diminish RenOne's graffiti "props" (respect) gained traction based on an accepted hetero/sexism too often used to bolster or repair the ego (heterosexual, cisgender male masculinity) of the person who started them. Instead of the rumor about her being (hetero)sexually available to graffiti writers, RenOne could have been labeled a lesbian, a dyke, or a queer—an experience many graff grrlz have, especially when they are new to the subculture. Rumors are one way that the politics of sexuality manifest in graffiti subculture so as to affect grrlz' sense of belonging, ultimately cutting them off from a subculture that thrives on its own brand of sociality. The ridiculous and tragic irony in RenOne's case is that the rumors about her being a fake and a jock were, in actuality, products of her commitment and determination to get up by herself. Now reconnected to the scene in Boston, RenOne would like to "send a big middle finger to the person who ever started the rumor [that] my boyfriend bombed for me. And a big up to all the lady writers from Boston from my day and before me. Ladies First, Dance wherever you are, Sun, Girl, Serv, Cuka, Aqua, Ladee Dase."

Writing Grrlz

Why are there so less female chemists, computer program-
mers and mathematicians? For the same reasons—women
are not conditioned to go out there and prove themselves intellectually. Why are there so many less women represented
in art galleries? Because we live in a society where women
are subversively encouraged to have no voice or expression
other than her body or image.
—Nungi (USA)

Listening to testimonies similar to Abby's and RenOne's at each stage
of writing *Graffiti Grrlz: Performing Feminism in the Hip Hop Diaspora*,
I have consistently revisited the feminist art historian Linda Nochlin's
1971 clarion call in "Why Have There Been No Great Women Artists?"
for scholars interested in theorizing and/or historicizing women's art-
making practices.

> Art is not a free, autonomous activity of a super-endowed individual,
> "influenced" by previous artists, and, more vaguely and superficially, by
> "social forces," but rather, that the total situation of art making, both in
> terms of the development of the art maker and in the nature and quality
> of the work of art itself, occur in a social situation . . . mediated and deter-
> mined by specific and definable social institutions, be they art academies,
> systems of patronage, mythologies of the divine creator, artist as he-man
> or social outcast.[34]

Examining the "total situation of art making" for graffiti grrlz illumi-
nates how heteropatriarchy functions within Hip Hop graffiti subculture
on both an institutionalized structural level (in books, social rituals, and
subcultural spaces) and on an everyday person-to-person level not only
to obfuscate the presence of graffiti grrlz throughout the Hip Hop diaspora, but also to create a sociocultural standard in which experiences
of sexualization, erasure, and discrimination are the expected—indeed,
anticipated—norm. Heteropatriarchal power relations materialize in,
on, and about graff grrlz' bodies (corporeal bodies and bodies of artistic
work), and those dynamics have produced an integrated but not equal

(and sometimes hostile) environment for grrlz as a "class" (if not on an individual level).[35] *Graffiti Grrlz* begins the important work of analyzing the visual, discursive, social, political, and digital aspects of contemporary graffiti art by organizing the grrlz' individual stories into a narrative about how they navigate their experiences as a collective within the subculture.

Writing *Graffiti Grrlz* required a kind of mashup methodology well suited to my training as a feminist performance studies scholar with a focus on queer studies working within Hip Hop studies (all interdisciplines). Because disciplinary boundaries only contain graff grrl stories, and my purpose is to liberate them, I engaged these grrlz, conducted my fieldwork, and analyzed my data with an array of methods guided by a commitment to feminist praxis, which seeks to document and contextualize graffiti grrlz' experiences and activities in order to incite social change.[36] I anticipate that some readers will find the interdisciplinary nature and mashup methodology of this book confounding, but I urge them to embrace my project as one that prioritizes intellectual goals over disciplinary demands. I am bound to my political commitment as a feminist scholar interested in how socially and politically disenfranchised individuals (and communities) fashion identity, imagine belonging, and stimulate empowerment, more than I am bound to the confines of disciplinary structures.

Graffiti Grrlz critiques and challenges grrlz' erasure from graffiti history by drawing from methods in performance studies and visual arts, such as thick description, aesthetic categorization, and consideration of method alongside bibliographic information for each writer and a chronological accounting of events. However, it is not a conventional historical account or a feminist recovery project that writes women back into an established subcultural narrative. Instead, this book examines the narrative frame itself and provides what Joan Scott refers to as a "history of difference" that explores how "difference is established, how it operates, how and in what ways it constitutes subjects" in graffiti subculture transnationally.[37]

I reject androcentric research practices and analytical methods that preserve "disembodied" objectivity in favor of ethnographic methodologies that situate knowledge, such as hiphopography and queer feminist ethnography.[38] From these methodologies in particular, I gleaned the importance of "giving back" to the grrlz—via commissions, talks, and gallery shows, for example—and "being down" with the grrlz while being careful and cognizant of how my desire to belong shapes my experiences and interpretations of those experiences.[39] Being "down" with these grrlz is something that came with time, patience, sincerity, and direct communication: when taking on the responsibility of sharing other's stories, being "straight up" is the only way to "get down."[40] That said, as a scholar making a queer feminist intervention, a professional "feminist killjoy" if you will, there are limitations to what I am actually "down" for; being down can sometimes actually hinder the work.[41] If I were to focus on those aspects of the subculture that scholars and participants have thus far deemed the most important, I would not be focusing on grrlz. Nor would I be writing about graffiti from a Hip Hop studies perspective.

Graffiti Grrlz does something most studies of graffiti subculture (and Hip Hop culture) published after the 1980s do not: explicitly link graffiti writing with Hip Hop culture. In *The History of American Graffiti*, Roger Gastman and Caleb Neelon refer to the relationship between graffiti and Hip Hop culture as an arranged marriage, packaged for mass consumption.

> DJ, please cue the debate about whether graffiti is a part of hip-hop, and loop it endlessly. . . . Rapping, DJing, and breakdancing were unquestionably the creation of black and Latino youths, so the faceless pseudonyms of graffiti writing were popularly assumed to be the same. . . . Following initial appearances in the background of early rap videos, graffiti was soon packaged as a part of the "four elements" of hip-hop. . . . With a dance, a vocal music, an instrumental music, and a visual art, hip-hop was a complete package of human expression with few parallels.[42]

When we concede that "hip-hop evolved from a variety of local expressive forms into a global enterprise" because of the way it was packaged by photographers (Cooper), filmmakers (Chalfant), gallery curators, and journalists (Sally Banes), we must also acknowledge that the writers themselves had a part in the packaging.[43]

A survey of canonical graffiti studies texts such as *Getting Up* (1982), *Spray Can Art* (1987), and *Subway Art* (1984) reveals that in these texts graffiti is implicitly tied to Hip Hop's other elements (rap, deejaying/

emceeing, breakdancing). In *Getting Up*, for example, Craig Castleman does not use the phrase "Hip Hop culture," but the musical influences are signaled when he describes scenes such as conga drum circles at live mural painting and explains that the messages seen on trains often drew from "funkadelic" music lyrics; also, Afro-Caribbean percussion and funk music are well-documented influences on early sampling.[44] In *Aerosol Kingdom*, Ivor Miller makes a point to discuss the pop-cultural influences on early New York City writers, including "urban music forms created by Kool Herc, Afrika Bambaataaa, and others"; he also highlights that DOZE, a Manhattan graffiti king, was a dancer with the infamous b-boy troop Rock Steady Crew and that Bronx-based Phase2 was the artist behind Kool Herc's early 1970s flyers.[45] The phrase "Hip Hop culture" may not have been widely used in those early texts because the culture—an amalgamation of diverse and nascent expressions—was still very much in the process of being labeled and circulated.[46] But the fact is, even if the relationship between these presumably autonomous forms of youth-driven self-expression was curated, they traversed the globe under the moniker of "Hip Hop culture." Denying the link between graffiti and Hip Hop's other elements is akin to forcing a divorce on one of the greatest polyamorous marriages of all time.[47] If we look to practitioners' performances across the diaspora, we can trace aesthetic, social, political, and indeed cultural links that come together as Hip Hop.[48]

To date, in the theater of Hip Hop culture's knowledge production, rap music/emceeing has taken center stage, leaving the other founding elements of b-boying, deejaying, beatboxing, and graffiti off in the wings. Subsequently, there is an unacceptable deficiency in the knowledge produced about the aesthetic interventions and political significance of graffiti as a component of Hip Hop culture. Graffiti art is Hip Hop culture despite the ways in which it differs from the other elements, and these differences introduce a new set of questions around minoritarian subjects using Hip Hop aesthetics to claim power and presence on a transnational scale. On a practical level, graffiti is the only "founding element" not fundamentally dependent upon, productive of, or related to music, nor is it always legal. On an ontological level (more in chapter 4), the performance is not located primarily on the artists' body (the body is a necessary, but temporary, component of the performance); the writers perform self by leaving a trace (the graffiti) on a surface (walls, bridges, trains). The writer's traces must act in order to become what they are: graffiti marks must circulate beyond the writers' bodies; in other words, peers must see the graffiti.[49] Unlike a rap, b-boying, beatboxing, or deejaying performance, the graffiti writer's audience (generally) does not experience the performance live, but rather after the fact—in the absence of the artist by way of the graffiti left on the surface. These differences offer opportunities to ask different kinds of questions around accessibility to the subculture, for example: How do minoritarian subjects become subcultural participants, members of a transnational community that functions outside of institutions like the music industry and mainstream media? How does the anonymity of the body effect participation in terms of gender, sexuality, race, ethnicity, and nation? The differences between graffiti painting and Hip Hop's other forms are not reasons to detach it from the rest of Hip Hop culture, but rather serve as markers that distinguish graffiti art as a particular aesthetic form requiring its own tools for understanding. Awakening the "dormant connective tissues" between graffiti and Hip Hop culture is a productive and necessary conceptual method for advancing the fields of graffiti and Hip Hop studies.[50]

Stifled by the lack of information in graffiti studies on graffiti grrlz, it was only because I began studying the feminist interventions in Hip Hop studies that I made real progress with my research.[51] In addition to their theoretical interventions, their first-person accounts of the spaces where Hip Hop culture thrived led me to wonder about the contemporary subcultural places writers might frequent. And since the books were no help in that regard, I took to the Internet—searching for any information I could find about graffiti-related events. At the time, Artcrimes.org (now Graffiti.org) had an "ongoing" shows and events page where people could post messages to one another.[52] Because my personal connections had failed to produce a single interviewee, I emailed the webmaster, Susan Ferrell, to inquire about posting an online call for participation. She responded affirmatively.

Female Writers
Hello all. My name is Jessica Pabón. I am a Women's Studies graduate student at the University of Arizona and I need your help on a research project. I am trying to find lesbian/bisexual identified graffiti artists. . . .

This research project is intended to create a resource for aspiring lesbian, or just female, writers. Participants will be asked a series of questions and will be asked for samples of that work. Whether the writer wants to be known/named in this project is up to the writer. NO PRESSURE ON "COMING OUT" PUBLICLY. . . . I think women need to know that there are other women out there just like them puttin' up pieces.

Naïvely, I was asking these grrlz to come out not only as writers (artists of an illegal medium), but also as bisexual or lesbian to a person whom they had never met (or even heard of) before. No one responded. I asked Susan to take that post down and replace it with a revised version:

Attn: female writers
What's up? Name's Jess: artist, activist, graduate student, looking for female graffiti artists for research project (aka master's thesis). Point: to highlight the females writing dope graf. What do I mean "highlight"? I want to document their contributions; I want to ask questions about being a female working in the graffiti culture; I want to give props where they are deserved and necessary. Long term book project will follow— more on that later. Interested? Get hooked up with my project by contacting me at pabon@email.arizona.edu. ANONYMITY ALWAYS A PROMISE.

Though I did not fully understand the dynamics of my initial request at the time, years later I know that the very term "lesbian" is regularly used to disparage graffiti grrlz who are "too good" or who assert themselves as writers without the help of a would-be heterosexual romantic partner. Many of the grrlz I have spoken to over the years have come out to me in conversation as lesbian, bisexual, or queer, but most refuse to put their nonheterosexuality on record to avoid the inevitable repercussions above and beyond the ostracization and sexual harassment they already face for opposing the conventions of gender performance set for "girls."

Letting go of the focus on lesbian, bisexual, and/or queer graffiti writers was a necessary decision to move the project forward that was nonetheless frustrating because graffiti art making is a nonnormative activity performed in resistance to and operating outside of the identificatory, temporal, and spatial registers of heteronormative patriarchal society.

In other words, though it (still) feels provocative to claim, graffiti writing is queer.[53] Framing graffiti writing as a queer subcultural practice is not an effort to organize all subcultural acts as "queer" or all writers as queer (and therefore erase any specific reference to queer sexual acts that ground queer theory), but rather an attempt to mobilize the challenges to normativity enacted by writers and to attend to some of the hetero/sexist misrepresentations embedded in the stereotypical Hip Hop body. If we are brave enough to cite "The Queerness of Hip Hop/ The Hip Hop of Queerness," we can make space for those queer bodies in Hip Hop graffiti subculture that refuse to come out publicly for fear of retribution (and perhaps inspire someone to pick up the research project that I let go).[54]

Six of the responses that the second call generated were teenagers who only provided basic demographics, some admitting they had not yet gone bombing: Merc/Elmo ("17, white, bisexual, England"); Lace One ("17, bisexual, black and white, FL, USA"); Dvine ("16, Puerto Rican, Bisexual, IL, USA"); Mel/Nasty ("19, white, straight usually, NJ, USA"); Erin ("15, Perugia, Italy"); and Desr ("17, Mexican and white, straight, CA, USA"). Three of the grrlz answered my interview questions and mailed photographs (using the Internet to send images was not yet commonplace): Nungi ("27, Caucasian, heterosexual, CA, USA"), Toots/2tsie ("old, Latina, CA, USA"), and Miss17 (author of this book's foreword). Miss17's participation radically altered the direction and scope of my project. Skeptical of my intentions, 17 kept a safe distance for years; she slowly trusted me with more and more information and eventually referred me to graff grrlz who had been in the game longer than she: Lady Pink, ClawMoney, and Mickey (Netherlands). My connections multiplied as graffiti grrlz began to trust me and refer me to their graff grrl friends.

Because I used digital communication technologies extensively to facilitate relationships with the grrlz, and because the "field" in which I conducted participant observation and interviews included spaces on the Internet, I refer to my primary research method as "digital ethnography."[55] What I call digital ethnography has also been deemed "virtual ethnography," "cyber-ethnography," "online ethnography," "netnography," and "online ethnography."[56] In my case, digital ethnography is the use of communication technologies (such as Skype, Facetime) and social networking sites (Facebook, Twitter, Instagram) to supplement the space between physical encounters—and to act as the encounter itself. My digital interactions with the grrlz differ from my "on the ground" interactions mostly in terms of intimacy, frequency, and depth, but contrary to the ways common sense might suggest. Imagine the difference between conducting an interview with a grrl in the middle of a paint jam versus having an online chat or Skype date after the event. In the former situation, because our conversation will delay her from finishing her piece it has the potential to be rushed. Also, there may be stories, explanations, or details about herself that she does not want to express in a public venue in front of other writers. In the latter, since we have both experienced the event (ideally), we can take the time to share and compare our experiences, I can pace the interview questions a bit more naturally, and she has the freedom to answer when in the controlled environment of a "private" online exchange. We can extend this example to think about frequency and depth as well. After the Skype interview—if we are not connected on social media already—there will be a "friend request" or a "follow request" that I will initiate or accept. From that point on, our interactions have the potential to be daily occurrences not always related to graffiti art. The symbiotic nature of the face-to-face and the digital interactions gave me a much better picture of the grrl behind the letters, and depending on the quality and tenor of those interactions, our interviewer/interviewee relationship can develop—as it did with Miss17—into an enduring friendship.[57]

When I began this project in 2002, scholars had just begun to recognize the capacity of the Internet and to account for the effects of digital spaces on ethnographic research methods and epistemologies.[58] In more ways than one, digital ethnography was a methodological experiment born of necessity. While the very nature of digital ethnography demands a cautious and vigilant response to results (how do we know the grrl is who she says she is, for example), for my research, the significance of the method cannot be overstated: these grrlz are subcultural actors who feel safer interacting with outsiders over email or chat; they live all over the world and physical interactions are limited by travel and sometimes by language barriers; and lastly, their stories literally cannot be found in books or archives. If I did not take the risk of an experimental mashup methodology dependent on digital technologies, I would not have witnessed firsthand what I like to think of as the graffiti grrl digital revolution—a shift in subcultural practice with profound implications for their visibility and belonging.

Digital Ups

In 2006 the photographer Nicholas Ganz published *Graffiti Women: Street Art from Five Continents*. The photobook showcases 130 street and graffiti artists, includes a foreword penned by the renowned street artist Swoon, and has an introduction by Nancy Macdonald (author of *The Graffiti Subculture: Youth, Masculinity and Identity in London and New York*). *Graffiti Women* was the first book specifically about graffiti grrlz and street artists; Ganz himself noted how despite incremental improvement the inclusion of grrlz in graffiti art publications remained sparse. *Graffiti Women* was followed in 2007 by the semiautobiographical "coffee table" book *Bombshell: The Life and Crimes of Claw Money*. Eight years later, two more appeared: *All City Queens* (edited by Syrup and Cyris) and *Women Street Artists of Latin America: Art without Fear* (by Rachel Cassandra and Lauren Gucik). *Graffiti Women* was an afterthought to Ganz's *Graffiti World: Street Art from Five Continents*—where women make up only 8 percent of the artists in his "world" (16 of 185, to be exact). The irony of being relegated to a follow-up book (with a hot pink cover in the U.S. version) did not escape the grrlz themselves. Foxy Lady, a graff grrl from the Netherlands, leveled her critique in a piercing book review published in issue #5 (December 2006) of her digital zine *CatFight: Female Graff Update* (discussed in chapter 3): "[*Graffiti Women*] is almost tasteless"; she and the other graff grrlz she surveyed for the review "had great expectations of this book. . . . But in the end it is a summarised vision, and leaves a bitter taste."[59] Graff grrlz want(ed) more: more evidence of their own voices, more in-depth analysis of their art, more consideration of their specifically gendered perspectives, and more of a distinction from street artists. Ultimately, graffiti grrlz want(ed) more power in how they are (re)presented.

In 2005—a year before Ganz published his book—an unknown graff grrl launched the now defunct but at the time wildly popular website GraffGirlz.com, the first website by grrlz for grrlz and about grrlz.[60] In contrast to the first graffiti art website to appear online in

1994—ArtCrimes.org—where the majority of tag names upheld the standard of anonymity via gender neutrality, GraffGirlz.com signified the writers' gender identities in the title. Utilizing the signifier "girlz," the site hailed participants and signaled, at minimum, that this was a community of people who could empathize with your gender-based experiences, people who would (hopefully) judge your graffiti art based on aesthetics and innovation, rather than gender difference. The site presumed the grrlz' agency, and desire for control over representation, by giving them the responsibility and choice to be included in this community. In English, Spanish, and French, the "Join Us" page explained the terms of inclusion and participation: "Send us a mail to graffgirlz@gmail.com with, your Name, Crew, Country, City, Website, and 25 pics minimum of your choice (only painting pics, no stickers or sketches) and a presentation in few words (beginnings, inspirations, lifestyle, projects . . .). You will receive your login and password as soon as possible." Each writer, once registered with a login and password, had control of the details that appeared on her own page; she could choose to include any combination of information, including tag name, crew, city, country, biography, website, MySpace profile, photos, and, sometimes, an email address.

Ignoring the basic "rule" of anonymity and defiantly identifying themselves as "girlz" on a public site changed everything. Suddenly, all grrlz had to do was click on "Interviews" to access a world of information about other graffiti grrlz: how they "presented" (demographics), how they got into graffiti and why, what inspired them aesthetically, what their experiences were as women, and, lastly, whether they were in contact with other graffiti grrlz. With one click, they were informed of the events grrlz were organizing in faraway cities, such as the 2006 "Pussy Powa" jam in Naples, Italy; the 2007 "B-Girl Be" Festival in Minneapolis in the United States; and the 2008 "We B*Girlz" Festival in Berlin, Germany. GraffGirlz.com went down sometime in 2009, but thanks to the Internet Archive Wayback Machine (www.archive.org/web) you can click through the site at the height of its usage in 2008 and discover that it showcased the work of almost 200 grrlz from twenty-six countries.[61] Catching what I call "digital ups," the writers who participated in GraffGirlz.com enacted the first digital performances of feminism in Hip Hop graffiti subculture.

I recently discussed the impact of grrlz making themselves accessible online with a graffiti grrl from the Czech Republic, Sany (of Puff Crew), who had just premiered her documentary *Girl Power* in 2016—the first documentary exclusively about graffiti grrlz to screen in the film festival circuit.[62] When she began filming *Girl Power* in 2008, Sany set her intentions on highlighting graffiti grrlz who "devoted their lives" to painting graffiti. She told me that in the process of making her film, she helped make "a network of women writers," connecting grrlz to one another online and in person.[63] The Internet made Sany's film possible because even the grrlz who chose to "stay underground" (i.e., keep a very low profile to hold on to some "real-life" anonymity) had an Internet presence.[64] Like the trains that inspired the New York graffiti writers of Abby's generation, the Internet is now the vehicle for communication and the destination of the message. Having realized the potential of blogs, social networking spaces, forums, and personal media sharing to generate a greater presence, writers have made public a subculture that was decidedly counterpublic; they have expanded the Hip Hop aesthetic of the local into the global and have consequently developed creative and affective ties to multiple peoples and places.[65]

GraffGirlz.com initiated profound subcultural shifts through the exposure it gave writers and the digital behavior it catalyzed. It was simultaneously precedent setting and a promise of more things to come. The web, it turns out, is an exceptional vehicle for the "more" that graff grrlz so desire (see chapter 3). Over the past decade, there has been a rapid proliferation of digital spaces specifically geared toward, focused on, and maintained by graffiti grrlz. Grrlz with access to digital forms of communication no longer have to experience a gender-based solitude. Instead, because of digital media, grrlz can choose to tap into a vast transnational network to connect across geographical borders, language barriers, and time zones. The site challenged expectations about the graffiti writer in regards not only to gender but also to race, ethnicity, and nationality— expectations cultivated by time-honored accounts of Hip Hop's origins that highlight a particularly gendered, racialized, and heterosexualized performance.[66] By taking the subcultural community "out of the shadows" to catch their "ups" in the digital public sphere, GraffGirlz .com demonstrated at least two interrelated points: grrlz wrote graffiti in numbers worth counting; and not all graffiti writers were working-class African American boys from the South Bronx.

Hip Hop Graffiti Diaspora

Though a great deal of rigorous debate within Hip Hop studies has attended to the fact that the culture is, and was at its origins, global and multidimensional, analyses still tend to pivot from the most commercially viable form of the four elements: rap music, a form predominantly understood and represented as the cultural property of heterosexual African American cisgender men.[67] Thus, the preconceived notion that people tend to have when you say "Hip Hop head" or "graffiti writer" produces a very specific Hip Hop "body," especially in the United States. Most conversations in Hip Hop studies, unless they are Hip Hop queer/feminist texts that directly address gender difference, center around the Hip Hop archetype perpetuated by mass media, or what Nancy Guevara refers to as the "hype fantasy image" of a young, urban, heterosexual, hypermasculine, working-class cisman of color.[68] But if Hip Hop culture (and by extension graffiti subculture) belongs solely to this group of individuals—what about everyone else?

In the same article in which she introduces the hype fantasy image concept, "Women Writin' Rappin' Breakin'," Guevara directly questions the evident gender bias in Hip Hop studies by focusing on Lisa Lee, Lady Pink, Baby Love, and Roxanne Shanté; this article was an exceptional and early attempt to thwart what has clearly become what T. Denean Sharpley-Whiting refers to as "women's footnoted status in hip hop."[69] A stagnant, Americocentric, racialized hetero/sexist metanarrative—featuring this very particular body as the one responsible for the writing on the wall—has dominated the lens through which some practitioners understand their art form and scholars have theorized Hip Hop graffiti studies. We have been told a very convincing story about the "who" in Hip Hop, and by extension in graffiti, especially in regards to race, class, sexuality, and gender: a story that I, too, believed until I transformed the lens with a critical queer, feminist perspective.[70]

I interviewed more than 100 graffiti grrlz from different generations (seventeen to fifty-six years old), all with different styles (wildstyle, public letters) and living in twenty-three different countries (Australia, Brazil, Canada, Chile, Colombia, Costa Rica, Czech Republic, Ecuador, Egypt, France, Germany, Italy, Japan, Mexico, Netherlands, New Zealand, Nicaragua, Scotland, South Africa, Spain, United Arab Emirates, United Kingdom, and United States). The amalgamation of places where Hip Hop thrives is often referred to as the "Hip Hop Nation": "a deterritorialized form that seems ideally suited for the current moment."[71] The concept of the Hip Hop Nation is a powerful tool used to name an imagined bond because it attends to how mostly marginalized youth around the world choose to build community beyond immediate geopolitical borders. However, the concept of the Hip Hop nation carries with it a patriarchal and heteronormative nationalist logic that imposes a limited framework of gendered and racialized presumptions on my research that hinders my theoretical interventions, misrepresents reality, and simplifies the complexity of this subcultural community.[72]

In the early stages of research, still tied to Americocentric ideologies about race, ethnicity, and expression, I found myself agonizing over how to make sense of the disjuncture between the bodies that I (and others) expected to find in Hip Hop graffiti subculture and the ones I actually encountered—the majority of whom were light-skinned, or considered "white" through the racial constructs specific to their country. Tellingly, the politics of race and ethnicity materialized most forcefully in my discussions with graff grrlz about graffiti's complicated relationship to Hip Hop culture. Though the reasoning varies and despite the fact that almost all of them professed a love for (mostly classic) Hip Hop music, some of these grrlz do not consider their graffiti writing *as* Hip Hop. During an interview in 2011, for example, ClawMoney (a Jewish American writer active in the boroughs of New York City since the late 1980s) explained that though there is a lot of old-school Hip Hop she loves, she thinks it is unfortunate that she is "lumped in[to Hip Hop culture] because of graffiti as an urban expression."[73] She then disassociated graffiti from Hip Hop culture by way of delivering a rather antagonistic question: "I mean, let's be real . . . where are the Black graffiti writers? And where are the Black girl graffiti writers?"[74] ClawMoney locates "the real" of Hip Hop in demographics that she does not fit into; she insists that Hip Hop and graffiti are "separate," and that for her graffiti culture (presumably in the United States) is mostly "heavy metal white boys."

ClawMoney makes thematic, demographic, and temporal distinctions as she tries to navigate her relationship to, and position within, Hip Hop, which she "used to be into" and has since "divorced" because the "message" changed.

According to Abby (who does consider her graffiti as Hip Hop), one of the primary reasons graffiti art is often imagined outside of Hip Hop's cultural boundaries is because people do not talk about the influence of musical genres (like heavy metal) overwhelmingly associated with "white" people on Hip Hop's founding practitioners.

> While graffiti started becoming popular, music started mixing . . . like rock music and the people from that environment started mixing a lot with people from the Hip Hop environment. At the time there was this huge influx of European influence in art and in music, and then you had these really poor people from the ghetto that were spinning records in the parks, and I think when you put them together in the club in Manhattan you suddenly had a new culture. . . . We were sort of a combination of all of that: the rock and the disco and Hip Hop, it all kind of mixed up together. . . . And people are surprised when they hear, like, oh you listen to Radiohead? . . . Inherently it's a part of the culture and I think a lot of people are like that and it's just that no one notices.

When I asked RenOne if she identified her graffiti as part of Hip Hop culture, though she is younger than Abby by ten to fifteen years, her response echoed the sentiment that, in terms of musical genres related to specific races and ethnicities, Hip Hop is "all kind of mixed up together."

> Hip Hop was the baby that soul and funk and jazz, R&B, blues, gave birth to, and similarly my musical genetics came from. My dad had an amazing record collection, and lovingly forced on to me an education of all these musical roots. His nieces and nephews educated me on Hip Hop in its early days; I devoured issues of the *Source*. . . . [A]ny Hip Hop song I forced him to listen to, he would laugh and then send me to his record collection and have me pick out the original they sampled it from. I consider all of this a valuable education in Hip Hop and as you put it "something I identify with." However being of the multicultural background that I am, I had a stepfather who had love for Black Sabbath and Jethro

Tull, a mother who loved all things disco and if not it was females like Diana, Chaka, or Janis. And then I somehow found my way into hardcore and the Riot Grrrl movement.

The more graffiti grrlz I spoke with, the more it became clear that the relationship between graffiti and Hip Hop was imagined through, and couched in, a racialized discourse of ownership based in the common origin story that elides how in its early stages Hip Hop was "all kind of mixed up together." Perhaps it is not that "no one notices," but rather that no one wants to speak the unspeakable and risk whitewashing or appropriating the culture in the process. "Basically everybody in the world believes that most writers are either from the inner city, from the ghetto, black and Puerto Rican," Lady Pink explained to Miller in *Aerosol Kingdom*, "but white is never really discussed."[75]

The precarious relationship between graffiti and Hip Hop culture seems to be due to a variety of factors: the differences between graffiti and the other elements; the conscious distancing from sexist, mainstream rap lyrics; and/or a lack of knowledge about graffiti's polycultural origins. But it is just as likely that the careful self-distancing I have witnessed writers perform repeatedly is an effort to make sense of the mismatch between the story they have been told about Hip Hop and the reality they have lived and experienced—an effort to make space in the subculture for themselves and their friends that is not overshadowed by the discourse of cultural appropriation.[76] This effort, interestingly, maintains Hip Hop's cultural ethic of "realness" and authenticity.

Graffiti scholars have managed the fact of the subculture's multiethnic makeup in various ways, from taking it for granted to using it as a way to explain how graffiti differs from rap. Addressing the politics of race and ownership in the introduction to *Graffiti Lives: Beyond the Tag in New York's Urban Underground*, Gregory Snyder claims quite plainly,

> white kids writing graffiti should not be construed as an act of cultural thievery or imitation; it is not the same as white kids playing the blues or rapping. Unlike most indigenous forms of American music, graffiti is not specifically steeped in African-American cultural traditions, and white kids, black kids, brown kids, rich kids, and poor kids have all participated in the creation and perpetuation of graffiti culture from the beginning.[77]

Like Snyder, I believe that well-intentioned cautions against appropriation too easily paint white, Latinx, and Asian Hip Hop practitioners as "cultural thieves" and artificial replicators; this kind of thinking is historically inaccurate and intellectually stifling.[78]

When it comes to acknowledging the contributions of "white kids" in Hip Hop, the dynamics are loaded—and rightly so—with the weight of privilege (e.g., who is most likely to be stopped, chased, arrested, shot, and/or killed), cultural appropriation, and monetary gain. But the question around cultural appropriation seems most critical in terms of music (which Snyder himself denotes by referencing blues and rapping); it boils down to who is getting the recognition and who is getting paid to do the cultural "thing" that is so popular. The concerns about cultural appropriation should rest on the shoulders of those with the power to fund or fuel the appropriation—those who are buying and selling art(ists) based on white supremacist, heteropatriarchal ideologies.[79] Most graffiti writers, particularly when they start, are not looking to get paid; they are looking to get up, and they do so by performing aesthetics that are recognized by the graffiti community.

The decoupling of graffiti from Hip Hop is also in part a manifestation of the anxiety inspired by the notion that Hip Hop is specifically African American cultural production, a notion that perpetuates the idea that performances of Afro-Caribbean aesthetics end at a racialized line of authenticity drawn to maintain ownership in the face of mass commercialization and a "new stage" of globalization.[80] Erasing or emphasizing the contribution of white and nonblack people of color in the days when the form was just emerging, or now, is unnecessary and even inappropriate once the conversation is removed from a U.S. context where racial constructs such as "white" and "black" mean different things.[81] Unlike Snyder I maintain and celebrate graffiti art's African American and Caribbean roots while acknowledging the fact that—most likely due to the anonymity factor—writing graffiti is, and has been, a highly accessible and attractive mode of Hip Hop expression for non-Afro-Caribbean individuals. It is not an either/or equation. Arguments to the contrary hold on too tightly to conventional and static Americo- and Eurocentric colonial discourses of race, ethnicity, and nation created and used by those in power to divide and conquer, to dominate and oppress.

Writers are not all Puerto Rican or African American Hip Hop heads from the Bronx, but the mode of expression they choose to cultivate is rooted in the Afro-Caribbean diasporic sensibilities that clearly influenced the early writers—who were by and large, but not entirely, Caribbean and African American kids. We need an approach that truly considers how a multiethnic artistic practice can be rooted in a specific ethnocultural tradition *and* be performed felicitously by individuals not of that ethnicity without it being considered appropriation.[82] We must make space for contemporary performances of Afro-Caribbean diasporic sensibilities and attend to how they are transmitted among writers in cities with oceans between them. Hip Hop graffiti is in fact "steeped" in Afro-Caribbean diasporic aesthetics, and those aesthetics are overwhelmingly characterized by hybridity, sampling, and "selection and fusion."[83] None of Hip Hop's elements are limited by a single move, shape, melody, or loop; thus, the way we study the culture should not be limited either. The static Hip Hop icon silences the dynamic Hip Hop community.[84]

Arguing that Hip Hop is both a Black and a multiracial cultural production in *Hip Hop Desis: South Asian Americans, Blackness, and a Global Race Consciousness*, Nitasha Tamar Sharma takes issue with the way "commodified Blackness" dictates the discourse of authenticity in Hip Hop. She asks, "How much more productive would it be if we were to reorient the ownership/authenticity debate by focusing on an artist's approach to Hip Hop, rather than on an artist's identity?"[85] Sharma "displaces hegemonic Blackness (along with maleness and a working class status) as the requisite(s) for 'real' Hip Hop" by focusing on approach rather than identity.[86] While I share her desire to privilege how participants engage and enact Hip Hop, I want to be clear that my analyses hold doing (performance) and being (subjectivity *and* identity) in a productive and difficult tension. In order to capture the complexity of the Afro-Caribbean sensibilities in graffiti art as they travel throughout the globe, I have come to understand that Hip Hop graffiti art aesthetics are learned, shared, and taught beyond conventional ethnoracial boundaries.

Understanding the cultivation of sampled sensibilities as performance emphasizes that they are something one does, or *can do*, rather than fixing them as something one "is" or is not. It is through performance, on- and offstage, that these practices are embodied, disseminated, stylized, and maintained.[87] Thus, to better understand the complexity of Hip Hop aesthetics in terms of authenticity and ownership, we need to first acknowledge how the powerful and well-intentioned rhetoric of "nation" erases, marginalizes, constricts, and simplifies the culture—and by extension the participants of the culture. Then, we can see that the cultural practices of early Hip Hop practitioners were transmitted through performance among individuals of varying ethnicities (and genders, classes, and sexualities) living in different boroughs in a city of immigrants.

Graffiti Grrlz contributes to the "strand of literature" in Hip Hop studies that challenges "the [gendered] African Americanization of hip-hop from a diasporic perspective."[88] Diaspora as discourse and as ideology is expansive; it not only maintains the Afro-Caribbean root of Hip Hop (itself diasporic), but also fortifies those roots—keeping the communities primarily responsible for its creation at the center while it grows, and reflecting the real-life way Hip Hop culture is transferred across all sorts of borders.

The countries that I listed earlier are the "mappable" places of Hip Hop diaspora where I locate the performance of feminism in graffiti culture, but knowing the mappable places does not tell us everything we need to know about these grrlz. In her introduction to *Difficult Diasporas*, which traces Black Atlantic feminist aesthetics through black women's writing, Samantha Pinto offers a striking conceptualization of the feminist aesthetic work in (and of) diaspora: it "scramble[s] the seemingly obvious knowability" of the subjects' representative identity in terms of location, race, and gender; "a diaspora feminist aesthetics can do more than represent 'black women' as an already known subject and object of study."[89] Pinto highlights the ways her texts come together in challenging representations of a static, knowable "stereotypical" black woman, instead presenting difficulties, contradictions, and complexity. I find common ground with Pinto because while *Graffiti Grrlz* is a project concerned with representation, I cannot (and do not intend to) ever "fully" represent them.

With each interview, I attempted to collect demographics (age, class, race and/or ethnicity, sexuality, religion), but as they were optional, more often than not the writers' desire for anonymity took precedent.

For example, to my question of race I might receive the answer "sure, where are we going?" Thus, the sociopolitical identity markers beyond their status as graff grrlz are both present and absent throughout, depending on the writer. Some readers will no doubt find the uneven theorization of race dissatisfying; theoretical attention is given to the racial/ethnic/national aspect of each grrl's identity whenever possible. That said, I did not attempt to balance those variations. Nor did I disregard a writer because she did not want to share her race, class, or sexuality. If a writer claimed a connection to Hip Hop (even if only at the outset of her graffiti career), or if I recognize a Hip Hop aesthetic in her work, she has made it into these pages; that also means that grrlz who distance themselves from Hip Hop (music) have also made it into these pages.

While I am certainly after a kind of representation for the grrlz as a social group, and an understanding of how knowing graff grrlz' activities reveals a shift in established epistemologies about Hip Hop diaspora, my main objective is to represent them through their aesthetics and sociocultural connections. Diaspora is messy and disorderly; that messy disorderliness reflects actual material lives rather than ideologies, desires, conventions, or fantasies. "Nothing about diaspora is easy to create, to define, to fix. [. . . It plays] between the known and the unknown, between recognizable forms of being, knowing, belonging, and acting in the world and the new forms that emerge as we try to understand its shifts."[90] I read the personal information these grrlz share with me alongside their artistic works in order to identify the performance of feminisms across a diaspora that is in and of itself "unknowable," in Pinto's terms, despite dominant narratives and expectations about the who behind the doing of graffiti art. The Hip Hop diaspora cannot be fully "known," but we can attend to the geographic, social, affective, aesthetic, and digital "places" where it is performed and innovated.

A logo illustrated by a Japanese graff grrl, Shiro, for the 2009 We B*Girlz Festival in Berlin, Germany (www.bgirlz.com), visualizes how affect and aesthetics are circulated throughout the Hip Hop diaspora. The image features four of Shiro's signature "Mimi" characters; each is identical in her full-lipped, Coke-bottled body shape but has distinctive skin color and hair texture. The grrlz sit on top of raspberry-colored public-style letters, performing Hip Hop culture in terms of not only arts practice, but also their attitude (e.g., postures and hand gestures) and attire (hoop earrings, matching T-shirts, baggy jeans, Nike sneakers). Students in my Spring 2016 "Gender and Sexuality in Hip Hop" class felt that Mimi was the "graffiti version" of the "demoralizing" video vixen phenomenon, as discussed by Sharpley-Whiting in *Pimps Up, Ho's Down*. They discussed how Mimi's sameness exemplified the "repetition of particular ideals of femininity," how her image depicted the collusion of an Americanized white beauty standard and the more ethnically ambiguous desires of Hip Hop moguls.[91] After they had made their case I asked them to look at the image through a feminist performance studies lens, to think about what they were seeing in relation to what was happening.

When we see hypersexual bodies being painted by graffiti grrlz, we must ask: What is the character doing? And what are the effects of that doing? To empower other grrlz in Hip Hop, Shiro paints her characters in action (if Mimi is not spraying with a paint can, she might be wielding a sword, carrying a child, or riding a motorcycle).[92] Mimi is

Figure I.3. Shiro, "Hip Hop Nurse" with Demer and Meres, 5 Pointz, Queens, NY, 2012. Photo courtesy Scott Barfield.

not a passive object lying about for consumption. In the We B*Girlz image she is spinning a record, holding a one-hand air-baby freeze, spraying a paint can, and spitting rhymes into a mic. A member of the Universal Zulu Nation (UZN; founded by Afrika Bambaataa), Shiro paints her Mimis in a way that is philosophically aligned to the concept of unity promoted by the organization; the Mimis are meant to unify Hip Hop heads across nations (indeed, across galaxies considering the UZN's commitment to Afrofuturism; www.zulunation.com). Circulated through print and digital means, the We B*Girlz logo interpolated grrlz from across the globe to come together, share their Hip Hop skills and styles, and build community. The image hailed them through an affective identification, a shared sense that "women in Hip Hop" should come together in celebration and competition (b-girlz-berlin. com). Shiro's logo is but one example of how graffiti grrlz perform feminism throughout the Hip Hop diaspora.

Performing Feminism "Like a Grrl"

Graffiti Grrlz: Performing Feminism in the Hip Hop Diaspora tells an alternative story about graffiti subculture—a story about "the art of getting ovaries" that considers the performance of feminism in everyday life as a graffiti grrl. Dona, a New York City–based graff grrl most active in the 1990s and early 2000s, painted this phrase on a wall as her "tongue in cheek response to . . . [*The Art of Getting Over*, a book], published in 1999, that barely referenced any women writers . . . coming from a circle where there were some girls really moving and shaking, I was bummed that he didn't give props. I was also very into calling out my female perspective. . . . I always threw something in my pieces, whether it be a tag or some imagery that called attention to the fact that I was a girl."[93] Dona's modification of "the art of getting over" is a feminist performance of difference that provokes recognition of her presence each time the image is viewed.

Without a declaration of gender difference, the gendered, racialized, and classed subject produced in the social imaginary would conceal Dona as the one who "got up." For example, when describing the reasoning behind the bow she adds to her letters, Mrs (an Italian-Puerto Rican

Figure I.4. Dona, South Bronx, NY, 1999. Photo courtesy Dona, taken by Diva (RIP).

writer from the Bronx) explained that even though she did not care, at first, that people thought she was a guy, she added the bow to make it "more girly."

> At first I didn't know if it was a good thing or a bad thing that people thought I was a guy. I guess I thought it was a good thing because girls are considered beneath men in graffiti. It's like, oh, you only want to paint because you want attention. So I wasn't getting *that*, so I guess that was cool. But also I didn't want to be thought of as a guy because I'm not, ya know?

Like Mrs, Dona wanted her gender acknowledged so she discursively removed the default subject of Hip Hop's cultural production from her painting. When the image circulates from one place to another (from the wall to the photograph to a website) the recognition for the doing (the getting up) returns, as it should, to her. The performative force of Dona's utterance on the wall demonstrates the power of declaring, rather than erasing or being ambiguous about gender difference.

Similar to my contention that we must imagine the boundaries of Hip Hop diaspora through performed aesthetics, my approach to feminism and feminist movement is also deeply rooted in performance.[94] I identify feminist acts by examining texts, gestures, and images through a simple question that characterizes feminism as a verb: what does it do? Like the fact that a woman does not a feminist make, not all acts performed by graffiti grrlz can be deemed feminist ones. Indeed, not all acts performed by self-identified feminists are feminist. I focus here on performances that expose and ameliorate the various injustices, biases, subjugations, and oppressions based on gender, sexuality, and race— based on difference—within the subculture. My contention that these performances are feminist is not meant to place the identity of "feminists" on them, which would be a kind of discursive dominance. I utilize the performance of feminism as a strategy for organizing the common "doings" of a large group of individuals with vastly different identities. No matter how they identify or disidentify with "feminism," what I am most interested in is the collective effects of their actions. Thus, when I refer to the performance of feminism, I am referring very specifically to acts (such as Dona's) that have the effect of creating solidarity in difference, fostering empowerment, cultivating community, promoting social justice, reclaiming pleasure and joy, asserting presence in public space, and restoring bodily agency.

Because there are so many writers, crews, and events discussed in the following pages, I included a brief timeline for readers. The timeline is not meant to be an exhaustive timeline of all graffiti grrl activity, but rather to act as a visual reference point for the information offered here. Each chapter identifies a site of transformation where graffiti grrlz elevate their subcultural status and resist hetero/sexist patriarchal oppression. Chapter 1 enters debates about the performance of masculinity in Hip Hop culture by characterizing graffiti grrlz' gender performance as "feminist masculinity"—a concept central to understanding how performances of masculine gender characteristics empower (rather than subjugate) graffiti grrlz. In chapter 2, I illustrate how they use that feminist masculine gender performance to sustain all-grrl crews (feminist communities) that enact the principles at the heart of feminist movement (collectivity, support, and empowerment) despite not always utilizing "feminist" as an identity marker. I address the tension between enacting feminism and not identifying as feminist further in chapter 3 by tracing how the performance of feminism has been circulated through a digital network, arguing that they have created a subcultural feminist sensibility through a kind of digital consciousness-raising. Chapter 4 examines how the relatively new phenomenon (dating back about twenty years ago) of graffiti subculture's online activity affects graffiti grrlz' "herstorical" presence in the production of the subcultural archive. The chapter interrogates the social and political potential of a digital existence for those who have literally been written out of history while it offers "transephemerality" as a conceptual tool for describing the ontological condition of an ephemeral art form that remains present in the digital world. Chapter 5 is concerned with how graffiti grrlz negotiate their precarity in terms of their subcultural value because their aesthetics *and* their bodies (thus, their peer recognition) are valued differently within this subcultural economy. Knowing this, graffiti grrlz choose to paint together, en masse, sometimes publicly, under a moniker signaling their gender difference and, in doing so, they temporarily restructure their subcultural position. I conclude by arguing that these grrlz perform a different kind of standpoint epistemology, one structured less by knowing and claiming a location on the grid of identification and more by doing something that *feels* revolutionary. In one last intervention, I close with a list of messages from the graffiti grrlz in the book to aspiring graffiti grrlz reading the book. The Hip Hop gesture of "passing the mic" amplifies the words and works of the grrlz taking public space across the diaspora.

Graffiti grrlz' performances of feminism not only positively influence the aesthetics and politics of Hip Hop graffiti subculture, but also demonstrate the transformative power of transnational feminist solidarity.[95] They show us how we can organize across difference (a perennial feminist concern), without trying to "become each other's unique experiences and insights"; grrlz share their experiences with one another, enacting a politics of "mutual stretching," while holding one another's feet to the fire.[96] The call has been sent out to writers across the globe: "We are here! We did this! Now, you!" They expect other grrlz to rise to the occasion, to get up without succumbing to seductive paternalism or the short-lived and individualistic benefits of tokenization or self-sexualization. In order to elevate their status as a group, they stretch to meet one another where they are at—this is feminism in action. As the proliferation of digital spaces, crews, and films created, sustained, and specific to graff grrlz illustrates, the community is rising. Graff grrlz are not only provoking one another, they are also relentlessly demanding recognition of their place in graffiti art's now-transnational community so that generations to come will know that they do, in fact, exist. More important, they will know how and why the experiences of graffiti grrlz matter.

1

Performing Feminist Masculinity in a Postfeminist Era

MISS17: Of course it's a masculine statement.

DONA: There's nothing feminine about graffiti.

MISS17: We're women: that's about all that's feminine about it. The rest of it is a masculine thing.

LADY PINK: Yeah, the whole thing we create. . . . And there's nothing feminine about it. Nothing at all, and if you're too feminine you're not successful.

CLAWMONEY: Well that's in terms of the traditional gender roles, if you are too so-called feminine. But it is very assertive, so if that's what is so-called masculine then . . .

LADY PINK: Aggressive.

CLAWMONEY: Yeah, and then you can call it masculine. Because people tend to generalize men as that, and women not as that. There are no societal customs now bringing boys into manhood, like hunting for wild cats or something.

DONA: Like rites of passage.

CLAWMONEY: So graffiti is a traditional rite of passage.

JESSICA: What do girls have, then?

MISS17: The prom! The menses, like you get your period and now you're a woman.

LADY PINK: You start, you know, tweezing hair and putting on makeup.

DONA: Learn how to walk in high heels.

MISS17: You learn to make yourself uncomfortable so that you can be what everyone else deems you to be.

LADY PINK: And you rebel. At one point we all rebelled and said: no more of these girl lessons. We're going to just do what the fuck we want.

During a group interview in Tucson, Arizona, in 2004, Dona, Claw-Money, Lady Pink, Miss17, and I discussed the relationship between Hip Hop graffiti writing and masculinity. Our conversation was inspired by the idea that (cisgender) boys and men do graffiti to construct and affirm their masculine identities, a theory offered in the then–recently published book *The Graffiti Subculture: Youth, Masculinity and Identity in London and New York* by Nancy Macdonald.[1] In response to my question, "What do girls have, then?," the New York City–based graff grrlz promptly voiced a list of various coming-of-age rituals capped effortlessly with Pink's assertion that they rejected the "girl lessons" mandating their behavior in favor of an expressive form defined by aggression, assertiveness, and defiance. Graffiti grrlz choose graffiti writing as an alternative to those obligatory lifelong girl lessons in "restraint, punishment, and repression."[2]

In order to get up, a writer has to exert the qualities of daring, confidence, and adventurousness as she dangles from an overpass, runs from the police, scales a bobbed-wire fence, climbs a highway billboard, or balances on an active train track—these are the masculine things Miss17 referred to in contrast to her identity as a woman. Her assertion—"We're women: that's about all that's feminine about it. The rest of it is a masculine thing"—illustrates the tension between graff grrlz' sense of self as women and their acknowledgment of the fact that they are performing

Figure 1.1. "Bitches 'n' Stitches" detail, Access Tucson, Tucson, AZ, 2004.

tasks and characteristics that do not correspond to the gender expression designated for women (femininity), but rather the one conventionally and ideologically secured for cisgender male bodies.[3] Further, it suggests how the politics of authenticity, belonging, and ownership in Hip Hop remain tied to a conventional Western sex/gender binary that not only positions grrlz as exceptions to the subcultural rule—enabling and furthering their tokenization—but also negates their agency to define themselves as women who take pleasure in the successful and sincere performance of masculinity through graffiti writing.

The hetero/sexist idea that only cisgender men can and do perform Hip Hop masculinity is a deterministic formulation wherein graffiti grrlz can only be understood one dimensionally: as tomboys (which implies a kind of permanently adolescent male mimicry) and/or as butch lesbians (which collapses the distinctions between gender and sexuality).[4] The consequences of this approach for grrlz are exemplified in Macdonald's research, which she described as an analysis of the "gender dynamics that emerge when women infiltrate subcultures that are predominantly male."

> The female writer's task is a difficult one. Male writers work to prove they are "men," but female writers must work to prove they are not "women." . . . [T]hey must replace all signs of femininity (incapability) with signs of masculinity (capability). . . . In this subculture there is little room for a woman to represent herself as a woman. . . . To be accepted, a girl must behave like a boy. She must act as if she has "balls." . . . Masculinity is upheld as her goal, so when she achieves this male writers tend to signal her worth in "male" terms.[5]

Macdonald claims that by acting "as if she has 'balls,'" the graff grrl denies her identification as a woman, and in so doing she undoes her ability to represent her feminine "woman" self. Regardless of the scare quotes she uses (e.g., "men," "women," "balls," and "male"), in Macdonald's rationale the balls that grrlz have are "as if," in contrast to the "balls" male writers have . . . naturally?[6]

In an interview with ClawMoney in 2011, I recalled our prior conversation about Macdonald's masculinity theory (created in part through interviews with ClawMoney and Lady Pink), and in her signature point-blank communication style, she asserted, "I have more balls than any dude I know." ClawMoney became known for her iconic paw-print "claw" in the late 1980s to early '90s, and now—drawing on the creative and aggressive energy of graffiti subculture—she is the CEO of Claw&Co, a major urban retail brand (clawandco.com). ClawMoney carries the attitude and posture she embodied as a bomber into her business: "You really have to be sort of like a tough bitch. [Graffiti] taught me my work ethic [. . . and] my aesthetic." Participating in graffiti culture is an outlet for her "tough bitch" personality, a way of being she attributes to coming from a long line of "tough motherfucking women"—a way she now shares as a mentor to newer/younger graff grrlz. "I like to nurture these girls," she said. "If no one is going to give them love, I'm going to give them love." Self-identifying as a "feminist, a tomboy, and a girly girl, too," ClawMoney defies one-dimensionality.

The way that ClawMoney performs masculinity includes and enables her vigorous advocacy for other graff grrlz. "I hold the same standards for girls that I hold for guys. The girls break my heart . . . because they

Figure 1.2. ClawMoney standing in front of "Bitches 'n' Stitches," 2004.

do have more of a hardship." When ClawMoney references her "balls," she actively manipulates and reclaims the use value and conventional meaning of an everyday colloquialism. Uttered in reference to herself, or while giving props to other graff grrlz, she exposes the gap between the anatomic sign referencing the cisgender male body (balls) and the metonymic function of the gendered colloquialism (balls = masculinity = hardness = realness). Leveled against grrlz on the basis of biologically determined difference, the "as if" rhetoric reproduces and reinforces the idea that graffiti subculture is a boys' club, an act that enables *only* cisgender boys and men to learn, practice, and demonstrate their (het-ero)masculinity.[7] In failing to recognize how the daring and courageous "doing" of Hip Hop masculinity is and has been done by individuals who are not interested or invested in constructing a (hetero)masculinity in order to become "men," Macdonald's analysis offers a limited rep-resentation of the gender politics in graffiti subculture that effectively (even if not intentionally) negates graffiti grrlz' participation.

Despite the topic's contentiousness and the multitude of approaches used, theories about Hip Hop masculinity are almost exclusively about heterosexual cisgender men—sometimes examining the performance of masculinity as a survival strategy, and frequently focused on the nega-tive affects that make girls and women victims of objectification, hy-persexualization, or internalized sexism.[8] In what follows, I will argue that Hip Hop scholars and graffiti lovers who want to advance "a truly alternative or progressive gender ideology and identity that resists rac-ism" and "challenge dichotomous understandings of gender" then have to make conceptual, social, material, and political space for graffiti grrlz who perform masculinity without expecting them to hide their feminin-ity or their identities as women, and/or assuming they are queer in terms of sexuality.[9] Moreover, we have to stop uncritically subscribing to—indeed, celebrating—a sex/gender binary in order to value and highlight women's graffiti art-making practices. Explaining feminine color choices or subject matter through gender conventions rather than as aesthetic differences between writers, for example, relegates graffiti grrlz to the realm of difference and otherness.[10]

Hip Hop masculinity needs a critical reimagining not only in terms of the present and future, but also in reference to the past. Graffiti grrlz were present as the performance of Hip Hop masculinity became the central mode of gender performance for graffiti artists; any claim to the contrary is historically inaccurate.[11] Recounting the early days ('70s) of graffiti writing in New York City's boroughs to Miller, Fuzz explained,

> Women writers were always put on the back burner; they weren't even on the stove. They were right out there in the trenches with some of the top dogs, and they were just forgotten about. Period. Most were black and Spanish. From day one, females were bombing; there were places you could go uptown, and broads were holding it down, bombing trains, insides. They did it to rebel, to be better than dudes. Me and POO-NI 167 we used to go racking together; I used to hang out with BARBARA 62, EVA 62 and CHARMIN [65]. These are girls that went just all out against the hands of time, and just crushed it. For a graffiti girl to get up, fix her hair, get a bag of paint, and go out to the train yards by herself and bomb, and you don't say "Hey, POO-NI 167, that Spanish girl is holding it down," then where does that leave you? She was in a true essence of top form from the very beginning. She should be before you. POO-NI 167 was one of the first to do block formation, pink pieces, black outlines with little eyes in the middle. BARBARA 62 was one of the first Scotch Guard, fat cap orange tank with black outlines, they were in it to win it, to bomb. But nobody ever shines the light on them. . . . These were among the forefathers of graffiti, only they were women.[12]

As "forefathers of graffiti," grrlz performed the masculinity that was both a behavioral by-product of sociopolitical conditions and a requirement of getting up. Here, I offer a frame and a model for understanding grrlz' performances of masculinity that does not position them as victims, posers, or reproducers of internalized sexism, one that attends to how their masculinity differs from toxic Hip Hop masculinity in terms of both intention and effect. I begin with this intervention because graffiti grrlz will remain on the margins for as long as scholars and practitioners refuse to acknowledge their masculinity as a sincere gender performance.

As a new conceptualization of an established way of being, I offer the term "feminist masculinity." Feminist masculinity is a gender performance characterized by the utilization of recognizably masculine traits (aggression, ownership of public space, braggadocio) for feminist means (community building, self-empowerment, peer support). As a concept, feminist masculinity can be imagined as a performance in line with the work of Hip Hop feminism—to "fuck with the grays"; that said, it is not axiomatic that graffiti grrlz identify as Hip Hop heads, feminists, or Hip Hop feminists.[13] Feminist masculinity is a kind of "female masculinity" in [Judith] Jack Halberstam's terms, but it is not always already a direct expression of homosexuality or a gender queer transidentity (the focus of Halberstam's theory). My conceptualization of feminist masculinity also differs from bell hooks's usage of the term because she uses feminist masculinity to make space specifically for cisgender male masculine individuals in feminist movement.[14] I locate feminist masculinity in how graffiti grrlz perform their gender, but it is a performance of self available to any *body*. Feminist masculinity does not come at the cost of femininity; it is a contextually specific enactment of self that embraces the complexity of gender expression, a way to conceptualize performances of masculinity in tandem with performances of femininity. The writers I discuss here—Are2 (USA), Miss17 (USA), Egr (Canada), Ivey (Australia), Jerk LA (USA), and Motel7 (South Africa)—exemplify feminist masculinity not because their letters are angular (instead of figural), or because they paint with blues (instead of pinks), or because they wear black hoodies, baggy jeans, and sneakers (instead of ruffled pastel sundresses and heels). A graff grrl could embody all of these traits (or their "opposites") and remain misogynistic. They exemplify feminist masculinity because they play with the gender binaries influencing our perceptions of color choice, letter style, and embodiment. Feminist masculinity attends to graffiti grrlz' everyday experiences as cisgender women who came into adulthood as part of the Hip Hop generation, an era increasingly marked by the neoliberal promise of "girl power" fueled by postfeminism.[15] Rather than imagining that their gender deviance, or rather defiance, goes unchecked, feminist masculinity is best understood as an ongoing performance, a constant negotiation with the "representations and narratives" that structure their place within graffiti subculture and society at large.[16]

Against the tired claims that feminism is dead, and that Hip Hop culture is detrimental for women and girls, I am committed to articulating the political potential and vitality of both Hip Hop and feminism as social justice tools by examining what the performance of feminist masculinity within Hip Hop culture can do. In *Feminism Is for Everybody*, bell hooks claimed that "if feminist theory had offered more liberatory versions of masculinity it would have been impossible to dismiss the movement as anti-male. To a grave extent feminist movement failed to attract a large body of females and males because our theory did not effectively address the issue of not just what males might do to be anti-sexist but also what an alternative masculinity might look like."[17] Graff grrlz have been providing one such example of an alternative to toxic masculinity under the "radar" of feminist movement by performing in and on public space; being assertive, aggressive, surly, risk taking, confident, and daring; dominant but not oppressive; exaggerated; hardworking; pleasure seeking, resistant to convention, and prone to deviation; and invested in both independence and collective activity. Each of the writers has her own take on the terms of engagement: they are not all self-identified feminists (more on this in chapter 2), they do not all consider themselves part of the "Hip Hop nation," and they do not all consider themselves masculine. That said, despite their social, economic, ethnic, political, and geographical differences, the feminism they perform is influenced by Hip Hop culture's aesthetics.

Are2 (USA)

Biologist by day, "vandal" by night since 1996, Are2 is a politically savvy, socially active, world traveling anticapitalist most often seen wearing a comfortable hoodie, T-shirt, jeans, and sneakers. Around 2001 she started painting on her surface of choice: metal, specifically freight trains. Her always-legible freight pieces exhibit one of two distinct variations—weighty, grounded, and all capitalized; or lean and buoyant with lowercased letters hanging midair. They are purposefully sloppy with "a lot of fades and doodads" filling each independent letter. The opening *A* of each Are2 is reminiscent of a social-cause ribbon, and the closing ends with a flourish. She is likely to embellish the piece with phrases such as "fuck society," "born against," "everyday struggle," and "all about destruction." The closest contemporary writers in the United States will get to seeing their work "run" on trains the way they did in the heyday of New York City's 1960s and '70s is on these freight trains. And for Are2, when the train moves, her declaration of presence and rebellion moves with it. Initially, Are2 painted "with about thirty dudes" in BA crew, "Burning America," for over a decade. She left BA after two sequential but not simultaneous events: with no regard for how it would affect her reputation, the crew invited a writer to join them that had called her a "graff ho" online; and on the occasion of a breakup with another member, the crew "took his side." She decided it was too much drama and went out on her own. In 2011, she joined Goonies (GNS), a "tight-knit crew" that is "a lot more of what [she'd] always thought of as a crew: a group of people that you put in work and play with, and in which everyone has each other's backs."[18]

When I met her in 2009, Are2 was actively using the Internet, specifically Facebook, as a second kind of "wall" where she could sound out her political concerns and also advocate for women. She was a regular contributor to the microloan nonprofit organization Kiva (www.kiva .org), which connects small-scale investors with entrepreneurs around the world to alleviate poverty, or at the very least to provide their borrowers with opportunities to build or grow their businesses. Using Kiva's Facebook application, Are2 shared her investment in a small, woman-owned business in Bolivia under which she commented, simply, "pro-mujer." Though her microloan donation was in line with what I knew about her philanthropic desires, the caption surprised me. During our email exchanges, Are2 had explained that she rejected feminism because she was taught that "we needed to correct the inherent bias against women with a bias TOWARD women. I thought this concept was flawed and never went along for the ride."[19] Are2 identifies herself not as a feminist, but rather "as an 'equalist' who rejects feminism as a political project that seeks to replace the patriarchal society with a matriarchal one." She is "not big on the whole girl power thing," but she recognizes that "women are most certainly marginalized, there is still a glass ceiling [and] we are judged by a different set of standards." Her "equalist" position is informed, no doubt, by her experiences as a gender minority, both at her day job in the sciences and in her painting. She wants there to be a level playing field on all fronts of her life, one in which gender does not influence one's social, political, or economic standing.

As "girls" and "women" in a male-dominated field, graff grrlz always have to go above and beyond normal expectations to prove their commitment: against hetero/sexist claims that they are writing graffiti to make their boyfriends happy (or to get a boyfriend); against claims that someone else gets up for them; against slut-shaming rumors exaggerating or falsifying sexual activity (being called "graff hos"); and against the idea that they are somehow exploiting their difference (which is only an issue if it works to gain them notoriety that surpasses their cisgender male peers). Fully aware of these dynamics, Are2 holds her peers to a higher standard of commitment, regardless of gender, and is vociferously opposed to graff grrlz using their minority status "as their 'look at me' factor, or a social-climbing tool, or an excuse," rather than developing their artistic ability and gaining notoriety through commitment and perseverance. Holding other grrlz to a standard, similar to ClawMoney, is an act that adds value to graff grrlz' participation without reinforcing the negative effects of their gender difference. As the "Others" of Hip Hop culture, grrlz must resist modes of power acquisition that simply reify their tokenization, marginalization, and sexualization. Are2 is a model in that regard. In her opinion, graffiti culture is "cheapened by chicks looking to get that extra leg up using their uterus."

Artists engaging in this precariously positioned art form become subjects of a highly contentious and competitive system whereby individuals compete with one another for the crumbs of stability, of recognition, of place in the (art) world. Historically, graffiti art has a messy, exploitative, and precarious relationship with the fine art world.[20] Having their place threatened, graffiti artists who gain a position of relative power in terms of gender (if not race/ethnicity) exert the sexist masculinity they deem necessary to maintain their stake in the subculture. It is easy to understand how those who do not hold a position of power precisely because of their gender subordination might succumb to the temptation to use their second-class status however possible to "move up" (but, of course, never to the top). Graff grrlz like Are2 take an uncompromising stance against that move; they do not take the bait of spectacular tokenization offered by patriarchal institutions—be they subcultural or mainstream.[21]

In her book *The Aftermath of Feminism: Gender, Culture and Social Change*, Angela McRobbie names the various subjectivities allowed under a "new deal" for girls and women after the incorporation of hegemonic liberal feminist ideals (of the 1960s and '70s): the global girl, mostly "Third World," earning wages, consuming femininity; and the phallic girl, who is sexually aggressive and presents herself as already equal to men. Neoliberalism promises both global girls and phallic girls that if they work hard, they can liberate themselves as individuals: free to buy their own beer, miniskirt, spray paint, and lipstick as long as they do not challenge their social and political position within imperialist settler white supremacist capitalist heteropatriarchy. In a 2007 article on the same topic, McRobbie explains that

> the taking up of the position of phallic girl bears the superficial marks of boldness, confidence, aggression and even transgression (in that it re-fuses the feminine deference of the post-feminist masquerade). However this is a licensed and temporary form of phallicism. And like the post-feminist masquerade, is predicated on the renunciation of the possibility of critique of hegemonic masculinity, for fear of the slur of feminism or lesbianism.[22]

The "superficial marks" that McRobbie attributes to the phallic girl are often attributed to hegemonic male masculinity. The phallic girl gains her freedoms by denying feminism, feminist gains, and feminist ideologies—by exploiting her body, using it as a "leg up," by making a patriarchal bargain to "emulate male behaviour as a post-feminist gesture."[23] Deeming characteristics such as boldness and confidence as "phallic" does the same kind of rhetorical work as Macdonald's "as if" discourse about balls—neither position leaves room for a performance of masculinity that does not make a bargain with patriarchy, that may reject feminism by name but ultimately performs feminism in inten-tion. Making a claim that graff grrlz completely escape the neoliberal postfeminist promise would be naïve: they are grrlz living in a globalized world where those promises are everywhere. Are2's feminist masculine performance informs her commitment to bucking social conventions, her advocacy for other grrlz, and her rejection of complicity with the demands of patriarchy. The destruction she is "all about," ultimately, is evidenced in her critiques of the social (discrimination based on difference), political (criminalization of art), and economic (industrial-ization) effects of neoliberal capitalism and globalization.

Miss17 (USA)

A New York City bomber, "mistress of mischief," and all-city graff grrl with a passport indicating her mission of "world domination," Miss17 has been writing graffiti throughout the United States, Europe, Latin America, and Asia since 1998.[24] Graffiti is "the longest running thing in [her] life next to eating and breathing."[25] She is probably best known for her throwies (aka throw-ups) appearing alone or in a "family" (a close group) and for popularizing the vertical tag as opposed to the horizontal (at least in the boroughs of New York City). Not afraid of contradictions, or one to be held accountable to socially inflicted conventions, she describes herself as both "fem[inine and] masc[uline . . .] and something else entirely all rolled into one!" She has a taste for fashion, but her daily uniform consists of sweatpants and a T-shirt—she is dressed to paint, most days. She loves to joke around, play with words, and especially takes pleasure in a well-played pun, but she is very serious when it comes to getting up.

In 2011, Miss17's lawyer estimated that she was wanted for over $600,000 worth of damages in New York City alone. Miss17 is so well known that her fans created a Facebook page (www.facebook.com/miss 17nyc) and a Flickr account (www.flickr.com/groups/miss17) to share and archive her work; toys try to copy/steal her tag with subpar throw-ups (in this world, mimicry is not flattery). The Hip Hop scholar, activist, and artist Danny Hoch includes a rather succinct outline of the tenets informing Hip Hop culture's aesthetics in "Toward a Hip-Hop Aesthetic: A Manifesto for the Hip-Hop Arts Movement."[26] He leans toward masculine descriptors such as "braggadocio," which is a kind of "empty, idle boast" according to the *Oxford English Dictionary*.[27] There is nothing empty about the prideful attitude that grrlz like Miss17 have about their work, and as a prolific writer painting for twenty years, she is hardly idle. Some graff grrlz are deemed, and occasionally self-identify as, "queens" (or, alternatively, "queenz").[28] Miss17 resists the second-tier status of "queen" and claims "I am the fucking king!" A graffiti king is named as such because of scope, command of mediums (spray paint, caps, and surface), and level of risk taken with each tag, piece, or production. Regardless of the "miss" in her tag, graffiti writers uniformly recognize her as a "king"—the highest status one can attain in this subculture.

Figure 1.3. Miss17, Athens, Greece, 2013.

In October 2013, we both traveled to Athens, Greece. She went first and left a trail of tags and throwies for me to follow, with the bonus at the "end" where she had spray painted my name inside the exclamation point finishing her "17!"[29] She provided an alternative map of the city, and in doing so she changed my relationship with the unfamiliar streets I would have otherwise avoided. The visual call-and-response experience generated by Hip Hop graffiti is a deeply affective one I did not completely understand until I began traveling abroad and finding her work scrawled across cityscapes. Three years before the Athens excursion, on a visit to Amsterdam, I found one of her tags near my hotel and experienced that same feeling: it was as if she was calling directly to me, saying, "Hey, I'm here, too!" By drawing an alternative map on each city she visits, she makes them feel differently, more welcoming because she has traversed and claimed the city streets for those of us who recognize her mark. Miss17 takes space for herself, but she also takes space for us. For those not "in the know," but who are paying attention, the "miss" in her tag modifies, if temporarily, a gendered sense of belonging to a public space, of feeling safe there, and taking pride in the ownership of a public space defined primarily by architectural features and urban planning. Without a bullhorn, she "takes back the night," takes back the streets, for herself and for others the moment that her marker, or paint can, alters the surface.

Miss17 is an experienced bomber who gets up and over in a matter of moments; her style is more often "gritty and raw" than not. She does not paint characters and rarely finds occasion to "pretty up" her 1s or 7s. "When I first came out I was writing MS.17," she explained, "and then that morphed into miss 17 and so I guess it was pretty obvious that I was a woman. Looking back I regretted that because everyone treats you and your graff so much differently when they know you are a woman. But as far as my throwups and blocks are concerned I don't think there's any obvious femininity to them."[30] With enough time at the right location, she may spell out her name—M-I-S-S-S-E-V-E-N-T-E-E-N—or use a color palette and pattern to match a clever theme. For example, in June 2012, Miss17 joined Claw, Are2, Anarkia, and Mrs for a "Summer BBQ All-GRRLZ Jam" at the Tuff City tattoo shop in the Bronx. It took a great deal of persuasion on my part, as Miss17 usually will not paint on a legal wall. On the back wall of a yard designed to look like a trainyard—complete

Figure 1.4. "Summer BBQ All-GRRLZ Jam" with Miss17, ClawMoney, Are2, Anarkia, and Mrs, Tuff City tattoo shop, Bronx, NY, June 2012.

with tracks, the side of a train, and a switch signal—Miss17 comple-mented Claw's hot dog, Anarkia's sundae, Are2's milkshake, and Mrs's ice cream cone with a quick, forest-green throwie highlighted with neon green, filled with watermelon pink, and completed with black doodads for seeds. She made an exception because it was an "all-grrlz" jam with other writers she respected and wanted to meet.

The "Summer BBQ" jam was my effort to connect two out-of-town graff grrlz—Anarkia and Are2—with the New York powerhouse PMS Crew: Claw, Miss17, and Mrs. From its founding by ClawMoney and Sho-Nuff in the early 1990s, PMS was the only all-grrl bombing crew not just in New York, but in the United States (until ClawMoney invited men to join PMS in the 2000s and then Few and Far emerged on the West Coast in 2011: see fewandfarwomen.com). Aside from its obvious signification, PMS also stands for Painting Mad Spots, Punchin' Many Suckers, Playing Man Slaves, Puffin' Marijuana Smoke, Powerful Mono-maniacal Sisters, and Power, Money, Sex. In 2004, when I first spoke with Miss17 about feminism during the group interview in Tucson ref-erenced earlier, I asked her if she was a feminist. She answered, quite brusquely, "No." I repeated my question in October 2009: "Definitely. In part due to my relationship and involvement with you on past projects as well as having friends like ClawMoney who taught me about being a feminist or rather that feminism wasn't a dirty word." Her relationship to feminism developed because of feminists who espoused and enacted the kind of ideology she was comfortable with, rather than the "man-hating" feminism she had been taught as a teenager.

Miss17 is one of a handful of graff grrlz consistently invited to show in galleries (though due to legal concerns she regularly turns these invita-tions down) and to be featured in video documentaries, books, magazine covers, and academic journal articles.[31] She has strong opinions about how writers attain fame, under what circumstances they are included in events, shows, and publications, and asserts that "putting bullshit bitches down takes away from the real women who get down"—they "take space that should be reserved." Balancing Are2's critique of women who use their sexuality to rise to fame, Miss17 places the onus on those who pro-mote writers who have not done the work to earn fame: "who should be doing shows all over the world? some bitch on her back or some bitch on the track?" With a harsh flourish of the tongue, Miss17 exercises her dexterity as a wordsmith and makes her opinion clear. Her feminist masculinity demands that graff grrlz who want respect work for it and meet a standard of excellence—this goes beyond writing the graffiti and extends to a kind of ethical engagement with the craft. Miss17 has no qualms generating beef with other graffiti grrlz whom she deems to be not worthy. She does not celebrate "girl power" for grrlz who do not earn it; Miss17 demands empowerment—respect, status, belonging—through action.

Miss17 separates her graffiti art from her other love, Hip Hop, though she admits that they have "somehow been married together." She thinks "these movements can be completely separate of one another" and finds no correlation "unless [she is] blasting some wu[-Tang] to get amped up!" Blasting Wu-Tang Clan to get motivated is emblematic of her hard-hitting, brazen, and raw graffiti aesthetic and, unsurprisingly, of her personality. Graffiti is an outlet for Miss17, a way to freely express the "something else entirely" that has brought her subcultural infamy. The something else entirely named by Miss17 is the feminist masculine gender performance born of Hip Hop culture and feminism.

Egr (Canada)

Based in Toronto and a member of the city's graffiti scene since 1996, Egr (pronounced "eager") paints an alternative model for grrlz and Hip Hop masculinity by exploring and exploding the bounds of sexuality through her use of the female form (www.facebook.com/EGRart). Often invited to attend events and participate in live-painting jams, Egr is also a fine artist firmly rooted within Hip Hop culture socially and aesthetically, producing works that are, in her own words, "fluid and bright, fresh or old school, with a reference to music, and the [other] elements of Hip Hop." While Egr firmly stated, "No, I'm not a feminist," she made sure to amend her response to my question by clarifying that, yes, she "believe[s] in equality." Often, she appears on my Facebook newsfeed performing the epitome of what I would deem high femme while she is painting a wall—rich red lipstick, perfectly coiffed hair (sometimes blonde), a corset, high-heeled boots of a thousand varieties, and sometimes a parasol. On #ThrowbackThursday, you might catch a picture of her from the '90s in a T-shirt, high-top Adidas, and a jean skirt. Her art "is a reflection of [her] thoughts and experience," and while she paints letters it is her characters that communicate her perspective and her sense of self—be they on a wall or on a stretched canvas. Egr's figures are hourglass shaped, made-up, accessorized, sexy, often politicized, and (depending on the context or purpose of the piece) painted with spray can in hand. They are also cool, calm, collected, and confident— armed and ready to defend themselves when their equality, autonomy, or belonging is threatened.

In *Thug Life: Race, Gender, and the Meaning of Hip-Hop*, Michael P. Jeffries offers his notion of "complex coolness," a theoretical extension of existing "cool pose" scholarship that provides a different perspective on "thug life" performances of masculinity—the kind that have sparked debates about the oppression of girls and women in Hip Hop since the '90s.[32] He argues, "Complex coolness, a descendent of both Thompson's cool aesthetic and Du Bois's undeniably painful double consciousness," "represents a new step in cool's evolution."[33] While Jeffries's complex coolness provides an interesting new take on thug life as presented in gangsta rap, his framework for the complexity of coolness prevalent in Hip Hop culture is not considered—even briefly—beyond its application to Black heterosexual cisgender male subjects. Nonetheless, complex coolness is instructive here because the Hip Hop masculinity that informs graff grrlz' performances shares characteristics with the same masculinity Jeffries is theorizing: the "hard," U.S.-produced version of Black male masculinity that consumers of Hip Hop culture know so well because of Tupac, the Notorious B.I.G., Jay Z, and Nas (to name a few).[34] Jeffries is interested in softening the "hard" and unpacking the "cool" by paying attention to how performing Hip Hop masculinity builds community through loyalty and signals vulnerability through love. Despite those "softer" aspects, complex coolness still relies on the tools of dominant heteropatriarchal masculinity, and this is the primary distinction between the masculinity he is describing and the feminist masculinity that graffiti grrlz perform.

Egr's Queen of Spades character is one example of how the masculinity that graffiti grrlz perform is a rejection of toxic masculinity. Wielding a pistol with her finger on the trigger, the "queen" in this piece is a woman of color wearing dominatrix-style black leather high-heeled boots with a black miniskirt and shelf bra that barely contain her curves. Her natural, curly hair suits her body language; with shoulders slouched, legs bent, apart at the knees and bowed at the feet, she is visibly at ease.

Yet she is at attention with a fixed, hard expression as she gazes into the eyes of her viewers. She is ready. She is comfortable with her sexual attractiveness and her femininity. She is an agent of her own space on the wall—she has claimed it; it is hers. Anticipating the precarity of that claim to space and belonging, Egr's "cool" characters come armed and angry—ready to fight their way into the picture and demand their place.

In Egr's work, aggressively claiming an empowered subjectivity and social positionality is not done at the expense of others. The feminist masculinity depicted in Egr's characters (and enacted by Egr herself) is not empowering because it can be wielded against "hos" and "homos" in an effort to claim or maintain power in a social hierarchy. The coolness of their masculine pose is not fueled by hegemonic heteropatriarchal masculinity, but by a complex version of feminist ideology—a self-proclaimed entitlement to equal space and a confrontational attitude fending off anyone who would challenge that claim.[35] In order to recognize that claim, and take it seriously, we have to flip the script whereby cisgender women are cast as victims of Hip Hop masculinity, *forced* to act like men against their implicitly "natural" gender inclination. Masculinity is a gender performance that graff grrlz throughout the diaspora stylize to assert presence and demand subcultural belonging to transnational graffiti culture. We have to shift our thinking so that the problem is not that masculinity is the primary mode of visibility (and the scapegoat for the sexism within Hip Hop culture), but where or on whom that masculinity is given credence and value as a felicitous performance. Certainly the iconic Hip Hop body is more than mere fantasy and the effects of the performance more than mere hype—critiques that recognize the oppressive aspects of dominant Hip Hop masculinity are crucial—but the negative effects are not intrinsic to the performance of masculine gender characteristics.[36]

Egr's "Army Girls" series depicts various female figures firing machine guns, wielding knives, and carrying spears while running and driving tanks through postapocalyptic war zones. In a 2015 interview with Fresh Paint Gallery, in reference to the series, she was asked what women should be fighting for:

> Aside from basic equality and freedom from violence, which is a lifelong
> battle on its own; we should first be fighting against societal pressures that

may hinder our confidence, abilities and achievement. I believe that the concept that women are inferior and nothing more than objects and child bearers began as a colonial tale, fabricated to give control back to men, as accusations of witchcraft emerged. I feel that if women were eager, hungrier and felt more deserving of positions of authority, our world might have a chance at being a safer, more harmonious and prosperous place. Here's a bold statement, it is mainly men that create and perpetuate war, and we need to use our influence and power to try to better the world or at least try; no matter what gender we happen to relate to.[37]

The militarism celebrated in the "Army Girls" series, or my claims to and about feminist masculinity, will certainly not appeal to those who prefer pacifism. But when we allow characteristics that are popularly recognized as "masculine" to belong to men, or rather to be understood only through Western heteropatriarchal gender conventions, we relinquish the political potential in aggressiveness, confrontation, deviation, and assertiveness—traits that are requisite in any struggle for liberation.

To counter positions of social and subcultural subjugation, graff grrlz like Egr perform the hard of Hip Hop masculinity. Other writers and passersby might not recognize graff grrlz' unconventional gender performances because gender can disappear through letters, handstyle, and color choices and also viewers have been taught to understand graffiti as a form of vandalism perpetrated by troubled boys of color from disenfranchised urban areas. Not one to let her gender difference go unmarked, or have her hard-earned claim to place in Hip Hop appropriated, Egr infuses her characters with feminist masculinity and in doing so exhibits her "confidence, abilities and achievement" as a graffiti *grrl*.

Ivey (Australia)

Writing in Australia since 1999, Ivey is a Hip Hop head who, aside from the forty-ounce beer in her hand and the extra-large textured hoop earrings, looks like "the girl next door." She was attracted to the culture through her self-motivated research into various media—books like "*Spraycan Art, Subway Art* and films like *Beat Street* and *Wildstyle*."[38] She took the inspiration for her tag name from a comic book supervillain, Batman's arch enemy Poison Ivy, who utilizes the assumed conventional femininity imposed upon her to her advantage. The character Poison Ivy shares qualities with Egr's Army Girl characters; both are fitting caricatures for "rebellious, determined, artistic, creative, socially aware, eternally young at heart, innovative, risk taking, street smart, ambitious, bad ass" graff grrlz.

Ivey describes her graffiti as akin to "New York public style" that is embellished with "elements of cartoon and tattoo culture." Her letters are funky yet legible, capitalized, and always finished with some combination of bubbles, bows, or stars—elemental patterns she considers "cute" and "feminine." She does not proclaim herself a feminist, but neither does she deny her feminist philosophies as she "most definitely believe[s] in, identif[ies] with, live[s] by and support[s] many feminist beliefs and ideals." While her graffiti art does not always have an overtly political message, the act of writing itself carries for her a "social message [about] equality, freedom, rebellion"—characteristics that resemble, at first glance, the "girl power" enacted by the "active, freely choosing, self-regulating" neoliberal postfeminist subject.[39] Like Are2's freight-train graffiti, Ivey's graffiti art reveals her negotiations with the discourse of "girl power" uprooted from U.S. "Third Wave" feminism (think Riot Grrrl) in the '90s and brought into mainstream popular culture in the early 2000s (think Spice Girls, Buffy, the Powerpuff Girls).[40] As I argued earlier, claiming that graff grrlz' performances of masculinity categorically escape the seductive narrative of postfeminist girl power would be a misrepresentation. It is more productive to conceptualize their feminist masculinity as an ongoing negotiation where graff grrlz enact masculinity to resist subcultural subordination and to navigate capitalist subjection. Graffiti grrlz understand that the "power" in girl power has been instrumentalized by capitalistic individualism and consumerism, and they have experienced how that power is limited by privilege (based on race, class, sexuality, and nationality) and allotted to those who perform femininity "properly."

An analysis of Ivey's piece *Real Chicks Paint, Fake Chicks Talk* exemplifies how graffiti grrlz' performances of masculinity differ from the masculinity offered to the postfeminist girl-power subject. The public-style letters of her tag name are outlined with a thin not-to-be-missed cherry red line, complemented by a thick maroon for depth, filled with three gradations of slate blue, and adorned with dots and five-point

Figure 1.5. Ivey, *Real Chicks Paint, Fake Chicks Talk*, Sydney, Australia, 2012. Photo courtesy Ivey.

stars. The top of the "E" in Ivey is cracked as if the composition of the word has challenged the elasticity of that individual letter. The style of *Real Chicks Paint, Fake Chicks Talk* is typical for Ivey, but the "caption" is what sets it apart; in both phrases, the word "Chicks" shares that same bold cherry red color. The piece is a harsh but poignant message for other graff grrlz—there are real chicks and there are fake chicks. Fake chicks take the bargain, the new deal; they excel at dismissing generations of feminist labor and revel in their celebrated tokenization without putting in the work. The choice between them, the piece implies, is yours. Ivey calls out to them: Want to be taken seriously? Do your work. Be real. Paint. Do not accept some fake version of girl power; make your own power.

When she hops a fence and tags her name on public spaces, Ivey is taking a risk and enacting deviant behavior; she is performing feminist acts of resistance against the constrictions of traditional Western white "womanhood" (i.e., passive, delicate, virtuous, domestic, moral, obedient, seen not heard, etc.). She is resisting the culture that defines her worth by how she measures up to the limits of conventional femininity. The kind of femininity that graff grrlz like Ivey perform transgresses norms and menaces expectations because it is performed in tandem with the feminist masculinity the grrlz have learned via graffiti writing. "Femininity is a demand put on female bodies," a demand that graff grrlz reject and reconfigure, whether they identify as "chicks" or not.[41] The feminine performance allotted to girls and women via a postfeminist neoliberal promise operates under "a new sexual contract . . . which encourages activity concentrated in education and employment so as to ensure participation in the production of successful femininity, sexuality and eventually maternity."[42] To be successful, girls and women must take the deal whereby they reject the tenets of feminism (resisting capitalism, colonially imposed gender binaries, hetero/sexism, and the reproductive demands of heteronormative time) in favor of performing a femininity activated by "Powerpuff girl power."[43] Acting more like her namesake Poison Ivy than the more popular Blossom, Ivey does not take that deal. She claims and performs an alternative femininity informed by feminist masculinity with her choice of tag name, the utilization of feminized signs and symbols (like hearts and stars) in her graffiti, and the outright call for realness to her graff grrl peers.

Ivey feels a sense of pride when she sees her graffiti up; her tag is a sign that she owns "a small piece" of her city. Being a graffiti writer provides her with access to one anonymous space where her work will be evaluated based on execution and dedication rather than popularity, gender presentation, or social standing. Hip Hop culture is largely defined by the expectation that participants use the elements of writing, dancing, rapping, and so on as a means of getting by in an ever-oppressive and isolating social environment—a narrative summarized by the phrase so often used to describe Hip Hop's development within a devastating economic context: that practitioners made "something out of nothing." Because of her activity in the subcultural world, Ivey is better equipped to manage the mainstream world. The masculine characteristics required for Ivey to be a writer transfer into survival strategies for everyday living. She credits her involvement with graffiti culture for getting her through "a challenging family environment," for motivating her to continue her education after high school, and for helping her get through the drudgery of a 9-to-5 job. Painting is a creative outlet, a "limitless passion," a space where she can feel "determined and focused yet cautious and aware"; it gives her a "rush of adrenalin" and "a sense of purpose, contentment and belonging." The mental and physical requirements of being a graffiti writer opened a world of limitless possibility for Ivey, a risky and rebellious world where she can explore her creativity and is empowered to express the many aspects of her identity.

Jerk LA (USA)

Jerk LA is a Chicana from Los Angeles who "always had an interest in art in general, including fonts," after attending "a lot of free after school art classes."[44] As a young, working-class teenager, she started getting up on the concrete flood-control channels of the Los Angeles River— hitting spots that are impossible today because the space is so policed. California has some of the strictest graffiti legislation and penalties in the United States because of the notorious gang-related graffiti, which predates Hip Hop graffiti culture in Los Angeles by decades. Jerk has been a member of a few crews throughout her graff career, but she now runs with CBS—a crew out of Hollywood that has been around since the 1980s.

Her graffiti varies in style; she explained that she gets "bored doing the same letters or color schemes and composition," but she does favor styles within particular genres. Her public letters are plump and crisp as opposed to her wildstyle letters, which are elongated and stretched like elastic, sometimes serpentine and true to the genre, difficult if not impossible for nonwriters to read (www.facebook.com/Jerk.LA213). She realizes this, agreeing that her "style will always look like [hers] but," she explained, "I definitely try to change it up and push myself to do better than my last piece, almost as if I am in a competition with myself." Jerk makes sure her graffiti identity does not feel stale or predictable, but instead fluid and variable.

In the 2013 short film *Jerk: Female Graffiti Legend*, directed by Eric Minh Swenson, YouTube visitors have the rare opportunity to see how this "competition with self" plays out.[45] Staged in a small, sparse white-walled bathroom in Chinatown, Los Angeles, the video opens with Jerk putting on a mask and talking about her graffiti career. When she started writing, she was "just fucking around," she quips. "It was no change-the-world bullshit."[46] She remains sequestered in this room throughout the interview. With a handful of different color and width markers in the sink, Jerk begins tagging her name all over the walls; some of the markers drip in excess of the boundaries of the letters. The image she is going over, or adding to, depending on your perspective, goes unremarked—the pencil-drawn vulva floating above the toilet is mere background. The questions asked are edited out. Her answers are stitched together throughout the three minutes in a way that disorients the viewer in time because the amount of tags does not follow a logical trajectory of less to more.

Later, with a markedly confused and surprised tone, she states "my favorite color? . . . I don't think I have a favorite color." Immediately following the question about color (which has gendered implications), Jerk is asked about gender in graffiti. Likely because her gender was hidden by her tag name for most of her career, she had never been asked questions particular to or informed by gender difference. Because "in most things, women are judged," Jerk took advantage of the opportunity afforded by a tag name to remain anonymous.[47] She did not want to "give away" her gender. After an adolescence of others trying to make her feel "inferior" by leveling statements such as "you run like a girl, or you this or that like a girl," the expressly not-feminist Jerk put in the affective labor of gender anonymity in order to be received fairly and her work was judged for years without gender bias. Now that other writers know who she is, she is glad she took advantage of the fact that "graffiti allows you to exist without a profile picture."[48] The tag name Jerk obfuscates her gender, but it is not an androgynous choice: it has a male "masculine" connotation, with synonyms that include brute (in the noun form) and (as a verb) to lurch, resist, combat, repel, buck. You can be a jerk, act like a jerk, and jerk someone around. You can also sound like a jerk. When Jerk speaks in this video, her tone is surly and often unapologetically profane.

As she answers the questions, she tags over her own tags, repeatedly, excessively: as if with each placement of the marker to the wall she is saying, "I am here. I am here. I am here. Not for your pleasure, but for mine." Acts such as this "register" as excessive in comparison to racialized, classed, and gendered notions of propriety, but they are *required* by graffiti subculture—one *must* produce one's self in excess—be egotistical, be noticed, be unruly, be dangerous, be "hyper," be in the places that good citizen-subjects do not go (e.g., dark alleys, dirty tunnels, underground), and do things that good citizens do not do (e.g., vandalize, disobey).[49] Her masculine gender performance in the sexist subcultural space of Hip Hop graffiti subculture—signified chiefly by engaging in an arts practice that aggressively takes place in public illegally—activates an alternative Latina subjectivity that revisits and re-values stereotypes about Latinas, particularly in relation to the value of our excessiveness. Meeting the expectation of excess for writers, which is grounded in the hetero/sexist social expectation that "boys will be boys," allows Jerk to outmaneuver these repressive stereotypes. Jerk's feminist masculinity does its work against sexism within graffiti subculture, but also as a performance of excess—*as a Chicana writer*—it allows her to embody a Latina subjectivity that complicates knowability in relationship to respectability and propriety.[50]

The expectation of *disciplined excess* within Hip Hop graffiti subculture, by which I mean the purposeful and repetitive performance of "too much," emerges from a working-class Afro-Caribbean affective social economy, one that differs greatly from the white supremacist narratives demanding the performance of restraint and respectability in order to access middle-class normativity, privilege, and place. The only way to escape the material consequences of reproducing these stereotypes and narratives about being "over the top," Latinxs are told to whitewash their excessive selves; they must be quiet, be respectable, be obedient: *cálmate* (calm yourself).[51] But as an active graffiti writer, Jerk abides by very different value systems and thus activates an alternative Latina feminist potentiality not only within the sexist subcultural space of Hip Hop graffiti subculture, but also against problematic representations reproduced about Latinxs by mainstream culture.

The video begins with Jerk refusing the audience a clear or "full" picture of her face, of her refusing knowability—another enactment of self that is foundational to illegal graffiti practice. Once layered, the individual (and legible) tags written on the surface of this bathroom with varying degrees of pressure applied—a thick peach-colored JERK, an almost translucent white thin JERK, a drippy cobalt-blue JERK with a curly cue, a black and angular JERK finished with an arrow—become messy, chaotic, illegible. The multiple layers through which she performs subjectivity make clarity in regards to her identity an impossible project. The video ends with her assertion that "by the time that *that* comes around about knowing who I am as far as gender, it becomes irrelevant." In her usage of the term "irrelevant," I read a confrontational assertion, an instance where again the performance of surliness obfuscates what we think we might know about her as a person, as a writer, as a Chicana. Her multiple performances of excess seduce the viewer into thinking we will finally know her, but in the end we are left with a partial knowing. Jerk's embodied excess—her feminist masculinity—redeploys the discourse of being "too much" away from the negative connotations of being Latina, indeed away from the negation of the possibility to enact a Latina subjectivity on its own terms.

Motel7 (South Africa)

"I don't think I paint 'like a girl.' I always try to defy that."[52] Sitting on the second-floor outdoor balcony at BeerHouse in downtown Cape Town on a perfect January day, Motel7—a Norwegian-English graff grrl down with the 40HK crew—first described her place in the city's graffiti community in relation to gender and then in terms of race. When she goes bombing, she dresses androgynously because it is "safer when going into dangerous situations without any obvious femininity." In addition to the safety that androgyny provides on the streets while painting, keeping her gender hidden shielded her from being treated and received differently by other writers. So while she enjoyed the fact that "people couldn't believe" that Motel7 "was a girl" at first, the loss of gender anonymity quickly became a hindrance. With skepticism in their voices, people began asking her questions such as how she received invitations to paint at high-profile jams (insinuating she must have pulled some strings); how she ended up painting with well-known writers (insinuating she was not up to par); or how she completed a complex piece quickly (insinuating she must have had help). At each turn, she has had to assert herself: "No guys helped me. The way I paint. And the way I approach a wall and be in that kind of environment . . . I can be sweet and girly and cute and that side of me falls away and I take my graffiti very seriously. I'm not here for a little side thing 'cause my boyfriend does it. This is my life and it's been my life for years and years. I'm obsessed with it."

She eventually stopped doing interviews because she kept receiving "girl questions": "I was tired of them and annoyed that everyone else was getting interesting questions." When I approached Motel7 in 2009 about interviewing for this project, she did not respond; perhaps my email looked too much like another person trying to ask her "girl questions." When graff grrlz agree to my interviews, more often than not, they are quick to explain they will not answer "questions for girls" about favorite colors or (believe it or not) bra size.[53] On the verge of my research trip to South Africa four years later—with a more careful understanding of how to navigate this "girl question" dynamic—I sent another email. In this version, I explained my project and dropped a lengthy list of graff grrl names, names of grrlz she was connected to, like Faith47 and Sany.

Writing was an escape from the world of modeling and beauty pageants that shaped Motel7's adolescence. When she first began in 2003, she tagged "Misty," hoping to "hold on to something" about her identity while she did "a very male masculine thing." Grrlz often start out identifying their gender by name or by painting "a fairy, or a heart, or flowers" instead of letters (more on this in chapter 5). But once she realized the thrill and power of anonymity, that she "could have this secret identity. . . . I kind of escaped into this world of people not knowing who I am." In addition to "Motel7" she wrote "Steak" for a while, saying "it doesn't get more masculine than steak. I think even the style was a little more rough." Motel7 feels that she changes her gender persona when she is painting: "I think I lose a little bit of my femininity when I paint. I stand differently. I paint the wall differently. I'm much more confident. I'm much more myself." I would like to suggest that what she loses, or better, what she let has go of when she is at the wall is not her feminine self, but rather that socially acceptable version of gender expression that forecloses the possibility that femininity could be performed alongside masculinity, in the same person at the same time.

Motel7's pieces all but assault the viewer with brightly colored geometric letters that are deconstructed to the point of animation. In the place of the "o," there is usually a character resembling one of the ghosts from PacMan with a face like a puppy, bringing humor, youth, and accessibility to the image. Her canvas work is strikingly different in affect from her graffiti letters, but you can locate the masculine and the feminine in both styles. While her letters are alive and joyful, her canvas paintings are composed mostly of excessively accessorized doll-like figures wearing Victorian-style dresses and ornamented by skulls and candy. Their big eyes seem to reach into dark souls, with a kind of Tim Burton-esque animated depression—too dark to be cute, but too cute to be dark (www.facebook.com/motelseven). "Most girls are not going to get their hands dirty and get up in the middle of the night," but as a self-described "tough, naughty" girl, graffiti writing is an activity to which she is well suited. "I think that's why graffiti stuck with me because it allowed me to have this strange identity I didn't have to explain to everyone. It was just my own. Just my little secret. It was such an escape." Like Ivey, what Motel7 escapes from through her graffiti writing is the pressure of normative, white Western femininity, and the social and political limitations grrlz experience because of their gender. The escape gives her a place to enjoy her little secret—that she is different from other girls.

Graffiti not only provides a subcultural space where she can express that gender complexity, but also where she can be proud of it—a space that provides her with self-worth and value through unalienated labor toward a more just society. Motel7 is one of a handful of active grrlz in the street art scene (including Faith47 and Nard Star), and she is one of the first white grrlz to paint Hip Hop graffiti in postapartheid South Africa (www.motelseven.com).[54] Through the invitation of friends who live there, Motel7 paints in townships, including Khayelitsha, Langa, and Cape Flats (the latter she described as "predominantly people of mixed race, often the forgotten race in South Africa"). Painting in the townships was "extremely dangerous" for her "as a white person . . . and even more so as a woman." Out of respect for the residents, and their continued race-based socioeconomic disenfranchisement and geographical displacement, Motel7 did not paint in the townships unaccompanied. She explained that "usually if we were going to go into the townships we'd go with Falko, who was well known locally, and we never had any problems, or with a friend of mine from Khayelitsha, who didn't paint."[55] Graffiti writers claim public space—that is part of the impetus—but as a white woman painting in a predominantly black township marked by a critical lack in resources perpetuated by systemic negligence under the ongoing effects of European settler colonialism, painting in these spaces was an entirely different gesture. Painting without local permission would be another kind of colonization, and Motel7 wants no part of that. "Painting in the townships had a sense of community, they were mostly friendly, and grateful for us painting their homes. They were proud of their places, and I think they saw us as decorating their homes into something unique." As part of a campaign to teach children about water conservation in townships across Cape Town, funded by the local councils, Motel7 painted murals in every school the group visited (while b-boys danced and actors performed skits). Offering her artistry to these communities for sociopolitical reasons, Motel7 enacted antiracist feminist activism through her graffiti writing.

While Motel7 is ambivalent about "the feminist thing," when she paints, she exerts self-described "female confidence." As the years passed and her skills developed, she noticed that she "can paint almost faster and better than most guys. I find that they find it intimidating and they don't know how to deal with it"—it bruises their egos. All writers have big egos when it comes to their graffiti personas—they have to; it is part of the confidence needed to get up and get over. But an elevation of ego has different effects on graff grrlz. To outsiders, it can be offensive, "bitchy" even. But when you are trained to squash your ego, as so many girls are throughout their lives, having a healthy ego is a good thing. Feminist masculinity undoes the training to make your self smaller, to become the "shrinking violet" with no self-worth, and instead demands that graff grrlz show off, strut their stuff, puff out their chests, and make their selves big enough to get up and get over.

Feminist Masculinity Takes Balls

I'm not the old school '70s hairy armpit, man-hating kind [of feminist]. I call myself a militant post-feminist. I embrace my femininity and sexuality, I don't hate all men . . . we should all be equal and go about doing a good job in anything regardless of our gender, not be afraid to speak up and if I want to wear a short skirt and lipstick to feel sexy, then I will! The militant part is because graffiti is a militant form of self-expression, as is my explicit rap and my loud, strong demeanor. In a way I've always thought me being dedicated to writing for so long is "revenge on a male dominated society."

You dis me, my styles and question why I'm writing, then
I'm never gonna stop as revenge on your/society's ideas.
—Queen MCTash

Based out of Queensland, Australia, and the editor of the (unfortunately) short-lived Hip Hop magazine *Hell Yeah*, Queen MCTash has been writing since 1991. She describes her graffiti as "funky public lettering," an easy-to-read style that she uses to "resist . . . the government, how society thinks women should act, conformity, the mainly sexist, dumb assholes in the Australian hip hop/graf scene, religion, fascism, the cops, and corruption."[56] When asked how she defines herself in relation to feminism, Queen MCTash uses the phrase "militant post-feminist" to indicate her conscious distancing from earlier versions of feminism associated with separatism; the use of the qualifier "post" here signals an epistemological break with feminism that also extends to her relationship with "the mainly sexist" Hip Hop scene in Australia.[57] In *Crimes of Style: Urban Graffiti and the Politics of Criminality*, Jeff Ferrell emphasizes how individuals gain a sense of both autonomy and community through graffiti writing because the genre's aesthetics are developed both individually and collectively.[58] The dialectical process between self and community allows individual prestige to accumulate not through mimesis, but through repetition dependent on innovative improvisation—or, in the words of the Hip Hop scholars Joan Morgan and Mark Anthony Neal, "Hip-hop pays reverence to and acknowledges its influences, but it does not necessarily conform to what those influences want it to be."[59] Like other graffiti grrlz, Queen MCTash is well aware that in Hip Hop, visibility and recognition depend on performances of masculinity, but the ways in which she performs that masculinity is anything but mimetic. Graffiti grrlz like Queen MCTash "militantly" resist conformity, sending a "message . . . that girls can be as dope/cool/hardcore as guys."

In an effort to assess the contemporary validity of her 2001 thesis in regards to masculinity and graffiti subculture, in "Something for the Boys? Exploring the Changing Gender Dynamics of the Graffiti Subculture," Nancy Macdonald asks if the Internet and the rise in street art might have "softened the boundaries of the subculture and invited more women to enter and participate." After briefly revisiting her original claims, she argues that because street art does not demand the performance of masculinity "the street art scene [is] an easier place for women to reside" and that "however the internet has benefitted women writing, it is ultimately going to benefit male writers too."[60] I analyze how the Internet has changed graff grrlz' experiences of, and place within, the subculture at length in chapter 3, but it is important to note that her declaration that the usage of social media, smartphones, and so on, equally benefits men flattens critical distinctions—the most obvious of which is the pre-Internet context that largely influences the "benefits." In my chapter for the same handbook, "Ways of Being Seen: Gender and the Writing on the Wall," I address the "masculinity is for graffiti, femininity is for street art" discourse directly.

> Scholars and documentarians of graffiti writing and street art have noted that more women tend to participate in street art (Ganz, 2006), rather than graffiti writing, because of the following: The juridical designation of street art as "art" versus graffiti as vandalism (the assumption being that women are less likely to participate in criminal behavior); the preparation of stickers, stencils, and posters in the private domain prior to being affixed to public surfaces (the assumption being that women are naturally inclined to be more comfortable in the safety of the private sphere); and the lack of an investment in "making masculinity" (the assumption being that women do not have the desire to exercise masculine behaviors) (Macdonald, 2001). These ideas, developed over time and in relationship to graffiti writing/street art history, have exacerbated the numerical minority status of female participants and grossly underestimated and over generalized their realities, desires, and potential.[61]

Organizing Hip Hop graffiti and street art along a strict gender binary is reductive to the art forms and patronizing (at best) to the participants. Reinscribing the "boys will be boys" narrative once again, Macdonald concludes her essay with a provocation I believe to be a sincere effort on her part to make space for women in the subculture: "Can masculinity be constructed alongside women writers without the need to physically and symbolically exclude their presence?"[62] Intentions aside, her inquiry can only produce a fruitful answer that is more representative of reality if we replace the "alongside" in the question with "along with." The hard of Hip Hop graffiti is what attracts graffiti grrlz; they are not waiting for an invitation, and they certainly do not want the subcultural boundaries to be "softened." Appreciating that graffiti grrlz are women who perform Hip Hop masculinity through graffiti writing requires an understanding that they are improvising and transforming gender performance through Hip Hop culture. Graffiti grrlz utilize the subcultural space of graffiti culture to "nourish, amplify, and salvage notions of masculinity," but the way in which they do so does not resist equity.[63]

Dominant Hip Hop masculinity is represented as a stubborn independence, a stoic singularity, an autonomous subjectivity that reads as tough and callous (Hip Hop's hard), simultaneously celebrated and criticized for the oppressive power it wields over women (be they straight, queer, cis, or trans). In contrast, feminist masculinity is characterized by a radical interdependence that challenges one to be better, steadfast, spontaneous, agile, bold, hard, and relentless—not at the expense of others, but for the empowerment of self and others. Graffiti grrlz break with the oppressive implications of heteropatriarchal masculinity by performing an empowering masculinity: a feminist masculinity. Rather than reproducing oppressive masculinity, hegemonic feminism, or a politically sterilized postfeminism, graff grrlz improvise—they take risks, deviate from norms, perform cool, heighten their alert levels, add something new, and play with the traits of masculinity to demand their place.

In reference to the power of Hip Hop culture, Michael Jeffries claims "cultural production has the potential to trouble social norms and dominant discourses" even if "there is nothing essentially revolutionary or progressive about hip-hop, despite its beginnings as the product of marginalized people."[64] Performances of feminist masculinity bring the most fundamental social, cultural, and aesthetic aspects of Hip Hop culture and feminist movement together. Because graffiti grrlz enact the basics of feminist movement—using their feminist masculinity to demand equity in terms of space and ownership through the cultivation of community—we must begin, as I do in the next chapter, conceptualizing them as actors in transnational feminist movement. Aggressive, competitive, independent, and confident performances of feminist masculinity throughout the diaspora activate the effects of Hip Hop's met potential, incrementally changing the dynamics of a hetero/sexist male-dominated subculture. Now this is a masculinity to celebrate, one that truly does take balls.

2

Doing Feminist Community without "Feminist" Identity

In my group, the only thing I'm in search of is the empowering of females in graffiti.
—La Kyd (Nicaragua)

Women as a group, or by ourselves, have overcome the things
that women are not supposed to do. I feel liberated now. I am
a feminist because I can do those things as a woman.
—Alma (Chile)

"I began experimenting with painting in 1999 and I take breaks only
when it is necessary to prioritize caring for my daughter."[1] Moments
after we sit down in her Santiago apartment, Chilean graffitera Solitas
is beckoned by the unmistakable sound of the Notorious B.I.G.'s "Big
Poppa" on her cellphone. As if on cue, the demands of motherhood take
precedent and we head out to pick up her daughter. Sitting at a restaurant a couple of hours later, the avowed anarchist explains that she
and her friends were exposed to graffiti subculture as an element of Hip
Hop alongside rap music. Making sure to first highlight the egalitar-
ian ethics of her current graffiti crew (Doce Brillos), she added that she
experienced resistance from "everyone" in her earliest years of painting (2003–2008). The standard sentiment then was that "*la mujer no
puede*"—women, they told her, cannot paint.

> Everybody thinks that! I became very critical about my position [as a
> woman], I was always thinking about women and about the discrimina-
> tion we encounter just because we are women. I paint to fight the re-
> sistance against girls doing graffiti. Everybody says women can't paint
> graffiti and I say NO—there are other women in other places who feel
> the same as I do. . . . Because *more and more* girls started painting, the
> boys are used to it now. Still today, here in Chile anyway, the men don't
> consider us *real* competition.

Figure 2.1. Solitas, Santiago, Chile, 2014. Photo courtesy Solitas.

Solitas attributes the social-subcultural attitude shift—from negative to neutral—to the "multiplication" of graffiti grrlz, grrlz who "feel the same" as she does about graffiti painting as an act of defiance in a heteropatriarchal subculture.

> I think that a woman has to be a *guerrera*! A fighter! A warrior! Women are always fighting—she is going to work, she is taking care of kids, she has to do all of these things. . . . And that is why I consider myself a fighter. I fight for equality. I fight the government! I fight for a better place to live. I fight for environmental issues. I fight for a mountain of things!

Instantly connecting with the energy she manifested when speaking about her activism, her liberation, and her struggles as a woman, I asked Solitas if she considered herself a feminist. "Am I *just* a feminist? [shaking her head] No, but I think men and women are equal." The spark that had ignited between us temporarily faded. What did it mean to be "just" a feminist, I wondered? In her conceptualization, the boundaries of the word could not contain her or the "mountain of things" she fights for daily. For me, feminism is the reason I can see the mountain of things worth fighting for; feminist movement gave me the tools to examine and deconstruct the white supremacist heteropatriarchal system and build a path to liberation. In that moment, the bridge connecting our commitments revealed itself to be built on a false premise and I had to check my U.S.-based queer Latina feminist expectations. I expected an affirmation based on our conversation, our shared enthusiasm, and our laughter. Prior to her utterance I imagined we were in sync as "feminists." Consequently, due to the politics of identification, in the moment of her disavowal the power line connecting us went down temporarily; or, rather, it was "let down."[2]

I begin this chapter on performing feminist community without feminist identity with Solitas for two reasons: (1) to share in writing the visceral experience I had as a feminist ethnographer whose desires, expectations, hopes, and frameworks for understanding were fundamentally challenged each time a graff grrl discounted feminism; and (2) to illustrate a significant tension built into the central argument of this book: graffiti grrlz provide an alternative perspective on the current state of transnational feminist movement and the potential in contemporary performances of feminism throughout the Hip Hop diaspora but the majority of the grrlz do not identify with the word "feminist" or as part of feminist movement. By the time I met Solitas, in August 2010, I had grown accustomed to holding space for the difference between my perception of graffiti grrlz as feminists and their rejection of the term. In one of my earliest interview sessions (in 2004), in reference to the fact that many graff grrlz do not claim feminist identities, ClawMoney explained that being a feminist graffiti writer meant "just being about it." I did not put too much thought into Claw's distinction at the time; rather than developing a particular methodology to navigate that difference, I purposefully left it bare. In the years I had spent researching graffiti grrlz' aesthetics, social dynamics, history, and politics, I could not integrate the full force of that difference until my fieldwork trip to Chile and Brazil where all-grrl crew formations were (relatively) common.

My initial thoughts on all-grrl crews were heavily influenced by my locale in the United States, specifically New York City, where the complicated subcultural dynamics of ownership, history, illegality, trust, and competition seem to affect writers to a greater degree; graff grrlz in the United States generally do not form all-grrl crews (the exceptions—as of 2017—being PMS and Few and Far). The sexualization, tokenization, and marginalization of graff grrlz breed a culture of misogyny that affects how these women relate to one another. Many of the writers I interviewed revealed their fear of being associated with weaker writers (read: other women and toys), their distaste for women rumored to be writing graffiti solely to gain sexual attention from male peers ("jocks"), and their disdain for women who exploit their minority status for "instant" fame (refer to chapter 1 on these last points).[3] All grrlz, per this logic, are suspect. Within this subcultural context, graff grrlz who participate in all-grrl crews jeopardize the respect and reputation they have earned from their peers.

Actively rejecting the misogynistic dynamic where graff grrlz are suspect is a revolutionary feminist act—the commonality of all-grrl crews does not simply amend the status quo (e.g., grrlz are not suspect, nor are they competition). Instead it creates a new politics of relation between graffiti grrlz and a standard for other writers to reproduce. Rather than expecting other grrlz to be "weak" writers, jocks, or exploiters, the graffiteras I will discuss in this chapter—Rede Nami (Rio de Janeiro), Crazis Crew (Santiago), and Turronas Crew (Santiago)—expect strength, commitment, and comradery. Except for Nami (which has become a nongovernmental organization [NGO] connected to transnational feminist movement), these graffiteras are not directly tied to the feminist movements in their countries, but their grassroots efforts are affected by earlier generations of guerrilleras, feminist activists, and revolutionaries.[4] They embody feminist ideologies in their all-grrl crew-making and community-building efforts. They build fierce community, and they do so largely without feminist identity and independent of transnational feminist movement.

The primary lesson about the importance of "getting up" is not limited to the act of writing graffiti; getting up is a subcultural ethos guiding writers' behavior in general. For a writer to be a writer, they must get up—actions over words. Or, in Claw's refrain, do not talk about it, be about it. Integrating this ethos, the question of who is or is not a feminist becomes secondary to what feminist actions are being taken in the subculture. Feminism is part of the performance of their everyday lives despite not always being their mode of self-identification. It was in these two countries, Brazil and Chile, that I accepted the fundamental and provocative reality that we need not call ourselves feminists to enact feminist change in the world.[5]

Rede Nami (Feminist Urban Arts Collective, Brazil)

"You must come to Brazil, I will show you." Anarkia Boladona was adamant. In the brief but informative hours when we first met face-to-face at the Diane von Furstenberg Studios in 2010 in New York, I realized her tenacity was fueled by a desire to share what she calls "her work"—her graffiti art and her personal mission to train graffiteras who "think like" feminists. Later that year, I was in Rio de Janeiro. From the moment we embraced at the airport, Anarkia (Kia) began feverishly detailing my itinerary. I was going to see "parts of Rio tourists do not see" and know everything there was to know about the organization she had founded several months earlier, Rede Nami.

Figure 2.2. Anarkia Boladona, Rio de Janeiro, Brazil, 2010.

Kia began her writing career in 2000 as a pixadora—a type of street artist who writes pixação (a thin, monochromatic, and illegible form of writing reminiscent of hieroglyphics and created by writers in Brazil). Pixação is associated with the "hardest" of street artists willing to scale a building's façade to paint a fresh tag over a window (or over *all* the windows); pixadoras go to great lengths to reach "impossible" walls, risking onsite execution by paramilitary forces (not uncommon for pixadors/as). She chose the tag name Anarkia and used a modified anarchy symbol for her pixação, "because [it] sounded like a symbol of freedom and rebellion."[6] The second part, Boladona, "is slang [for] an angry person with power who does not accept being down. And my images [have] the face of 'boladona' to express power." She integrated what she considers a Hip Hop style around 2005: "I am from Hip Hop, I have to represent my world in it. I believe in the essential ideas of Hip Hop and here in Rio de Janeiro [it is] used against war, drugs and all sorts of problems generated by our current society." In his 2008 ethnography of Hip Hop culture in Brazil, *Brazilian Hip Hoppers Speak from the Margins,* Derek Pardue argues that, "for the most part, feminism in Brazilian hip hop has been limited to a discourse of 'inclusion' rather than one of epistemological 'critique' . . . while Brazilian hip hoppers take aim on criticizing and opposing much of what 'the system' offers in the way of race, class, socio-geography, national history, and art, they seem to turn the other cheek with regard to gender critique."[7] Representing "her part" in her Hip Hop community meant bringing that feminist epistemological critique to structures that oppress and dominate girls and women, not just through words but through actions rooted in aesthetics. Kia has mastered the gamut of graffiti genres—characters, tags, throw-ups, and productions—but her characters' faces are how I came to interview her. In her earlier years, her characters had this intense look about them; they stared directly at you. They were hard and serious; they not only returned the gaze, but also initiated it. Today, her characters have a more ethereal and expansive quality; one character's hair knotted together with an equally enchanted mirror image while both initiate the gaze in true boladona style.

Rede Nami is a feminist urban arts collective with an official membership of approximately thirty women and an extended network of more than 500 girls and women who participate in their programming. Nami has a three-part vision: "using art as a promotional tool for women's rights"; "fostering female leadership in urban culture"; and "creative economy and economic empowerment of women."[8] One of Nami's most consistent efforts has been to teach women living in favelas about Brazil's Maria de Penha law (legislation enacted to reduce violence against women) through lectures and public mural painting.[9]

According to their 2014 annual report, since Nami's founding in 2010, at least 5,000 girls and women have participated in their actions and over 50,000 individuals are connected to their social networking campaigns. At the time of my visit, the collective was a mere three months young, but Anarkia had been actively engaged in social justice work through urban arts for approximately three years prior to founding Nami. In her eyes, Nami is the next generation of feminist graffiti activism in Rio, following in the footsteps of TPM and under the mentorship of Prima Donna (see chapter 4).

After meeting and working with Prima, Anarkia began to see the oppression around her—on both personal and social/institutional levels. She began to think about the domestic abuse she had survived and how her motivation to "just keep painting" earned her status as a respected graffitera, not just in Brazil but increasingly around the world. Although founded as a grassroots collective, Nami was run from the outset "like a feminist business," where hierarchy is utilized for organizational purposes. Anarkia always intended for Nami to become an NGO. She realized this dream in 2012 (the same year *Newsweek* named her one of "150 Fearless Women in the World"), and she manages the organization with an expanded governing structure (a president, vice president, three directors, and ten consultants) supported financially with the assistance of VitalVoices Global Partnership, UNWomen, and the Avon Institute. When she explained her vision to me, she stopped, looked me directly in the eyes, and spoke with such sincerity that I was moved to tears:

> How can we sleep at night when women all over are being beat to death every day? I thought that, with my visibility and status, I could help the other girls fight against discrimination and make society more equal. When they start with Nami, a lot of the girls don't know what feminism is, but over time they start to think about what feminism is, they remember what they have done and experienced, and then they come to believe, they come to feminism on their own.

Nami is not a conventional graffiti "crew," though its leaders are graf-fiteras. Not all Nami's members are feminists, though its founder is one of the most vociferous feminists I know. Anarkia founded Nami as a collective open to anyone willing to learn and not just play around with paint—to paint with the group attendance at a lecture or workshop is mandatory. Rede Nami builds their feminist political community upon an aesthetic base; members enter the organization not necessarily as feminists or graffiti writers, nor with the expectation that they must name themselves feminists or graffiteras. But all participants gain a fem-inist education through the pedagogical style of a feminist graffiti grrl; their teachings are collective, unapologetic, empowering, and public.[10]

During my interview with Injah, one of the original Nami members and the first codirector of brand management and product develop-ment, we discussed the strategic and critical space that Nami provides. Participating in Nami gives Injah the chance to act as a kind of mentor to the newer members, working together with other graffiteras to im-prove women's lives while reinvesting feminism with a contemporary meaning suitable for "women in the community." "It's very difficult" to manage how feminism as a concept circulates, she explained:

> Many of our girls are afraid of this label "feminism." I think because of the
> history of it; in the beginning it had a need to be that kind of revolution—
> dress like a man, be tough, break all the patterns. And today we don't
> want that anymore. We are at a different stage, but it doesn't make the
> feminists of the past wrong. The girls just think back to that time, with
> the burning of the bras . . . and they say it will hurt if I don't use the bra.

Injah is adamant about the importance of providing a space in which women, no matter their stance on feminism, can come together and "talk to other women about being women"; for her, and many others, this is the most beneficial service Nami provides.

A graffitera activist since 2005, Injah chose her tag name to reflect her spiritual beliefs in *jah*—in God. Injah identifies unequivocally as a feminist artist. Her definition of feminism is grounded in a recognition of the ways her everyday life is affected by gender difference. "I live in society as a woman and that is different than living as a man; . . . I try to think about what I can do to live better, and how other women in the society I live in can live better, too. How can we make it better for us?" She made a point to give an example of one of the ways in which gender difference affects her graffiti making—the physical danger involved in the act of painting itself. She navigates her fear of lingering in dark alleys or dangerous places alone by preparing stickers and posters at home ahead of time. Interestingly, the imagery on these stickers and posters (and in her aerosol work) is very sexual, very sensual: a direct reflection of her aggressive interest in empowering women in regards to their sexuality. When I asked her to elaborate, wondering if maybe this would be a chance to talk about lesbianism or bisexuality in graffiti subculture, she replied nonchalantly, "I think of the way a woman *feels*. The object of her desire is not specific in my work; it is what she is feeling about her sexuality that I am trying to convey." Injah's nude female figures, whether painted on walls, canvas, or made into stickers, provoke women to "liberate" their sexuality from social and moral restraints; legs spread, breasts uneven and exaggerated, Injah's women defiantly touch themselves with heads thrown back in ecstasy (facebook.com/injah.debora/). Nami is a network that facilitates and "authorizes" members to discuss taboo subjects like sexuality and the body, topics typically understood as private or inappropriate for discussion within a group.

When I spoke with Kitty, at the time seventeen and one of the youngest active members of Nami, she expressed that in contrast to her non-Nami friends (who consider her to be very outspoken and a little "crazy"), the network of friends she has made in Nami makes her feel normal. She spent years during her childhood in drawing classes that were focused on "landscapes, flowers, and fruit"—which for her was "so boring." Wanting to find a different way to express herself, Kitty researched Anarkia online and then enrolled in the next graffiti art course she offered. An avid reader, Kitty considers herself a political person and, prior to her involvement in Nami, worked with children in various arts organizations. Kitty claims her feminism, but qualifies it by saying, "I don't want a woman's world; I want equality."

Nami's role as a space for "crazy girls," a descriptor that many graffiteras use to identify themselves, is part of the countercultural force that attracted N30 to the group. As an editor of an arts magazine and an aspiring graffitera when she joined Nami, N30 was a natural fit for the communications committee. She explained that she does not "suffer prejudice because of [her] color," or class, but because of her gender presentation. While N30 had a long way to go in terms of her skills as a graffitera when she joined Nami, she has always had the determination to fight against poverty, racism, and women's rights—qualities that made her a welcome addition to the organizing team.[11]

Jups is one of Nami's most dedicated members. She came to the group in 2010 with three years of graffiti writing under her belt. Anarkia and I met with Jups at her home, where her mother, aunt, and grandmother greeted us with a homemade buffet of delicious Brazilian cuisine. While we ate, I commented on the matriarchal structure of her family—noting at least three generations of women present—and asked her to explain her views on feminism. Jups pondered her response as she spoke: "I am a feminist because I am part of Nami's capacity-building group. I am still learning; I am in process. Before Nami I did not know what [feminism] was, but I come from a long line of strong women. I was one, I just didn't name it. To be feminist is to know that men *have* to respect women." Like many of the Nami women, Jups was learning through participation how to articulate her intuitive conviction that she was worth respect and deserved just treatment. Part of Jups's feminism is also rooted in her need for autonomy and personal power; as a silversmith she makes jewelry, purses, and accessories for a living and requires that kind of agency to thrive. Having had some experience with arts-related social justice activism, Jups found in Nami the freedom to paint her own unique imagery. She also had agency, as a valued member of the collective, to propose ideas and see them through to production. The day before our interview at her home, I asked Jups about the "little monsters" she painted; she corrected me, saying that they are not monsters, but her "ghosts." She went on to explain that women usually paint, and are expected to paint, flowers and "feminine" things, but she was more interested in transferring the "ghosts" in her life onto the wall, to exorcise them from her body and mind. The ghost that caught my eye was a rather lighthearted one—it had a big goofy smile that exposed misshapen teeth. The ghosts she exorcises are not always meant to communicate a dark message, she noted with a big smile: "that day I was happy!"

We were all happy the day she painted her goofy ghost: painting, laughing, and chatting in Lapa. Anarkia had organized and scheduled this event as part of my itinerary so that I could gather as many interviews as possible in one day. The wall was situated on a street that ended at the Escadaria Selarón, an impressive multilevel staircase made of one-of-a-kind handcrafted mosaic tiles. When Anarkia and I arrived around 1:00 PM people who had heard of the production were already waiting. The audience arrived before the actors—an audience of friends, family, photographers, journalists, fellow graffiteras, pixadors, and passersby who would increase in number steadily throughout the ten-hour event.

Sitting on the curb taking a break, Anarkia and I spoke to Si Caramujo. A graffitera since she was fifteen (in 2004), she started painting alone, primarily doing throw-ups on the trains. Si has always styled her graffiti imagery (long-haired goddesses in natural settings) to mark her gender; her clothing, however—jeans and T-shirts—is chosen specifically to avoid attention. Her tag name reflects her independent character and Zen nature as it directly references the simple, slow, self-sufficient life of a *caramujo* (snail). "Yes, I am a feminist, but only in the streets. When I go home I am a traditional mother. I take care of everybody." Curious about this split, I asked her to talk about being a mother. In her explanation, the break she articulated between feminism and motherhood, between private life and public life became more nuanced, revealing that the split was perhaps more like a braid. She told me that she makes it a point to share care-giving responsibilities with her mother, her in-laws, and her husband (a graffitero), saying that "it is not healthy for a baby to always be with the mother and it is important for the mother to have her own life, her own time to do things she enjoys." Despite her "traditional mother" self-identity, Si's opinions on caregiving, motherhood, pregnancy, work, fun, and alone time reflect (and are reflected in) her commitments to Nami's feminist goals. In "taking care of everybody" she still makes time to take care of herself, and this includes her participation within Nami.

That day in Lapa brought a few graffiteras out of "retirement" (including Prix, Aila, and Cuca) to join this collective event with women who are actively involved in the urban art movement in Rio (N30, Jups, Anarkia), as well as women just finding their place within the culture (Gabi, Kitty, TMB, KR, Si, and Alexia). After three years of painting alone, seventeen-year-old KR met the women of Nami. She started out painting pixação, but now as a member of Nami she was transitioning into painting what she characterizes as "crazy" cartoonlike characters that are specifically "*not* feminine"—despite sometimes being adorned with bows. While she believes that women have to fight for equality, she was adamant about her position regarding feminism: "I am not a feminist. I am a woman." An independent person from a very early age, determined to do what she wanted when she wanted with whom she wanted, KR had experienced quite a bit of turmoil in her personal life. Her aggressive confidence and guarded vulnerability, born out of the challenges of being judged for acting "differently" than a girl should, are evident in her personal interactions with people and her aesthetic choices. Unlike other artists, KR did not mention anything about her graffiti purposefully reflecting her persona. And yet KR's Frankensteinian characters, reminiscent of Jups's ghosts, illustrate her complex response to feeling "different." The character she painted that day was an unsmiling, red-faced figure complete with a forehead scar, purple hair, and a dainty blue bow—a motley amalgamation of parts and pieces that come together in a figure that ultimately looks uncomfortable. I wondered if this monster was uncomfortable with the bow (signifying femininity and youth), the visible scarring (signifying potential weakness or past injuries), or both. KR says that women make graffiti for the same reasons men do: "it makes me feel calm, it is pleasurable." When I asked why she participates in Nami, she said that it is because she "simply wants to paint." In my estimation, KR's membership in Nami is anything but simple. Nami not only provides her with a physical space (the wall) to express herself aesthetically, but also embraces her rebellious character and in doing so offers her a community of women who also feel crazy or different and do not expect that difference to collapse into sameness.

Once a majority of the women had arrived, the group began casually dividing the wall space in order to get a general sense of who would be stationed where. Huddled in a tight circle, sketches in hand, N30, TMB, Jups, KR, Si, Anarkia, Gabi, Alexia, Prix, and Kitty delegated background roller-painting duties, plotted the space, and talked through how best to use the single ladder. Most of these graffiteras were still learning how to wield a spray can and work together to create a single image. Si spray-painted a larger-than-life goddess adorned with a starfish-shaped crown (which she embellished with actual seashells) and a powdery blue gown darkened with hints of sea foam green toward the bottom where she inscribed "earth mother forgive these people" in Portuguese.

She completed the picture with her tag: the letters "S" and "I," and her signature caramujo. Taking up a mostly horizontal position on the wall, Prix stenciled layers of a modified version of the "woman" symbol used for restrooms—the figure's arms extended into a loop with a heart shape at the end. Kitty painted a woman's head that took up half the wall vertically, the entirety of which, aside from the blonde hair, was filled in with solid black, with negative white space for the eyes, nose, and mouth. N30 was experimenting with layers of quasi-geometric lines and ended up with a multicolored half-human figure that resembled a doll made of innumerable layers of yarn. Jups painted a dark, cloudy blue, off-kilter ghost head (with no body), diamond-shaped eyes, an exaggerated nose, and misshapen teeth. Alexia and Gabi painted together, using stencils, spray paint, and a bit of acrylic to produce what might best be described as a psychedelic tree. TMB used a mixture of acrylics with a brush and spray paint to design a hypnotic eye with curvy, candy-red entrails that connected to the tree. Toward the end of the night, when all the other women were done and at their fervent request, Anarkia painted her soft yet serious eyes at the top of the composition. The eyes looked protective, as if they were watching over the images below.

While this was not the most impressive image I had ever seen in terms of group cohesion, handstyle, color palette, use of space, or overall composition, the production *process* itself was fascinating. For a well-known graffitera like Anarkia to put her work next to writers who would be considered "toys" is remarkable. When I mentioned this to Anarkia, she stated quite frankly that "we do not call people toys when they start painting because we do not know who they will become." The relinquishing of ego and reputation in favor of experimentation, support, and encouragement produced an overwhelming sense of community. Witnessing the empowering effect Nami has on women and girls and the community that formed around their graffiti making reawakened my "communal" feminist sensibilities and further validated my unwavering belief in the revolutionary potential of graffiti art.

After the Lapa production was complete, everyone was hanging around chatting. I was joined by eight-year-old Luna and her mother, Gisella. Gisella is not a graffitera but participates as a lecturer in Nami's seminars. She brings Luna to Nami's productions to paint with the other girls. Luna was clever enough to notice that "Nami" is an anagram of the syllables taken from the street slang word *mina* (meaning woman); she took the same liberties with her given name to create her tag name, Nalu. Nalu joyously painted a heart and "made friends with the adults." When I asked about the heart she painted, she pouted, explaining that "it was so small," but her expression changed instantly when she added, "Anarkia promised me more space next time!" The first time Gisella brought Nalu to a Nami event, she painted her name, the name of her school, and a "much bigger" heart on the wall so that, as she proclaimed, "if someone that knows me passes by the wall, they will know that it was me that painted it." A true graffitera in the making, Nalu wants recognition for her work, is confident enough to boast about her efforts, and even made a point to represent her school. Feeling like "an artist painting with other artists," Nalu sees her artistic future as clearly as an eight-year-old can. She asserted, "The older girls are better than me, but one day I will be like them!" Nalu is but one of the children of Nami. As a daughter of one of Nami's directors, Nalu is probably one of the most consistent students, but there are many more children who witness or participate in Nami's events.

The day after the Lapa event, Anarkia and I met with another budding graffitera, Ale, who lives in Rocinha, Rio's largest favela. After the interview and an exhilarating (and frightening) "taxi" motorcycle ride to the uppermost area of the favela for a birthday party in one of the *casitas*, we went back to Ale's studio. The plan was for her and Anarkia to paint together on a wall near the studio, but by the time we arrived and they got set up it began to rain. Undeterred, they painted anyway. While they worked, a young girl of no more than nine years old named Jennifer wandered over and was invited to join them. Ale, who was just learning how to control a spray can herself, experimented with figurative lettering as she taught Jennifer how to hold the can and helped her press with all her might on the cap.

Anarkia translated a majority of the twenty interviews I completed during my eight-day visit, and in the final interview with her she said that although it was exhausting, she gained a lot of knowledge about Nami's growth and place in the members' lives.

> Nami recruits by word of mouth. We don't want to work with all girls, but girls with whom we can see potential . . . the potential to be a feminist.

Even the girl who wants to just paint—we just need time to transform this kind of girl. Like KR, she said she is not a feminist, but she doesn't know what it is. She doesn't think about it. She said she just wants to paint but I know she is a feminist. One day she will be a feminist. I believe that we can transform the girls. Especially the young girls.

When Anarkia came to visit me in New York in March 2012, she told me that indeed KR had begun to call herself a feminist. Once KR realized it was up to her to determine what feminism meant, she was happy to lay claim to a feminism defined by her actions. Nami helps grrlz come to feminist movement as they are, and if they do come to a feminist identity it is a self-directed result of their actions.

Anarkia's passion for her work is what Augusto Boal calls an "'enacted' faculty, a faculty that [has become] a concrete act," as demonstrated by the consistent performance of feminism in her behavior, her discourse, and her graffiti.[12] The production in Lapa and the smaller work in Rocinha depend on some of the tactics outlined in Boal's *Theatre of the Oppressed*, practices, which Nami often employs in their capacity-building activities. Taking graffiti making out from under the cover of anonymity and the dark of night allows the experienced and aspiring writers of Nami to develop a participatory audience that is conscious of the feminist concerns of the collective. The crowd that gathers on the street as they paint is almost always invited to attend the next lecture or activity. Anarkia purposefully structured Nami, with the help of the director's team, to "change the ways the girls think about feminism by showing them how to do it themselves."

Performing feminist community in this way produces a moment that Jill Dolan describes as a "utopian performative"—an event or action where the "audience" is lifted "slightly above the present, into a hopeful feeling of what the world might be like if every moment of our lives were as emotionally voluminous, generous, aesthetically striking, and intersubjectively intense."[13] This "temporarily lifted" community recurs with each action Nami produces—the audience comes back to reexperience just such a moment, which has profound implications for the social justice work Nami is trying to accomplish, whether those in attendance officially join Nami or not. The feeling, the affect produced by Nami's actions, translates into social action because the stage is set by friends and neighbors; the stage of everyday life is altered by the participation of everyday people. A utopian performative is called forth by aesthetics and by performances of identities that allow participants to play with the potential of making a space that is their own.

With every project Nami brings to Rio de Janeiro's streets, the women perform their artistic identities and the girls practice the adult identities they desire—"one day I will be like them." As N30 explained, "It is important for people living in the slums, the favelas, to have [a medium] like graffiti that communicates quickly and can be political. We want to use graffiti to claim the streets, our neighborhoods and to inspire others to do it, too." Taking place in the public sphere, accessible and welcoming to onlookers and passersby, Nami provides not only the time, space, and materials needed for these women and girls to *feel like and become* agents in making Rio de Janeiro more beautiful, but also the confidence needed to *feel like and become* valuable culture makers resisting heteropatriarchal juridical, social, economic and political systems that restrict their safety and civil liberties. Nami teaches girls and women about feminism by giving them an opportunity to *feel it first* through performance.

Crazis Crew (Chile)

"Crah-zis Crew," Naska corrected my mispronunciation, "not Crazys Crew! Although we are loca!"[14] Surrounded by the bohemian vibe and décor of the Galindo restaurant in Santiago's breathtaking Bellavista neighborhood, graffiteras Naska and Shape punctuate their explanation of their crew name with fits of laughter, the kind borne of a private joke between friends. Founded in 2000 as Chile's first all-grrl graffiti crew, in 2010 Crazis Crew included Naska, DanaPink, Shape, Bisy, Cinemas, Eney, and Adri. The original Crazis, Naska and DanaPink, began painting together because they shared both the experience of isolation as graffiteras among men and the unrelenting desire to "write their voices on the walls of the city." Crazis Crew prioritizes collective projects; their works are painted to convey an attitude of personal and collective expression, to both integrate and distinguish the different styles of each graffitera.[15] The crew's group productions have a light, cartoonish quality, with rotund characters and highly stylized organic beings (such as insects, plants, animals) and people of varied ages wearing indigenous clothing—all part of a pleasurable surrealistic natural landscape that they describe as "marked by very feminine characteristics."[16] Naska elaborates: "The importance of taking part of an all-grrl crew is not just about coming together and going out to paint graffiti in the street: it is something that leads to organization, an exchange of ideas, opinions, projects, et cetera." For the members of Crazis, having a network, a working relationship with peers, and access to mentors are all critical. In their collective statement, which they developed and emailed to me the year after we first met, the grrlz explained to me that while they do not identify as feminists, either individually or as a crew, they acknowledge that they are perceived that way because of the gender composition of the group and because of their expressed intent to demonstrate that they "do not need to have the mind of a man" to paint graffiti with style and innovation. "With respect to feminism, we value our gender difference as it provides an opportunity to paint with more freedom because we take advantage of that quality which presents us as less suspicious than a man graffiti writer on the street. . . . Our perspective and intention is to grow together through mutual respect and appreciation, generating even more powerful ideas to enrich our graffiti." They distance themselves from a feminist identity while simultaneously articulating their awareness of sexist stereotypes about graffiti writers. Rather than dwell on the detrimental effects of gender difference that play into that stereotype, they redefine the terms of engagement into a means of proliferation (i.e., their perception is that they can get up more, with less risk, because as women they are not imagined as criminals). The value and allure of building an all-grrl crew is clear, particularly if you trace the development of Crazis from a two-person "tag" team to a group of seven sustained over a seventeen-year period (and counting).

When Naska began painting at sixteen in 1999, there were no other graffiteras in her circle, so she painted with her male friends. She says she wished for a female friend, "a partner," to paint with. She met Dana-Pink, a graffitera who shared Naska's skill set and abilities with a spray can. DanaPink and Naska became partners in crime, literally and figuratively, a partnership Naska identifies as truly beneficial for their artistic and personal growth. Not only did they grow as graffiteras, but they also matured together as women on the fringes of acceptable social behavior. Realizing the benefits of being in a peer mentorship/friendship, the two women decided to form Crazis Crew to foster deep personal connections and encourage open artistic exchanges with other graff grrlz. Explaining how this exchange functions, Naska described a "chain" of learning and mentorship: Naska learned from Bisy who in turn learned from Naska who taught Dana who then taught Shape who also learned from Naska, and so on. Out of shared experiences of isolation, the members of Crazis built their own support network.

The formation of crews, which function as small communities, is a point of pride throughout the graffiti subculture. The difference worth noting here is the concerted effort by Naska and Dana to find a common ground based on gendered life experiences from which to build this network. Generally, when people enter graffiti subculture they hang out with more experienced mentors, perhaps an older brother or friend, who then mentors their stylistic and cultural development. Entrance into the culture is often different for graff grrlz. Experienced male writers may not want to "waste" their time mentoring a woman for fear she would not be truly committed. In addition, if a graffitera's male peers do offer to train her, there is also always the risk that, due to hetero/sexist assumptions, the work she produces will be contested by the subcultural rumor mill: "she didn't do it," "she had sex with him," "she just copies his style," and so on. While Naska says that she felt no direct sexism, sexualization, or marginalization among the group of friends who taught her, I gathered from her tone and phrasing that being the sole grrl in a crew of men was extremely isolating.

Like most graffiteras, Naska began by experimenting with letters, but she has since become more focused on her passion for developing new styles in figurative work. She describes her style as feminine and intends for her graffiti to communicate a message that is not confrontational, but rather soft, fluid, and suave; the overwhelmingly pastel color palette combined with the animals and environments she chooses to depict realize her objective. Her signature big-eyed birds and fish are never grounded— they fly and float freely through rose-colored skies and apple-green waters. Naska's dreamlike worlds make visual her affective experience of writing graffiti: "When I paint, I feel better. It feels good. It is a relief. I feel calm because it is like a moment in the day when I can concentrate and take it easy. Taking time for graffiti is very important. The feeling that graffiti, and painting with Crazis, gives me is sentimental." Naska found

her artistry in her joyous, dreamlike images. In a subculture where notions of authenticity are rooted in aggressive imagery and handstyle, her
stylistic choices may not have been fostered or given the space to develop
without DanaPink's support—without a writer who shares and, perhaps
more importantly, *values* Naska's aesthetic.

Despite a common root in U.S. Hip Hop graffiti aesthetics, Latin
American graffiti productions tend to differ from the North American
or European productions that are most often perceived as representative examples of graffiti subculture. North American and European Hip
Hop graffiti art is centered on letters of varying degrees of legibility, and
if there are characters or landscapes they tend to emphasize photoreal-
istic imagery with an aggressive composition (e.g., wildstyle); these two
aesthetic imperatives combined often produce a more "menacing" (read:
masculine) impact. The majority of the writers I have spoken with—
including in Latin America—characterize this style (along with the use
of spray paint) as authentic or "real" graffiti (implicitly and directly) and
consider anything else street art—an unflattering characterization in
this context.

Throughout my interview with her, Naska advocated for gender
equality and emphasized how empowering Crazis had been for her and
for the others. However, when I asked if she identified as a feminist she
said without hesitation, "I am not a feminist. I am a graffitera. Here in
Chile the woman feminist is a protester, she is passionate about equality.
I started an all-girl crew to empower the women through graffiti. I am
not a feminist, but the part of feminism I like is to empower women in
work. It is not about women's power; it is the power of women." Naska
makes an intriguing distinction: "I am not a feminist. I am a graffitera."
Her striking nonfeminist feminism is located specifically within the
realm of artistic labor, which for her is different from who feminists
are—protesters. The empowering work Naska accomplishes with Crazis
is a form of unmarked social protest that takes place in her everyday
life and is a valuable contribution to the attainment of gender equality
particularly because the methods and means utilized are specific to graffiti's subcultural framework. By doing the work of a graffitera among
graffiteras, Naska engages in and instigates feminist action: with every
mint-green line sprayed on the wall she protests her invisibility, claiming
space in a subculture where the walls "belong" to men.

Shape started writing graffiti after going to a Hip Hop party with Dana, Naska, and Adri in 2002; after the party, the grrlz went out tagging. Shape tried it out, tagging "Kary," and was hooked. She was in college at the time, studying painting and training to be a contemporary dancer. She incorporated those formal lessons into the less-formal street knowledge she gained bombing and b-girling with Bisy. Her modes of artistic expression transitioned "from the studio to the street": "Graffiti is more urban, less formal . . . and that is what I love. I love the urban; it is on the street. Let's go to the street and paint! . . . Getting out of the studio and onto the street, you have more experiences."[17] Shape joined Naska and Bisy on their graffiti missions and began experimenting with tile mosaics, but ultimately acknowledged her attraction to spray paint and adopted it as her primary medium. As her tag name implies, she describes her style as a continual process of investigating shapes that are "psychedelic, feminine, and colorful."

Shape's experience with graffiti and breakdancing differs from most Hip Hop practitioners. Due to the numerical gender disparity, and the consequent and coreproductive lack of representation and notoriety for grrlz, it is unique for *anyone* to be brought into Hip Hop culture by an experienced practitioner who identifies and presents as a woman. Shape recognizes that her experience is atypical, and her introduction to Hip Hop through the influence of strong, like-minded women informs her take on feminism:

> I am not a feminist, but I hate machismo. I am the opposite of machismo! I believe that women and men should walk together; men should not step all over women. We think of feminism as having an active part in politics, activities, and protests. I don't go to the feminist activities. It makes me happy that they are doing it and I feel secure because of the progress women have made, but I don't participate in it.

Like Naska, Shape indicates that the activities she engages in do not count as feminist because they are not the standard "politics, activities, and protests." Shape's self-empowerment comes from painting with an all-grrl crew, an activity that provides her with "an opportunity to represent female writers in Chile, to grow and advance as a woman doing what you love . . . [and to make] friends [who] form a bond that goes beyond graffiti"—it provides her with a powerful community to tap into personally and professionally.

Representation, friendship, and empowerment are the effects of her participation with Crazis. The difference she feels personally, and makes as a member of the community, is performed feminism—feminism being done through the aesthetic realm of graffiti. Graff grrlz' performed feminism is the "street" version of feminism: it provides the grrlz with the organic intellectual knowledge that can only be gained by doing graffiti as a grrl in a hetero/sexist male-dominated subculture. Though this feminism "moves" differently, it remains feminist movement loaded with politics and a protest positionality.

After almost a decade of painting and breaking, Shape became pregnant. She continued painting at the beginning of her pregnancy—wearing a face mask—but her activity decreased once the baby was born. Shape spent a good portion of our interview explaining why having a child changes everything, even when you have a partner who shares parenting responsibilities. Because graffiti is traditionally framed as a male-centered youth culture, the topic of parenting (never mind of mothering) is one that has yet to be investigated and included as part of this subculture's story. When I began this work it was a concern I had not considered; now it affects many of the women whom I work with and informs their stories significantly. These women do not neglect their parental responsibilities to focus on their artistic careers, or vice versa, but rather spend a great deal of energy balancing the responsibilities of both roles—like most working women who are primary caretakers. For Shape, if too much time passes between getting out to paint with her crew, she feels that something integral to her quality of life is missing.

At the time of our interview, her daughter, Carmen (named after a Crazis member), was almost two years old and had attended quite a few Crazis productions. Shape intends to continue bringing Carmen with her to expose her to new ideas, people, and places, and also to teach her how to paint—an alteration of the "average" subcultural initiation rituals. At the wall, Shape always has help from the other Crazis, who care for the little girl as if she were their own. Aside from childcare there is the larger issue of finances—when you have to buy food and clothing for your child, buying paint is a luxury expense. To supplement the family income and perhaps buy paint for the next Crazis production, Shape spends her time at home fashioning various *artesana* goods to vend.

DanaPink has also been balancing motherhood with her commitment to graffiti making. DanaPink's son, Clemente, was born the day we were supposed to meet for an interview, and while she obviously did not make it, she managed to orchestrate my meeting with Naska and Shape from the hospital. While Dana enjoys painting with both her husband and her crew, she also cherishes the temporary disconnect from everyday responsibilities that painting alone provides; she uses this alone time to "release her energy" on the wall. For Dana,

> Graffiti is life, it is love. I paint graffiti because it is a part of my life that makes me feel special. I like being able to give my work to people. I love to paint graffiti as much as I can, but now with motherhood I do not have as much time to paint graffiti on the streets. So I settle for drawing and continue painting at home until I can return to the streets.[18]

Like Shape's artesana, DanaPink transfers her graffiti aesthetic to canvas and fabric, painting on premade textiles like jean skirts and jackets, and hand sewing pillows and dolls; both women use the artistic skills they developed as graffiti artists to earn extra money.

Dana started painting in 1999, watching and practicing with her brother and friends. Admitting to the poor quality of her initial work, Dana shared that in Chile there is a colloquialism that says you cannot learn without failing, so she soldiered through those bad first attempts and came out a highly skilled visual artist whose work is "soft and feminine with a focus on children, flowers, and animals." Sharing a bit of herself each time she presses down on the spray-paint cap, Dana offers a kind of self-portrait with each of her wide-eyed *muñecas* (little doll-like girls). If her muñecas are reflections of herself, then this is a woman who has her eyes wide open to the workings of the world. Her muñecas are not hyperstylized in their bodies, but in the adornment of their dresses, their environments, and the scale and color of their eyes. The large-scale eyes at first read as "cute," lighthearted, and warm, but they also gaze directly at you, calling for your undivided attention. Dana primarily uses pinks with female characters to "note the difference . . . [,] that it was made by a woman." Knowing full well that what "marks" graffiti as made by a woman is both specific and arbitrary, Dana qualified that, in graffiti art, gender difference is never absolute: "In Chile there are many women who paint [in a style] that has nothing to do with envying a masculine style. You can walk down the street and see wildstyle or a throw-up that looks like a man did it by its aggression, but it will be done by a woman." Dana navigates her place in this subculture by consciously marking the gender of the artist producing the graffiti. I asked if she considered that to be a political statement and she responded rather tentatively: "maybe subconsciously." Dana's ideology regarding graffiti, as an "art [that]

Figure 2.3. DanaPink, Santiago, Chile, 2016. Photo courtesy DanaPink.

connects you to the community; as a gift of life to a polluted city, at no cost, with just a little color," resonates with a kind of anti-industrial, procommunity Hip Hop ethic that, when combined with the deliberate marking of her gender difference, makes a political statement out of the least likely aesthetic: cuteness.

Dana does not immediately identify with Hip Hop culture, but she does recognize the "original connection," stating that "in the beginning graffiti was a branch of hip hop, but nowadays it is not necessary to be in the world of hip hop to do graffiti." While plenty of writers use "soft" imagery like Dana's prepubescent girl characters, with Dana (as with Naska) the style is not immediately recognizable as, or intended to convey, a Hip Hop attitude. And yet the influence of Hip Hop in Dana's work is evident, especially in her lettering (despite not being wildstyle). When I asked Dana if she felt any hindrance being a woman in a male-dominated subculture, she replied, "Not really." Through her participation in Crazis Crew, Dana feels secure, empowered, and at home as a graffitera. However, Dana continues to guard herself against the threat of displacement or disrespect by signifying her gender difference on the wall—a reminder that it is always necessary to mark her presence lest she become invisible.

Joining in 2011, the newest addition to Crazis Crew is twenty-six-year-old Eney. She chose her tag name as a way to "keep a part" of herself, creating something that was legible, "friendly, female, and curvy" when written freehand.[19] She describes her free forms, which are often flying through the air (or floating in water, similar to Naska's), and her characters, who are "very rounded and outside the stereotype, with small breasts," as exemplary of her stylistic preference, which is "linked to nature" and her mestizo roots in Mapuche culture. In order to create texture in her pieces, she waters down the paint, which makes it drip freely and act more as a translucent ground layer that she then contours with definite spray lines and volumizing effects. Eney finds inspiration in her urban surroundings: "Temuco is a very gray city . . . surrounded by nature and culture." At first she wanted to capture the natural elements and paint them in unexpected places to disrupt the monotonous cityscape, "like a gift," but when she discovered the impact of those images she expanded her repertoire to embrace an ideology, using messages of "girl power," for example. Eney started altering public space with stickers and wheat pastes in 2005; shortly thereafter she was introduced to aerosol—a medium that opened an entirely new window of possibility and inspired her to "capture the streets." The same year that she was introduced to spray paint, she learned about Crazis Crew.

When I asked how painting made her feel, she replied, "A diluted paint and a fine line . . . in a single word make me orgasm." The orgasmic pleasure in graffiti writing for Eney comes from the feeling of unity with her crews, the connection to and communication with her city, and from belonging to a larger (Hip Hop) family "on which [she] can always rely." In her elaborations on the power of the erotic, Audre Lorde famously claims that the erotic is the "assertion of the lifeforce of women," "creative energy empowered," and "is not a question only of what we do; it is a question of how acutely and fully we can feel in the doing."[20] Eney's claim reminded me of a statement in *The Art of Getting Over* by Stephen Powers, where a male writer, Crayone, also makes use of the erotic to define his relationship to graffiti (albeit in regards to the debate regarding gallery vs. street graffiti art): "Some graffiti artists think that hitting canvasses is like jacking off and wiping their cum with a napkin; putting their art on a napkin. Why not get off on a wall? Why not fuck the real bitch?"[21] The misogynistic language used here in relation to the orgasmic and the erotic is quite different in tone, intention, and effect than Eney's use of a similar metaphor and illustrates the extent to which the wall, the streets, and the act of painting are gendered. For a graffitera to unapologetically claim the erotic in describing the affective component in painting, as Eney did, is striking. When Eney asserts the pleasure she takes in deviant, public self-expression, she redefines the hypersexualized and problematically gendered dynamics within graffiti subculture. She offers a discursively feminist take on the feeling of writing that is fueled not by domination, but rather liberation.

The community the Crazis grrlz build with one another is tied together through feminist affect: feeling connected, feeling empowered, feeling erotic, feeling liberated (to explore color, texture, medium, and form), and feeling validated as graffiteras with something to offer the subculture. The grrlz' distinctions between feminists and themselves as graffiteras—we do this and they do that—reveal the limitations of feminism as a compulsory identity. Feminism as a noun becomes a static knowable entity, defined by conventional associations that vary by geographic location but ultimately rest on an archetype most people do not identify with. If we imagine feminism as a verb, as something one does, a host of new connections reveals itself. To expand our perceptions of what feminism is and does, we must expand our perceptions of what counts as protest, what counts as a political act. Performing graffitera in the way that Crazis Crew does demands a shift in those conditions of isolation, neglect, and hostility that graffiteras experience—that is a shift in power relations within the subculture and *that* is a political act.

Turronas Crew (Chile)

In 2006, Chilean graffiteras Antisa (Los Ángeles), Gigi (Villa Alemana), and Mona (Santiago) founded the all-grrl Turronas Crew after meeting one another at Conce Graff, an annual graffiti event hosted by El Departamento de Jóvenes del Municipalidad Concepción (the city of Concepción's youth department). Over time, Dninja (Belo Horizonte, Brazil) and Pau (Cologne, Germany) joined, making Turronas a transnational crew rooted in Chile.

I met with Antisa on the last day of my visit to Santiago. Sitting at a picnic table, nestled in the verdant front yard of La Chimba Hostel in Bellavista, our hours-long conversation began with Antisa describing her ties and commitments to the kind of Hip Hop that has a "conscious" relationship to community and the people, distancing herself from the corporate "bling bling" Hip Hop everyone loves to hate. For Antisa, Hip Hop is "un estilo de vida" (a lifestyle) that she does not consciously enact—in her words, "I just am it."[22] A painter since childhood, Antisa recalled with some humor how her father always encouraged her to paint because that was the only way to keep her peaceful. She traces her love for graffiti back to the '90s and her instant affection for Hip Hop music and culture in high school, where graffiti writing was taught as part of the arts and culture curriculum to promote appreciation and proliferation of mural work.

Already active in the Hip Hop scene as an emcee, around 2000 she began doing tags and throw-ups with her first crew, Taxi. She was the only woman. During that time, she noted, she was not cognizant of graffiti culture or of its history, she "didn't know any graffiteras" and simply

"did it because it was Hip Hop." In 2003 she focused her creative energies on her graffiti, developing into one of the most virtuosic wildstyle
writers I have met. As I have noted with Naska's pastel surrealism and
Dana's cute pink muñecas, the choice of style itself is loaded with gendered implications. Not many women paint wildstyle graffiti, so Antisa's
style preference is uncommon. When asked to describe her style, she
said, "I am a graffiti purist. I only use spray paint. I listen to Hip Hop. I
think if I claim to be a graffitera, I need to be able to do a tag, a throw-
up, a piece. . . . Anything else is street art. I like the challenge that wildstyle brings. You have to control the pressure, technique, and style. I
love letters!" Antisa's relationship with wildstyle and her identification
with Hip Hop go hand in hand; wildstyle is the hallmark graffiti form
of Hip Hop—a solidified relationship that can be partially attributed to
the success and notoriety of the 1983 Hip Hop film of the same name
(*Wild Style*), produced by Charlie Ahearn, which is now a cult classic
among graffiti lovers. Antisa uses the raw energy and often-illegal status
of graffiti as an outlet; by day she works as a graphic designer creating
"acceptable images." Since she is restrained in her "day job" to the literal,
the legible, and the socially acceptable, in her graffiti she expresses her
outlaw energy through complicated, illegible, and aggressive letters. Despite the vigorous, seemingly unreserved kinetic characteristics of her
style, now as before, when Antisa is painting she is "quiet, calm, focused,
and relaxed."

Figure 2.4. Antisa, Santiago, Chile, 2012. Photo courtesy Antisa.

Antisa began her graffiti career as the sole woman in a sea of many men limited in their graffiti expressions to tags and throw-ups. Now, she is part of Turronas, a crew of women who go beyond the tag to challenge the boundaries of the letter, the human figure, and the natural world. Painting graffiti with her friends is a state of being that she described as "delicious." In contrast to Naska's experience of isolation among all male friends or Dana's certainty that Crazis assisted in her creative development, for Antisa, painting in a crew with all women does not offer anything different or better for her physical or emotional experience in graffiti culture. "When I started, I never felt different. They came to get me to go paint. I jumped walls, I climbed the fences. I did everything they did to make tags. They were my friends." That said, she had at least one memory at the ready: a moment in which she was "put in her place," reminded that she was a woman, and realized that gender identity had consequences. "When my friend came to visit, I said let's go paint the [concrete walls of the open-air drainage channels on the] river. And he said, no you are a woman, you can't do it! It is dangerous; there are drug addicts and it's dark and bad people go down there. And I said to him, you are the first person to say this to me in my life!"

She did not go to the river when her male friend told her not to, but she did choose to go on her own terms, explaining that she had plans to paint with Solitas later that week. Wondering how Antisa made sense of her male friend's paternalism, I asked her what she thought about gender equality, graffiti culture, and feminism. "Feminism is extreme. Just like machisimo is extreme. Both with closed minds. I am not a feminist. I believe in equality. I have never felt discriminated against. Only the one time, and one time as a graffitera is *nothing*." She may not have felt gender discrimination more than once, but she still recognizes that consistent discrimination is a common experience for graffiteras—so much so that she punctuated her comment with this observation: "one time as a graffitera is nothing." Antisa knew that Solitas would not try to deter her, but rather provide companionship and solidarity as a graffitera just trying to get up.

Gigi, a founding member of Turronas, turned her childhood nickname into her tag name. Twenty-nine years old at the time of our first email exchange in 2011, she teaches and produces visual art for a living. She is also a member of the Viei, WDR, and BBC crews. She began writing in 2003 under the mentoring and friendship of the acclaimed writer Acb, who was in her early twenties in 2006 when she died of stomach cancer.[23] Eight years later, Gigi described her graffiti style as a mixture of pre-Columbian and religious carnivalesque imagery meant to celebrate her Latin American culture and identity. Her multicolored, voluptuous female figures are often lounging in a landscape replete with flowers, trees, and small animals. When asked how graffiti affects her, she responded that in doing what she loves—"painting her opinion in the streets," making herself "appear"—she feels "free, happy and in touch with the city, people, and landscapes." Being a graffitera makes her "feel alive, awake, and free"; it is part of her "dream lifestyle."

Gigi attributes her growth as a writer, in both skill and knowledge, to her relationships with other graff grrlz—painting with friends made her "a better artist." Like Antisa, Gigi does not identify as a feminist "at all." Like most, she qualifies her rejection of the word as identity by using the language of feminism. She believes that women and men are equally capable of "art, science, politics" and is grateful when her work is approached and appreciated without either a gender bias or a preoccupation with whether it was made by a man or woman. "Being girls doesn't mean our work is less important or bad; we have the same skills if we work hard for it." In a "female-friendly crew" she has the space to create in a competitive but friendly atmosphere, an atmosphere where her opinions and feelings are respected. She thinks of Turronas as her family, a chosen family of friends in which communication is paramount. Despite the geographic distance between them, they "stay in touch all the time about work, troubles, art, and life."

In the summer of 2015, Antisa, Gigi, and Pau emailed to ask if I wanted to join them on a panel for the 2016 Latin American Studies Association annual conference in Manhattan as a discussant/moderator. For various logistical reasons, ultimately Pau and I presented on a different panel about our own work, but originally our panel was to focus on Turronas's sociocultural work from the framework of vulnerability. The grrlz wanted to discuss how their work as graffiteras, in a crew and in their personal and professional endeavors, affected their vulnerabilities as women—how it secured them to a community, enabled them to thrive as professional artists, and challenged them to prosper beyond their graffiti careers. "Turroneando" is the word they use to describe their actions: it roughly translates to "doing Turronas." Turning the proper noun (the identity of the crew) into a verb, these writers affirm that Turronas is not just who you *are*, it is what you *do*. Turroneando may not be considered "feminist" by these grrlz, but in being there for one another, in accepting no less than hard work and commitment, and in helping each other thrive as artists, these grrlz demonstrate how feminist teachings are embodied, how they have concrete results in terms of shifting one's sense of vulnerability to one of security, capacity, and notoriety.

What Does Your Feminism Do?

There is shit among us we need to sift through. Who knows,
there may be some fertilizer in it.
—Gloria Anzaldúa, *Making Face, Making Soul / Haciendo Caras,* 146

The aesthetic communities produced by Rede Nami, Crazis Crew, and Turronas Crew articulate a continuity dependent upon virtuosic singularity: each graffitera must contribute her best for the "production" to be successful. In *Crimes of Style*, Jeff Ferrell comments on the relationship between building community and doing graffiti: "As they add pieces to a new wall of fame, or tag their way down a dark alley, [writers] not only alter the face of the larger community, but develop an aesthetic community among themselves."[24] What Ferrell does not consider is how gender affects one's capacity to participate. Throughout their testimonials, these women clearly communicate a shared, collective ideology grounded in the value of equality and the necessity of doing the work. The "work" here, while not defined by the "direct" feminist action traditionally associated with feminist movement, instead activates the ideologies of feminism through ways of being—both personal and collective—that foster empowerment, pleasure, and supportive relationships. They perform a feminism that is rooted in friendship. This dynamic reverses one mode of feminist collectivity whereby individuals gather to address an immediate yet external social concern, like reproductive justice, and then form friendships based on that group identity. These crews flourish through their camaraderie, which in turn informs the structure of the crew in ways that promote pleasure, give individuals the freedom to imagine, and create a space for taking personal time to mature as people and as artists.

Writing about the future of feminist movement and the place of feminists of color in it, Gloria Anzaldúa, in her oft-cited anthology *Making Face, Making Soul / Haciendo Caras*, offers an unusual metaphor for hope—finding something useful in the "shit" produced by the "failures" of feminists. I find Anzaldúa's words of hope particularly salient for thinking about the politics of naming something a feminist act, a feminist performance, when the actor refuses that designation. Tracing the complicated negotiations with which the graffiteras of Rede Nami, Crazis Crew, and Turronas Crew reconcile their desire for equality with their perceptions of feminist identity has fortified my refusal to accept the perennial debate that feminism itself has failed because women who have made tremendous strides toward gender equity in graffiti subculture refuse to be called feminists. In *Affective Mapping: Melancholia and the Politics of Modernism*, Jonathan Flatley explores various conceptualizations of melancholia from Aristotle to Lacan, arguing that melancholizing is a performative affect that provides information and an orientation, a direction toward something lost.[25] Similar to Dolan's utopian performative, but different in the affect produced (sad, not happy), melancholizing does not figure as a depressive (immobilizing) affect, but rather as a performative antidepressant. Melancholizing over our feminist failures to connect, to build, to name, and to recruit is one way to affectively map how our vastly different experiences and feelings can also be shared experiences and feelings. Affective mapping requires that we hold on to our losses so that they become objects we can analyze— that is the muscle behind melancholizing.

As I looked at how many women nominally rejected feminism, I tried to understand how we (feminists) had failed. Repurposing the failures of identification and affiliation as starting points for seeing more clearly what was actually happening in these communities enabled me to draw an affective map without borders, one that demonstrates, as Chandra Mohanty suggests, "how differences allow us to explain the connections . . . and how specifying difference allows us to theorize universal concerns more fully."[26] The concerns relating to finding a place in public spaces, equality in work and at home, support and encouragement, and artistic respect are just some of the issues that these crews actively address through their performances of everyday life. Are these not feminist concerns?

Hanging out with grrlz who demonstrate what feminism can do when enacted, knowing they reject that affiliation, allowed me to hold failure close enough to be affected by it, to be affectively moved by the work—not despite but because these graffiteras fail to be legible within a feminist discourse that privileges a clear or outright declaration of feminist solidarity. The failure is a performative pedagogical tool, a productive resource for articulating contemporary and future feminist praxis—which in fact is actually *present* in the subcultural now.

To grasp the value of action deemed nonfeminist for the future of feminism (without succumbing to the seduction of postfeminist rhetoric) requires that we make way for the praxis developed by a new generation of individuals who enact the principles differently. In *Against the Romance of Community*, Miranda Joseph approaches the dynamics of community by shifting the conversation from questions of sameness and difference to considerations of social processes. She argues that scholars interested in identity-based communities (in this case, all-grrl crews) must not erase the performativity of individual labor practices—the forms of production and consumption—that construct those communities. The "it" in Claw's refrain "being about it" is a direct reference to the physical and emotional labor required to achieve subcultural, social, and political justice and equity. Graffiteras perform feminist acts on the stage of everyday life when they take public space, exceed gendered expectations, raise each other's consciousness, and support one another's artistry. The acts of production and consumption that develop crews such as the Stick Up Girlz (discussed in the next chapter), Maripussy Crew (Peru and USA), Few and Far (USA), Ladies Destroying Crew (Nicaragua and Costa Rica), and the Girls on Top (UK; discussed in chapter 5) are performed in ways that challenge the traditional invocation of community and thus can profoundly alter the end results.[27] Their crews are feminist communities formed regardless of feminist identity, regardless of individual subjectivity, and in contrast to the ways in which some graffiti communities function.

The failure is not necessarily that feminist movement fails to attract them, nor is it in their refusal of affiliation; the failure is in our acceptance of that disconnect on the grounds of delimiting "what counts." What we have not done is make room for truly alternative performances of feminism, despite years of scholarship and activism demanding that very thing. Our feminist failure, or mine in this case, can be repurposed as fertilizer; with the knowledge we gain from analyzing our shit, we just might grow alternative strategies for recognizing the abundant performance of feminism occurring everyday. Affectively mapping the failure of feminism to appeal to people who embody feminist ideologies, the failure of individuals to identify their acts as feminist, and, perhaps most importantly, the failure of self-identified feminists to claim a connection to and theorize nonfeminist feminist movement allows us to see what has thus far been obfuscated in the construction of our "we": contemporary feminism "lives" in embodied acts that are inherently feminist acts.

Performing feminism through mentorship, taking public space, promoting pleasure, and the collective imagining of something better: these are all forms of resistance in the everyday struggles of the oppressed. If recognized as such, these acts have the power to render moot the limiting stereotypes of feminist behavior depicted and exploited by contemporary media. One does not have to already be a feminist to join Rede Nami; in fact, the nonfeminist members who participate assist in what Butler calls the "more insidious and effective strategy" of rendering categorizations "permanently problematic," of fostering the kind of feminism that is "located within the possibility of a variation on that repetition."[28] The nonfeminist participants provide a constant challenge to the structure of Nami; as an open collective, it cannot settle into a static feminist form lest it push potential participants away. The feminist leaders of Nami embody and perform a feminism that is then transferred through the repertoire to the members, the spectators, and the onlookers who experience their events. The writers of Rede Nami, Crazis Crew, and Turronas Crew perform a feminist aesthetic community among themselves within the larger aesthetic community that is Hip Hop graffiti culture.

Feminism is too often defined by Anglo Western, liberal feminist politics; this is the "feminism" these graffiteras reject, a "feminism" with borders. The point is not that they do not know what feminism is, but rather that they are not aligning their ideas and actions, developed in response to the systems of domination under which they live, with a kind of "feminism" that in fact reproduces those conditions. I have come to realize that my desire for graffiteras to call themselves feminists (the reason for the "let down") is misdirected energy. It seems more productive to focus my energies of being "let down" on those people in positions of national and international power who claim feminism as an identity and then enact policies, foster relationships, and/or promote ways of being that participate in the subjugation of women positioned differently in relation to imperialist, settler white supremacist, capitalist cisheteropatriarchy. In her 2016 book, *We Were Feminists Once: From Riot Grrrl to CoverGirl®, the Buying and Selling of a Political Movement*, Andi Zeisler discusses the drawbacks of celebrity feminism in the United States—the kind of feminism that gets to represent all feminism because of cultural, geopolitical, and economic global hegemony. She argues, "Media and pop culture have to help change the narrative whereby simply claiming an identity that's feminist stands in for actually doing work in the service of equality. It can no longer be about who says they stand for feminism, but about how they stand for it."[29] Because these graffiteras are not pop-culture celebrities but subcultural figures, the ways in which they are actually doing the work are simply not on the radar. Politicians and pop-culture celebrities use the word, but spoken by them the word makes a promise in its utterance that it often does not fulfill—that is the failure we should be most concerned with remedying. Instead of seeing the various modes of feminism being performed differently as a hindrance, and instead of seeing the failure of feminism to attract a unilateral following in name as an "end," with the example set by Nami, Crazis, and Turronas we can reinvest feminism with the dynamism of movement.

By being about it, these graffiteras model a kind of being through doing that disrupts static hegemonic representations of what feminist movement "is" and what a feminist "looks like"; they provoke one another to perform the kind of subcultural space they desire, the kind of world they want to bring into being. For these graffiteras, feminism exists in the doing and the doing produces a performative being that enables their participation in graffiti subculture. Passionately produced against static hegemonic feminist identity, the crews these graffiteras create exemplify the future of feminist movement. From their subcultural vantage point and through their artistic ways of doing and being, graffiteras around the world have effected an extraordinary surge in the transnational presence of grrlz in this male-dominated subculture. I will address the tense and uneven relationship between "being about" feminism yet not claiming feminist identity in a different way in the next chapter by analyzing the digital spaces where graffiti grrlz enact feminist masculinity to build and sustain themselves as a *transnational* community connected by feelings of difference and dissonance. These grrlz perform feminist masculinity to build up the subculture, but also one another, through analog and digital call and response: do your work, prove your worth, and join us.

3

Cultivating Affective Digital Networks

The website is mainly to show each other and anyone else who checks it out who we are and what we've been painting. . . . [I]t's also a good way for people overseas to contact us if they're coming to any of the countries we're in and want to paint.
—Fluro (New Zealand)

The influence of the Internet and social media is doing crazy things to the world of graffiti. It allows writers to network with each other from around the world; it allows us to see what pieces are being painted in countries we have never been to.
—Hops (USA)

Something remarkable happened between 2005 and 2006 that would forever change Hip Hop graffiti's transnational subcultural landscape. Graffiti grrlz went public, via the Internet, en masse, ultimately creating what danah boyd calls a "networked public."[1] Since then, the presence and visibility of graffiti grrlz have mushroomed; it feels as though every day there is a new digital space for, about, and by graffiti grrlz. Traveling from one digital space to another, you can easily witness their art, impact, and connections. What is less obvious is the motive propelling those connections—what would prompt these grrlz (especially those threatened with imprisonment) to take the risk of exposure? In "Affective Solidarity: Feminist Reflexivity and Political Transformation," Clare Hemmings contends that "feeling that something is amiss in how one is recognised, feeling an ill fit with social descriptions, feeling undervalued, feeling that same sense in considering others; all these feelings can produce a politicised impetus to change that foregrounds the relationship between ontology and epistemology precisely because of the experience of their dissonance."[2] Over the last decade, grrlz with access to the technological communication resources required—uncensored Internet service, a computer/tablet/smartphone, leisure time—have utilized various digital platforms to act upon the feeling that something was "amiss" in how they were being treated, represented, valued, and documented. On these platforms, grrlz who have chosen to hide their gender difference came together with those who proclaim it. In what follows, beginning with how I experienced it firsthand, I will trace how taking the risk of going public online together facilitated a solidarity inspired by shared "experiences of discomfort" and of dissonance—a subcultural digital revolution of sorts with the power to change graffiti grrlz' subcultural status.[3]

Though I had been in contact with grrlz via digital means before 2005, our interactions were limited to email exchanges and AOL Instant Messenger (AIM) chat sessions. I tapped into what is now a vast digital

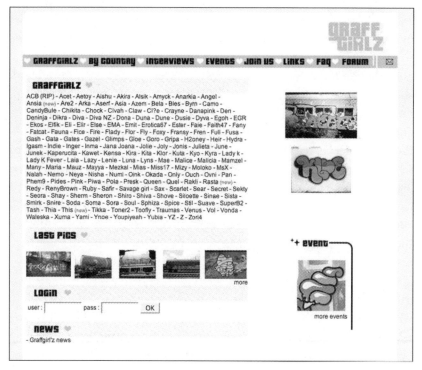

Figure 3.1. GraffGirlz.com homepage screengrab from the Internet Archive Wayback Machine.

network when I first visited GraffGirlz.com in 2008. I clicked on the link for Sinae's page and navigated my way to her crew's website, StickUp Girlz.com, finding (as far as I know/knew) the first *transnational* all-grrl graffiti crew in existence. Founded "as a one-woman crew" in 2003 by Sinae and then joined by Lady Diva in 2005, SUG's members are from Aotearoa/New Zealand (Fluro, Oche, and Lady Diva), Spain (Sax and Eire Gata), Portugal (Rafi), Japan (Shiro), and Australia (Spice).[4] Visiting SUG's website, visitors were met with the crews' moniker "StickUp-Girlz," which topped the page in a style that mimics a drippy, sparkly, pink, yellow, and purple throw-up. The page also included a "ticker" sidebar listing the latest image updates, a toolbar to navigate to additional pages (History, Members, Walls, News, Downloads, Links, Contact), and a series of hyperlinked boxes for joining their mailing list, reading the latest news, and seeing the latest page updates. In case one wants to know, "Who are da STICK UP GIRLZ?" the "History" tab offers a brief herstory. SUG's website offered the visual, and linguistic, discourse of graffiti subculture but did so in an atypical way for the period by marking their gender difference. The central image on the homepage was a young woman with olive skin and blueish-black hair fitted with a gold three-point crown reading "SUG." With spray-paint can in hand, she was fit with sneakers and a "feminine," but not hypersexualized, one-piece jumper. She had an air about her, communicated in stance and facial expression, that she had just made her mark somewhere in the urban background—the illegality of her act signified by a gang of searchlight helicopters closing in behind her. Transgressing gender roles, legal boundaries, and safety concerns, SUG's representative stood on a riverbank with one foot propped on a skull and bones; she did not look concerned about the search party and her confident posture assured us that we were not concerned for her either. To the contrary, her presence commanded the viewer's affirmation.

When I asked them how they felt about writers being online in relationship to their crew SUG, both Sax and Fluro emphasized connectivity—to writers both affiliated with SUG and not. For Sax, the Internet is "the future! Some years ago we only had contact by writing letters sending photos etc. . . . but now you are millions of photos with one click and contact with all [the] world['s] writers."[5] And for Fluro, "It's cool to be part of an international crew, you get to see a whole lot of diverse styles and see what's going on in the other countries. I'm lucky to have members of both crews to paint with in the city I live in and also the opportunity to travel and paint with crew members overseas."[6] Performing belonging to place grounds Hip Hop practitioners and maintains the impetus to stay connected to the local, to the history, and to the foundations as the culture continues to develop aesthetically and geographically.[7] One of the earliest examples of Hip Hop graffiti's performing place aesthetic is the addition of numbers to a tag name as a way to reference a specific geography; the street a writer lived on or a notable area in their 'hood became a part of their graffiti identity. The popularization of this aesthetic is often attributed to Taki183, a Greek writer from Washington Heights, New York, who worked as a bike messenger—the first writer to be acknowledged by the media.[8] The number(s) signified the place and the people to which that writer "belonged." Surpassing the popularity of performing place through numerical locators (street numbers), performances of community in contemporary graffiti culture often take the form of an acronymic "shout-out" to one's crew, usually in tag form on the outer edges of the piece (or inside a letter). In *Getting Up*, Craig Castleman notes that the "saturation techniques and wide-ranging coverage" of one of the earliest groups formed specifically for graffiti writing, the Ex-Vandals crew from Brooklyn, produced a model for other graffiti writers. The Ex-Vandals demonstrated the positive attributes of crew membership: companionship, assistance with larger pieces, the availability of lookouts, and *the capacity to get up via proxy.*[9] When a writer in a crew paints, it is not just *her* tag or *her* spot on the wall—she shares it with her crew by representing it publicly. Getting up allows one to mark your presence and claim your affective ties. However, because the experience of the local, the history made available in publications, and the conventional ways of learning and participating are different kinds of experiences for graffiti grrlz, they have taken it upon themselves to make connections beyond the local, to write and circulate their own histories, and to circumvent barriers to belonging (such as mentorship) through digital media.

Part of acquiring artistic skills, attaining fame, and becoming part of the community for graffiti writers is participating in (some or all of) a variety of collective activities such as exhibitions, jams, walls of fame (popular walls where writers paint to demonstrate skill), and writers' corners ("secret" meeting places). The exchange of ideas and techniques at these events and in these places, combined with the competitive nature and bravado motivating writers, functions "to accelerate the technical precision and style of their work, [and] to create a sort of collective aesthetic energy on which they all draw."[10] The exchange of styles and methods happens primarily through the showing and sharing of a blackbook (also called a piecebook or a bible, depending on local vernacular) at these events. By showing your blackbook to another writer—especially if you are a new writer (aka a "toy")—you are not only accessing knowledge about techniques and practical aspects of writing graffiti, but also encouraging a connection: be it a friendship, a mentorship, or crew membership. Crucial connections and innovations occur in these various social spaces, but these spaces are not always welcoming or positive experiences for grrlz. A lot of the grrlz I spoke with expressed hesitancy to attend these events at all, particularly when they knew they might be the only grrl (discussed in chapter 5).

Before writers went online, access to the subculture's "collective aesthetic energy" could be affected not only by their gender presentations in person, but also in terms of whose images were prized, kept in personal archives, and circulated in magazines. Falling "somewhere between sketchpad and archive," a website is different in physicality, but similar in purpose to a blackbook.[11] Grrlz can now self-archive; they can choose to then share that archive with other writers through a website or social media page (more on the effects of hetero/sexism on the graffiti archive in chapter 4). Ian Bourland points out that "the vast majority of writers document and study their practice through DIY journals, websites, and piecebooks."[12] The Internet has not replaced a marker and a clean piece of sketch paper, but it is an added space where writers can practice, share, critique, and communicate with one another. For example, by building an all-grrl crew and then sharing that crew's graffiti publicly on a website, SUG made a statement about the vitality, necessity, and benefits of ties between graffiti grrlz. The affective investment performed through crew membership in graffiti subculture is often described as an empowering relationship, a familial bond (grrlz often referring to one another as "sisters"), or a means of authenticating identity and proudly rooting oneself in a local community, in a "place." "Crew = Unity and family," Sinae explained, you "can show and produce way greater things in a group, it has a big and powerful vibe."[13] On their website and in our email conversations, the members of SUG used the language of family to describe their relationship to one another. Theirs is a chosen family of individuals born across oceans. Against a hailstorm of hetero/sexist stereotypes and ideologies representing graff grrlz as unskilled, isolated, unmotivated visitors to graffiti culture—or not representing them at all—SUG provides a counterimage of the graff grrl in a tight-knit transnational crew comprising tenacious grrlz skillfully and proudly getting up. Counterrepresentations, such as the ones on SUG's site and GraffGirlz.com, matter to not only how grrlz experience the subculture, but also how the culture is perceived historically and ideologically.

Graffiti grrlz have cultivated their affective network in, on, and through the digital zine *Catfight*, the GraffGirlz website, the *Chicks on Powertrips* blog, the "Female International Graffiti" Facebook group, and the "FEMALE CAPS" Tumblr microblog.[14] In these spaces, they performed feminism by producing counternarratives, challenging aesthetic value structures, defying "commonsense" quantitative accounts, presenting their feminist masculinity, and providing new "ways of being seen" to navigate the gendered politics of visuality within the subculture.[15] By (literally) "sharing" these aesthetic and social practices, they have created a subcultural feminist sensibility amongst grrlz who are involved and invested in these digital platforms throughout the diaspora. Moving from one digital communication platform to another, I draw a discursive topography of the rhizomatic graffiti grrl digital network in order to illustrate the previously inconceivable system of support, wealth of information, and conduit for sharing that graff grrlz have nurtured over the past ten years. They have changed the perspectives and expectations that graff grrlz have about themselves and each other in regards to their social belonging, their subcultural roles, their aesthetic possibilities, and their historical (herstorical) presence. The notable increased presence, visibility, and respect for graffiti grrlz attest to how their digital revolution gave "feminism its life" in Hip Hop graffiti subculture and how Hip Hop graffiti grrlz give life to transnational and digital feminist movement.[16]

Catfight: Female Graff Update

After seven years of writing "graphic, tight, candy color[ed], funny, funky" styled graffiti, Dutch graff grrl Foxy Lady (sometimes F. Ladi) created the zine *Catfight: Female Graff Update* in 2005.[17] She represents multiple crews, some simply for fun and community (TM aka Top Models), some to engage in legal artistic endeavors (BIC aka Bitches in Control), and still others to go bombing (AFC aka Altona Female Crew, of Germany; www.facebook.com/AFClique). When we first emailed about her zine in October 2010, she explained that after graduating from art school she wanted to further develop her graphic-design skills by working on a project of importance to her: "there was no medium yet that highlighted female graff. The sites that were there had outdated info and pictures and only a few female writers were really internationally known."[18] With *Catfight*, F. Lady broke ground by claiming subcultural validity for graff grrlz on a transnational scale.

Like many of her peers, when asked if she was a feminist, she replied with an emphatic, "No, not at all." Why would a writer who purposefully distances herself from a feminist identity create a zine that does important feminist work by only and specifically highlighting graff grrlz? With her zine, F. Lady was acting upon her sense—her feeling—that something was not right. The status quo at the time felt inadequate, the information "outdated," the level of international representation unacceptable. F. Lady was certainly not the first to feel those feelings, but she made those feelings public by putting them in a zine that existed primarily online (catfightmagazine.com); further, she established a norm for sharing those sensibilities with a networked public and thus across time and space—a kind of infinite distribution "to reach as many people as possible."[19] Ultimately her zine—first distributed through the website graffitishop.nl—was the starting point for various and rhizomatic digital forms of subcultural feminist life based on "structures of feeling, sensibilities, everyday forms of cultural expression and affiliation that [do] not take the form of recognizable organizations or institutions," fostering feminist sociopolitical progress within Hip Hop graffiti subculture.[20]

Her first goal was "to show the diversity of female graffiti," and while she was the sole editor and producer of the digital zine it was a community endeavor. In preparation for Issue oo (April 2005), she asked every writer she knew personally for photos, stories, and current information; they, in turn, asked their friends and so on. "[Ninety-nine percent] of the pictures [were] sent in by writers from all over the world. Without them, there [would have been] no *Catfight*!" Some notable contributors to the ten issues include Anarkia Boladona (Brazil), ClawMoney (USA), Faith47 (South Africa), Indie (USA), Kif (Mexico), Lady Wave (Denmark), Mickey (Netherlands), Miss17 (USA), Queen MCTash (New Zealand), Toofly (USA/Ecuador), and Nina (Brazil). F. Lady sorted and organized submissions into sections that varied depending on what was available for each issue: Intro (a brief note from the editor with contact info and calls for participation); Places to Go and See; Tags and Throwups; Stickers and Posters (street-art genre); Bits and Doo Dats; Legal Walls; Walls; Contents (a figure list to help decipher the graffiti, later replaced with captions under some of the photos); Silver (silver paint or markers used); New Media (books, DVDs, CDs related to street culture); Expo (exhibitions); Reports; Steel (trains); Thumbs (thumbnail pictures); and Action (grrlz in the act of writing). At the time, mostly due to the fact that graffiti is often an illegal activity, the Action section was spectacularly innovative because in most graff media made for mass circulation (websites, magazines, books) more often than not the documentation is the final result (the image) and not the process (the making).

A survey of the books on graffiti published before F. Lady put up her zine reveals that with the exception of Murray and Murray's *Broken Windows*, while there are numerous pictures of male writers (mostly from the back so not to expose their faces) there are *none* of graff grrlz actually painting.[21] As mentioned in the introduction, *Broken Windows* is one of the only books out there that treats graff grrlz in the same manner as their male peers, featuring images of Muck, Acet, Dona, Lady Pink, Peak, Diva, and Blue in action.[22] That said, the impact of these images on graff grrlz' collective memories is nonexistent in comparison to three iconic images of Lady Pink. When I ask graff grrlz (particularly grrlz under thirty) what images they saw of other grrlz writing, they overwhelmingly refer to *Subway Art* and *Spraycan Art*. In the former, Pink is standing next to a bookshelf stocked with aerosol cans, holding a Chihuahua and wearing paint-covered overalls and a signature-style '80s jean jacket; in another image in the same text she is sitting, legs crossed, hands folded, on a bench in a train car covered in tags, holding a can, which suggests that she had just painted the white "Pink 82" tag to her left. In the latter text, Pink is shown painting on one page and on the opposite page AbbyTC5 is standing in front of her piece and smiling. Nothing like the poses we see of kings like Lee, Futura, or Dondi (in both texts) where they are in action—straddling the space between train cars, dangling from fences, painting in a dark alley. When I questioned the lack of images of grrlz in action in my 2004 group interview with Dona, Claw, Pink, and Miss17 in 2004 (mentioned in chapter 1), they told me that I simply had not seen enough pictures. At the time they were correct. However, the images I *had* seen were the ones that could and still can be easily accessed through canonical books. These are the images that shaped the representation of graff grrlz until the era of Google Images. These are the representations that established conventional thinking about graff grrlz: there are not many of them; they are not as daring; they do not claim space aggressively. Because grrlz' bodies were not seen in action, and especially in the case where gender is not signified in the piece itself, the maker of the graffiti often becomes the default male writer. Thus "seeing" the process and recording the graffiti grrl in action challenges the representational deficit and raises subcultural social awareness in the same way that consciousness-raising groups did (and do) for disenfranchised and oppressed individuals.

In her article "The Personal Is Political: Feminist Blogging and Virtual Consciousness-Raising," Tracy Kennedy outlines the features of U.S.-based, 1970s-style consciousness-raising groups in order to make the case that similar work continues today in the form of feminist blogs. She argues that the Internet is a "new vehicle" for the "intimate interaction" needed for social transformation.[23]

> First, many women think that the discontent they feel in their lives is a personal problem that is not worthy of a more public recognition or discussion, which in itself can lead women to feel isolated and alone. In the past, consciousness-raising groups helped women understand that experiences were often shared. Second, these feelings and experiences are not self-inflicted, but instead can be attributed to a social system laden with cultural and institutional ideologies that dominate and subjugate women. Third, consciousness-raising groups not only named the issues, but worked to build a community of women who could then collectively advocate for social change.[24]

Catfight was not a feminist blog in the same sense as those that Kennedy considers: overtly feminist in name, journal(istic) style entries, and born-digital writing; it was instead a specifically "not feminist" zine that lived on a blog space used not for daily or even weekly entries, but rather as a mechanism of distribution. Those distinguishing factors aside, *Catfight* offered a digital space where consciousness was raised through the collective efforts of graff grrlz sharing artwork, opinions, and experiences.

In the Intro section for the first issue, F. Lady sets the blunt and unapologetic feminist masculine tone for *Catfight*: "The first *Catfight* magazine filled head to toe with the meanest cleanest female graff and streetworks that we could get our hands on. The contents shows graffiti in all its aspects. *Catfight* is not a feminist magazine, it is here because female graffiti is not documented or published (well) enough. Female skills are often underappreciated and underestimated. So it's time for a magazine that really shows what we can do: It's time for a *Catfight* ladies!"[25] The name of the magazine redefines the traditional derogatory gendered meaning of catfight: "a fight between women," according to the *Oxford English Dictionary*, or "an intense fight or argument especially between two women," according to Merriam-Webster. Hetero/sexist (and sexualized) images of two or more women, "claws" out, pulling hair and screaming in high-pitched voices over some trivial issue (such as a boyfriend) abound. The catfight that F. Lady initiated was between graffiti grrlz and the other writers, conventions, and (mis)representations that suppress them. *Catfight* fostered a sense that graff grrlz can and should inspire and challenge one another, showing the graffiti zine-consuming public what they can do—no claws, just cans. The publication of these feminist sensibilities particular to Hip Hop grrlz forges a community among them on the basis that what the magazine features in its pages is worth reading, sharing, and reproducing. *Catfight* shifted the consciousness of those who imagined and accepted a personal failing, or rather a personal feeling, not only that they lacked the skills to be great graffiti writers but also that the graffiti-writing community would not support them.

Tired of their second-class status, the grrlz decided it was time for a catfight with the "establishment," time to take action on the behalf of their selves and each other—a commitment F. Lady describes as a DIY ethic: "Since the '80s [Eindhoven] has had a vibrant Hip Hop & graffiti scene. It is not a big city, so the kids organised all kinds of stuff themselves. By the time I moved to Eindhoven these kids were all grown up and organised big parties and every one had developed their own talent within Hip Hop or art. The mentality they had (D.I.Y.) . . . was such an inspiration to me. I learned that Hip Hop is so much more than just the music."[26] Doing it yourself with a group seems like a contradiction in terms, but not within the context of a culture that values individual innovation as an assumed component of collective worth, like Hip Hop. Hip Hop culture samples from many genres and geographies, but it distinguishes itself as a culture through specific aesthetics—the countercultural aesthetic of doing it yourself, together, is one of them.

On the zine's one-year anniversary, F. Lady announced, "We are proud to say we at *Catfight* have achieved one of our goals: to grow! . . . [W]e have a new website [and forum] where you can contact other female artists and where you can chitter-chat about this and that."[27] In just one year, *Catfight* had garnered enough interest among graff grrlz to invest in its own domain name and extend its mission through a chat forum (a joint effort with GraffGirlz.com) where asynchronous discussion occurred among participants with registered usernames. As of February 2016, the forum (graffgirlz.easyforumpro.com) had 3,130 posts made by 490 registered users. Despite those numbers, it is now basically deserted, with new users and posts appearing few and far between. The forum's desolation can be attributed to at least three factors: the zine is no longer producing new issues, the website that directed major traffic to the forum (GraffGirlz.com) is down, and social media platforms have made the networking function of the forum all but obsolete.

When I asked why *Catfight* was important to her, F. Lady responded, "It was important at that time. Now it is much more common to see female writers. And I feel the magazine has no purpose any more. People already know female writers can kick ass. So there is no need in telling them anymore." The last issue that F. Lady put together had a specific theme (unlike the others): "Ladies of the '90s." She introduced the issue by writing: "Inside this issue you can see the legacy these ladies have left behind . . . for us to find."[28] F. Lady may have decided it was unnecessary to continue producing *Catfight*, but in her final move to pay respect to the legacy of writers who came before her, she (perhaps inadvertently) signaled the ongoing need for recognition—of the ladies of the '90s and the ladies of today. Suggesting that readers utilize the forum to continue sharing their work, it is clear F. Lady realized the power of the space her zine afforded to other women. Reading through forum posts today, it is easy to discern the dismay users felt when they realized GraffGirlz.com had gone down, new issues of the zine were no longer being published, and the forum was abandoned. Clearly, the desire for digital space specifically for graff grrlz persists. Graff grrlz have expressed their concern on other platforms as well. On March 6, 2011, a Facebook user based in the United Kingdom asked the other 289 users subscribed (at that point) to the invite-only "Female International Graffiti" Facebook group page: "does anyone know what happened to the graffgirlz website?" The handful of comments share a sense of nostalgia, confusion, and longing for the site even though at that point it had been down for about two years.

As a free and accessible archive focused on graff grrlz, *Catfight* had a value that is timeless and a purpose that remains relevant because the images and the information in the zines exist in digital spaces for others to discover beyond the zine's "end." The network that *Catfight*, GraffGirlz, and the joint forum fostered when they joined forces in 2008 quickly became a community of graff grrlz armed with a knowledge of self and each other. Once realized and galvanized, it did not simply disappear, but instead continues to enable the development of a transnational network. The transformative results of F. Lady's labor are evident in the fact that today graffiti grrlz can "surf" their way into spaces where they can publicly share experiences, revel in their newly formed affective solidarity, and challenge one another to bring their best battle strategies to the (cat)fight against hetero/sexism in the culture.

"Chicks on Powertrips"

In 2009, upon receiving a Facebook friend request from "Chicks on Powertrips" (*COP*), Anarkia Boladona suggested that I "friend" them as well. The *COP* "crew" plainly stated their mission in the About section of their Facebook page: "to meet more of the new guard." The new guard they reference and invite to join them in their endeavor are the same network of graff grrlz initiated by GraffGirlz.com and *Catfight*— *COP* picked up where *Catfight* left off. Both publications, despite their differences (free versus for sale, DIY zine versus high-end magazine) produced, performed, and circulated feminist sensibilities not only in print(able) form, but also online.

COP began in 2008 as a small full-color print magazine out of Australia dedicated to providing space so that "all female writers have the opportunity to showcase their work."[29] In the launch issue's "Welcome from the Editor," the inaugural name for the magazine was put in context: "I'm not saying any of the girls featured in this magazine [literally] have balls, but these are some gutsy bitches. Jumping fences, copping chases, and running up criminal records in the name of doing what they love. These are crimes of passion."[30] "*COP*," the magazine name they ultimately chose, functions both as an ironic play on the word "cop"—meaning both police officer and to steal or take something—and is also a purposefully promiscuous acronym, signaling many phrases: Crush on Posers, Can't Overstand Pussy, Check Our Pages, and Chicks Out Pimping. The magazine evolved quickly, claiming within two years that they were not just a graff mag, not just for Aussie girls, but the kind of magazine that highlights all the "chicks out there doing rad stuff," making them "easier to spot."[31]

COP founders I. A. and E. J. took the sections of a mainstream women's magazine and restyled them to fit the new guard—the advice is definitively tough love; the recipes require illegal ingredients; the interviews are with strong, outspoken, sexually explicit, successful women; and the how-to's are hilarious, unexpected, and practical (e.g., how to place bets on a horse race or bake with marijuana).[32] Over six years, they published four full issues, two special issues, and developed a very active blog presence on their website, www.c-o-p-magazine.com. The blog, subtitled "Shut Up: The World's Worst Magazine for Girls," offers the "Dirt" on the magazine and its contributors:

> Pronounced "cee-oh-pee," the three letters of our name stand for a bunch of different stuff and we are for the girls that most other girls don't really get. Now up to our third (nearly fourth) issue, we include anything that could be classed as "dope shit for sick bitches" and are gaining a quietly snowballing following across the United States, Australia, Canada and Europe. While other chicks are happy to read articles called What He's

Really Thinking or devour three earnest paragraphs on the social rami-
fications of The New Pencil Skirt, the C.O.P. girl is learning how to forge
someone's handwriting, lose all her money at cee-low or start her own
cult. . . . Not to mention she's having way too much fun to just sit on her
ass and read second-rate girls' mags all the time.

Signaling their cultural affinity with graffiti subculture with the titles
of their blog pages, they also give some information on the "crew":
I. A., the art director and a "degenerate" who "refuses to grow up" while
"lurking in Sydney's back alleys" and "bumpin' some NWA"; Erika,
the editor "responsible for 99% of the swear words on this blog"; Elle
Aye, the subeditor, photographer, and "a dope bitch all in one fly package"; D. L., a writer, blogger, designer, and "one of Australia's smartest
femcees"; and Rio, a writer, blogger, designer, and "tamale-loving desert-
dweller located on the west side of the U.S." Reading through their
self-descriptions, blog entries (from "the Iggy Azalea controversy" to
"the Occupy Movement" to "a haiku for the single girl"), product adver-
tisements (a bedazzled COP forty-ounce beer coozy), and the editorials
("Special Shit"), one is hard-pressed not to notice the abrasive tone, the
vulgar language, and the performance of feminism. When I ordered
issues 4 and 4.5, my package came with a stack of stickers that eventually
inspired this book's dedication: "For All the Girls Who Never Wanted
to Be a MotherFucking Princess." A callous descriptor using one of the
crudest expletives, this sticker says it all.

   COP engaged in a continuous effort to construct an identity both for
themselves and for their readers. I. A. and E. J. found it difficult to define
the kind of reader COP caters to; she is hard to explain in a way that does
not automatically fall into static stereotypes of gender-deviant girls. "For
a while there, the only term we could throw at people that they could
semi-wrap their heads around was that we're a mag for 'tomboys.' . . .
But 'tomboy' is off the mark."[33] Without the language to describe themselves and their readers, I. A. and E. J. took to calling themselves, and
the women in their magazine, "sick bitches." Calling on the trope of the
"hysterical woman" and the "nagging overbearing woman" in one fell
swoop, COP was a magazine/blog that highlighted women so sick (styl-
ish), so ill (cool) that they belong in the headlines. Sick bitches might be

Figure 3.2. "Top 10 Hazards," *COP*, 2012. Photo courtesy I. A.

"trying to put out a mag, run a label, go all-city or get a PhD."[34] Some of the blog entries, "Christmas Gifts for Dope Chicks," for example, define their readers/the new guard indirectly, but others hail them through shared experiences, providing an opportunity through commenting and digital sharing functionalities to respond affirmatively and often with a similar sense of humor. By not defining their reader by who she "is" but rather by what she does and how she feels, *COP* kept its identity fluid yet specific.

In September 2012, I. A. posted a blog entry that resonated with graff grrlz because of its truth and humor. "Lady Problems: Top 10 Hazards for Female Writers" was a half-serious, half-humorous post that briefly described the hazards of writing illustrated graphically with Barbies. The hazards were tetanus (the risk of stepping on a rusty nail in the train-yards if you are wearing the wrong shoe); (stepping in) poo; hookeritis (being mistaken for a sex worker because you are in a dark place, alone, at night); pee (having to squat in the bushes with guys around); (getting hit by) trains; (getting a) sunburn; (being surprised by) Aunt Flo; (inhaling) paint fumes; (going to) jail; and (dealing with) angry bums. The "Hazards" post was shared widely: links appeared on Facebook pages, screengrabs were shared on Instagram feeds, and crews reblogged the entry. Creating images using her signature mix of blunt and comical, I. A. struck a nerve and triggered an affective sensibility that connected grrlz across these various platforms. Examining the proliferation of humorous feminist Internet memes in response to the 2012 U.S. presidential Republican candidate Mitt Romney's statement that he had "binders full of women," Carrie A. Rentschler and Samantha C. Thrift contend that the creation, circulation, and distribution of memes created a "technological, cultural and affective network that enabled participants to *build feminism* and, importantly, *an experience of feminism, together,* across their differences, in shared spaces of consciousness raising on-line."[35] The widespread circulation of I. A.'s captioned graphic demonstrates the power of performing feminism to build affective solidarity across the diaspora, engaging those who may not *identify as* feminists for whatever reason, but who nonetheless *identify with* the sentiment in and of digital feminist cultural productions. The "Hazards" post elevated some graff grrlz' common experiences to points of playful conversation and carefree sharing: experiences that are otherwise shrouded in shame fueled by misogyny—such as being mistaken for a sex worker and bleeding through your underwear.

Always true to their goal of making space to represent graff grrlz, *COP* had a recurring post titled the "Piece of the Week"—my personal favorites. Though the blog is no longer active, it is possible (though admittedly a bit onerous) to locate these posts on the Internet Archive Wayback Machine by typing in the URL, selecting a date range, and then surfing interactive page grabs. Keeping readers up-to-date with the various styles and techniques that graff grrlz were developing across the diaspora, and providing grrlz an opportunity to put themselves and their work out there, these entries were posted on their Facebook page and then, of course, circulated an incalculable number of times through shares. Each piece was representative of what these sick bitches were capable of, captioned with information about the writer, location, and the occasion (when applicable). Not only did this particular series highlight individual writers, but it also provided information about the scene when the piece chosen was a production—the result of a collective effort at an all-grrl jam (more on these in chapter 5). *COP* offered its readers a chance to connect to the "dope shit" graff grrlz were doing as individuals and in collectives. Other graffiti blogs, websites, and social media pages spotlight "burners" (pieces so well executed in terms of color and style that they "burn off" the wall): www.graffiti.org features a chosen writer on the front page, www.12ozprophet.com has the "Forum Shot of the Day," and www.puregraffiti.com and www.fatcap.com both feature artists and crews. Though similar in terms of purpose, the "Piece of the Week" posts differed from these because the editors of *COP* featured only grrlz—a purposefully defiant and radical move.

Like *Catfight*, *COP* produced something for women, to be consumed by (mostly) women, which broke all the rules about what the word "woman" is supposed to signify. Rooting themselves and hopefully their readers in their shared experiences of dissonance due to gender difference within graffiti subculture was a much more successful strategy for inclusion than if they were to position themselves in terms of identity politics. Their approach enabled them to reach across difference and build a new guard of individuals working collectively to change their second-class status in graffiti subculture.

Though I. A. and E. J. ceased all *COP* production in 2014, the new guard they hailed and nourished for six years remains connected.

"Female International Graffiti"

Since Facebook became available to anyone over the age of thirteen with a valid email address in 2006, writers have struggled with the public nature of this social media platform—it is way too easy for anti-graffiti taskforce police officers to connect a writer's real name with a tag name, which means arrest can be imminent if you are not careful.[36] Clearly deciding the digital ups were worth the risk, writers have created countless Facebook pages for themselves, their crews, and their cities—each acting as a kind of digital writer's bench (meeting place) for sharing work and connecting to the subcultural diaspora.[37] But none of these pages made a concerted or collective effort to connect graffiti grrlz in particular—not until "Female International Graffiti" (FIG) was created. Since 2011, FIG has existed as an invite-only "secret group."[38] A heterogeneous group of graff grrlz populates this secret page, posting images of artwork, promoting events, and announcing travel plans (often in hopes of finding a couch to crash on). The majority of FIG's graff grrlz live in the hemispheric Americas and across Europe, and most posts are in English and Spanish (Facebook provides imperfect but satisfactory translations). Feminist performances of various kinds are shared on this page, validating the grrlz' cultural production and creating a transnational diasporic community that would be inconceivable without this digital networking platform.

The group page is now moderated by the user Yo Geisha, a writer from Murcia, Spain, but it was created by Kif, a writer from León, Mexico, who started painting in 2001. The "About" section reads,

> This group has been created to know and to promote the female international graffiti, and so know between we, and share our works. It will be interesting to see the different styles of graffiti according to their country and their evolution. We will be contacted, too. Is only for female writers, you can invite more girls! Este grupo ha sido creado para conocer y promover el graffiti internacional femenino, y así conocernos entre nosotras y compartir nuestros trabajos. Será interesante ver los diferentes estilos

de graffiti de acuerdo a su país y su evolución. Además estaremos en contacto para lo que surja. Es sólo para mujeres escritoras, ¡podéis invitar a más chicas!

On the FIG page, grrlz can receive constructive and generous criticism on their latest throw-up, tag, or production, if they choose to. When it comes to some of the most frequent users, like Kif, you can witness their style progress over the years—*almost* as if you were in the city with them. With each piece she posts, it is clear that Kif's writing skills have improved substantially from basic block-style letters adorned with multidirectional arrows and a timid, often muted color palette (2011 style),

Figure 3.3. Kif, Salamanca Guanajuato, Mexico, 2015. Photo courtesy Kif.

to a rounded block letter boasting layers of "textured" fill-ins in a very bold, almost fluorescent, colorscape (2017 style).

FIG was a natural extension of Kif's documentation and networking labor, which first manifested in a hot-pink and jet-black Spanish-language blog in 2006—LadysGraff.blogspot.com. Understanding all too well the gender-biased isolation and neglect that most graff grrlz experience, Kif used the blog format to show "the works [made by] women within graffiti."[39] Making her intentions clear during our email exchanges, she explained that "there is no interest to foment the feminism. [The blog satisfies] the simple necessity to know the work and . . . points of view of female graffiti writers." For Kif, her blog was a necessary space where graff grrlz could be credited for their role in keeping graffiti subculture alive and dynamic. FIG serves a similar purpose with a wider reach on an easier-to-find platform kept alive by a network of grrlz posting information, images, and introductions. Claiming a space on Facebook specifically for graff grrlz, Kif and the other 311 members of the group are "doing feminism in the network."[40] Through their performances of feminist intentions (community building, peer support, resource sharing) and sensibilities, they foster a larger network of graffiti grrlz in the subculture. Again it is important to note that these grrlz are not connected based on their identity as feminists (per se), nor their nationality, class, gender expression, or sexuality—they are connected through a shared sense that their togetherness in digital space is a relevant and necessary strategy for combating the isolation and discouragement they may feel offline in their local scenes.

The sense of community they build is protected by the kind of Facebook group they have chosen—a private page is a "safe" space because membership is invite-only and posts are moderated. In the five years that I have been a member, I have never seen an inappropriate post or a post get "trolled" with an inflammatory off-topic comment. This is not to say there are not internal conflicts among members in real life or in personal messages, but the interpersonal "beef" that no doubt exists is not posted to the group's wall. The majority of posts come from a place of love, friendship, advocacy, and transnational sisterhood. For example, on February 28, 2015, a Cameroon-based user posted a video of the Egyptian women's street art and graffiti collective "Women on Walls" with a comment (posted in English), "Love it! They are fighting for women [sic] rights . . . they are the voice of women in their cultures. . . . I hope you like it."[41] On April 5, 2014, Kif posted on behalf of another writer planning to travel to the States:

> SEARCHING GRAFFITI WRITERS FROM MIAMI: hello how are you? I'll be in Miami on April 16 to May 6. I am an artist from Argentina, I paint murals and paintings with paint markers and stencils spray. I would like to take 4, 5 days of class because I don't now [sic] to spray thin lines . . etc. . . . do you know of someone who can give me some lessons? [. . .] I hope your answer [sic].

Here, an Argentine graff grrl makes her request through a Mexican graff grrl (Kif) in the hopes of finding a Miami-based graff grrl willing to train her. Locating a teacher, and potential mentor, is just one piece of her post that fellow graff grrlz can empathize with. She is tapping into the common experience that finding someone to teach you in your own city can be a major obstacle. That common experience, rather than an identity as a woman or a feminist, is the grounds for an affective solidarity. As I argued in the introduction, it can be intimidating to approach an older brother or cisgender male friend for help for various reasons, such as the potential for hetero/sexist rumors about your sexuality and/or sexual activity (e.g., the assumption that you are sleeping with your mentor), and the risk that the writers dominating your local scene may be outright hostile to your presence because you are a girl. Both of these realities are experienced as obstacles that run counter to graff grrlz' own sense of commitment and capacity. Tapping into those shared experiences of affective dissonance makes it possible to connect across difference; it also makes it possible to create a collective that can take action, at least digitally, to disavow the dissonance.

Members of the FIG digital network are also avid jam organizers. Without fail, year after year, they post their calls for participation on the group page. Even if an individual Peruvian graff grrl cannot attend an event in New Zealand (or vice versa), for example, she can share it with her network and support the organizer's labor. On January 25, 2013, on a thread related to a call for participation in an event in Peru (Nosotras Estamos en la Calle; We are in the street), an Uruguayan user posted, "Felicitaciones a todas las mujeres que nos jugamos la vida por hacer arte, con las dificultades que ello conlleva en sitios tan machistas" (Congratulations to all the women who risk their lives to make art, with all the difficulties that chauvinistic places entail). It is fair to admit that the large majority of grrlz do not join FIG because they are specifically looking for a way to challenge their subordination within a sexist, male-dominated graffiti culture, but because they are performing feminism within this digital space—and across the digital diaspora—that is exactly what is happening. Graffiti grrlz are taking the opportunity afforded by the social media platform to network with a purpose—to foster collective strength and visibility by offering one another support, respect, praise, and admiration across individual differences.

"FEMALE CAPS"

"FEMALE CAPS: Girls Get Up" is a Tumblr page purposefully designed as a visual hodgepodge of imagery that seduces the digital public to browse, offer a "heart," and reblog the colorful and dynamic graffiti art posted (femalecaps.tumblr.com).[42] The purposefully anonymous "artist/feminist/asshole . . . from north eastern USA" who created "FEMALE CAPS" prioritized images over words, so viewers will not find contact information, and the images are not organized by country, style, or crew.[43] Upon navigating to "FEMALE CAPS," you are greeted by a jet-black background offset with text in a bubblegum-pink easy-to-read straight-letter font. In the upper left-hand corner is an image of the blog name that looks like it is a scanned-in sticker, with spots of light pinks and moss greens, accessorized with a knife, a U.S. dollar symbol, some smiling and frowning faces, the woman symbol, and an exclamation point. There are six menu options: About, Posts, Links, Ask, Submit a Post, and Archive. The About page says, "This blog is dedicated to graffiti and other vandalism art done by females as well as feminist/socially conscious graffiti. Not everything posted is illegal. Most photos are not mine." The Links page is a rather sparse blog roll of "other dope blogs for female/feminist/socially conscious graff," which includes OFFMural-es ("feminist/antiracist/anticorporate street art in Montréal 2013–2014"; offmurales.tumblr.com), Bustoleum (an earlier name for my research blog), Few and Far (www.fewandfar women.com), LAGraffitiGirls ("a blogumentary documenting the lives of female graffiti artists in Los Angeles, California"; lagraffitigirls.tum-blr.com), and *Catfight*. If you want to contribute, you can go to the Submit page to show "your own work or others—it doesn't have to be spectacular—just do yr thing!" The performance of feminism in this instance mirrors how *Catfight* and the GraffGirlz site functioned— graff grrlz have to submit their own work, "spectacular" or not, to the collective oeuvre. And when you visit the Archive section, you can scroll through everything that has ever been posted to the blog; all the way down at the bottom sits the very first group of posts, from August 2012, including a descriptive introduction. "Welcome to Female Caps! I wanted to create a blog dedicated to female graffiti writers. It can be tough being a girl in a boys game but these queens are doing it and doing it well."

The circulation of feminist sensibilities and the development of an affective solidarity in the digital network that I have considered thus far occur a bit differently on "FEMALE CAPS" —mainly because of its out-right politics. "FEMALE CAPS" is a curated collection (the page creator chooses what to post from open submissions) with a *specifically* feminist mantle (unlike the other sites discussed in this chapter) that invites "fe-male" vandals (regardless of their relationship to feminism) and street artists with a political message to submit their work. Usually, in online spaces designed by writers based in the United States and Europe in par-ticular, the line between legal and illegal is enforced as is the related line between spaces for street artists and graffiti writers. It is interesting and telling that the moderator makes allowances for street art vandals of dif-ferent kinds. The moderator understands the multitude of subculturally imposed limitations, tied to an economy of worth and belonging, that may obstruct her purpose: legal versus illegal, graffiti versus street art. Rather than reproduce them, she keeps these lines of value flexible; in keeping it flexible, she gives those on the boundaries the space for inclu-sion. Writers who do not have a specifically feminist presence or iden-tity are included because they are writing graffiti, and street artists who may be doing legal work because they are women. I assume she receives submissions that do not follow her parameters because she occasionally reasserts her curatorial position. For example, a 2015 post states:

I'm not here for porny pictures of women with spray cans
  let's be empowering
  let's give artist's credit
  let's be here for the girls getting up.

The "artist/feminist/asshole" who moderates the page takes the importance of feminist values such as empowerment, respect, and support for granted—as standards of behavior toward graff grrlz that simply should be. The foregrounding of these feminist sensibilities about the way graffiti subculture *should* be is a politicized position that we might imagine as a cumulative effect of digital performances of feminism that came before ("FEMALE CAPS" emerged seven years after GraffGirlz .com). While "FEMALE CAPS" is not necessarily the kind of medium that enables direct connections (e.g., you cannot "friend" other users), because sharing and reblogging is easy the page moderator often reposts items found elsewhere online—further enriching the digital graff grrl network. For example, a post from Mrs's blog appears on "FEMALE CAPS": "Dear women who are into graffiti, You don't have to put on a sexualized show to impress anyone. Do your graffiti and enjoy your spray paint. You don't have to lick a spray paint can for attention. . . . Unless that's what you are into."[44] Additionally, while graff grrlz may not feature prominently on a popular subcultural news outlet like 12ozProphet.com or WhatYouWrite.com, when there *is* a post related to the "FEMALE CAPS" audience it can easily be reblogged and thus redistributed. The continued circulation of these feminist sensibilities, though fairly insular in the grand scheme (it is a subculture after all), broadens their networked public because it affirms the desire and need to be seen, to share thoughts, to compare images, to have their presence and participation "liked."

As one of the youngest digital outlets for graffiti grrlz to perform their feminism, the impact of "FEMALE CAPS" on graffiti subculture is still unknown. For now it is enough to recognize that it is a space to collect—to come together, to share work—that does not require an invitation (like FIG), a PDF download (like *Catfight*), a registration process and username (like the GraffGirlz and *Catfight* forum), or a rather difficult search through an Internet archiving application (like *COP*). "FEMALE CAPS" is currently the most accessible *active* digital platform for graffiti grrlz, and in that regard it is an important step in the digital revolution for graffiti grrlz begun by GraffGirlz.

Graffiti Grrlz' Feminist Techné

The Internet is putting all people in contact. Graffiti travels the world, but unfortunately, people are doing graffiti only to put it online. New generations are thinking that they should paint for fame on the Internet! When I was starting, I didn't have a cam, I tried to capture my work with my friend's cam. We were more concentrated on our work!
—Kif (Mexico)

There are a lot of new females, and it's international. Graffiti has never been more international than it is now. I feel like the Internet has really sped that up and despite my hesitations about us being so public as a society, I also think that the international element is *really* cool. And what's really cool is that graffiti is a skill like dancing or anything and you need a reference. So you can just Google your favorite graf writer and sit there and learn. But back in the '80s and '90s, we were not doing that. We were really just practicing with our friends in blackbooks and just relentlessly practicing our letters and going out in the street and trying to innovate in any way that we could. But the Internet has just accelerated all of that and the amount of people who can learn and organize their own jams worldwide . . . it's just ridiculous.
—Queen Andrea (USA)

Uploaded, scanned, or otherwise turned into data, the multiple, material, local (and mostly criminal or socially deviant), anonymous signatures that grrlz produce in the "real" world now circulate on a transnational scale as digital reproductions. Queen Andrea, a U.S. writer, attests to the fact that before the Internet and the digital revolution, the circulation of graffiti art and graffiti writers' exploits was limited to personal anecdotes, published works, artists' private blackbooks, gallery collections, and personal photographic collections, but now the potential for the circulation of those traces has increased exponentially.

Unsurprisingly, writers express both the positive and the negative effects of graffiti being online—interestingly, both "sides" of the argument have to do with exposure. Spice points to one negative of instant communication and availability when she says that "meeting a pioneer from New York [used] to be like 'Ohmygod.' Now any kid can hit 'em up on Facebook."[45] In Spice's estimation, the excitement of coming across something or someone unexpectedly has been replaced with an assumption of finding who or what you are looking for online. An "oldschool" Hip Hop head from the '80s, she admits that her viewpoint stems from her experience pre-Internet. Within her nostalgic "negative" there is a testimony to the ease, relative accessibility, and intensified usage of the Internet (and related contemporary technologies) to communicate across local and national borders, enabling graffiti writers to connect. I, too, am hesitant to wholeheartedly celebrate the move to digital spaces,

Figure 3.4. Jessica Pabón-Colón interviewing Queen Andrea, Welling Court Mural Project, Queens, NY, 2012. Photo credit ©Martha Cooper.

but for different reasons.[46] The writers' concerns revolve around authenticity, proof of work ethic, and paying dues by doing graffiti illegally. They are concerned that writers are gaining fame for "ups" that the great majority of their fans are only seeing online and so are unable to verify, or gauge, the daring of the act or the quality of the ups (though Miss17 did offer one trick in this regard: is the piece on a "clean" or primed wall?). There are writers seeking fame through the digital *image* that remains, not necessarily for the *act* of getting up. Similarly, the founding principles of getting up for one's local geographic community and developing a style of one's own are losing their import because of the unlimited availability of graffiti imagery circulating digitally—styles can be imitated without giving credit to the source (graffiti plagiarism?) or acknowledging where and how the graffiti was made. Digital images cannot always be traced to a specific locale.

While I am empathetic to these concerns, I recognize them as issues for the subcultural participants to negotiate among themselves and hope they do so without reproducing the hetero/sexist bias that has long been directed at graff grrlz. For example, instead of disregarding graffiti posted in a digital space that is made by a grrl (and signified as such) because of a comment such as "I'm a writer in this city and I don't know who she is," writers might perhaps ask the question, "Well, why don't we know who that is?" There are all sorts of reasons that might explain why a writer may not be known or respected by her local peers (recall RenOne's experience). I challenge writers to think through the easy assumption that just because a writer is not well known (or, specifically, respected and appreciated) in their local community, that her work should not be considered if not appreciated (in and) beyond that locale based on stylistic innovation and proliferation. At first, I hesitated to claim that the Internet is providing a kind of subcultural revolution in agency and equality for graff grrlz. However, after years of delivering "bad news" about the isolation, sexual harassment, and devaluation of graff grrlz, when I started analyzing the effects of social media in particular I finally had good news to report. I want to value that transformation without glorifying it.

Thus, my concern is less with questions of authenticity and more with unintentionally bolstering the idea that "greater visibility of the hitherto under-represented leads to enhanced political power," that digital representation is an uncomplicated solution to graff grrlz' social subcultural precarity.[47] The visibility and presence of graff grrlz—representation in and of itself—is not a magical solution to the misogyny in Hip Hop graffiti subculture, any more than the "fempowerment" campaigns brought to you by companies like Dove, Verizon, or Always are solutions to the ways that consumer culture exploits and abuses girls and women the world over. Expecting that once your identity is represented and made visible that you will be liberated from the oppressive effects of that same identity is risky (if not a failed project to begin with) if/ when the identity being represented is rendered "essential," if it is offered as stable and knowable; it is more productive to be strategic about your representation, the ways you are made visible.[48] It is even better to control your own modes of representation. Graffiti grrlz do not expect that their digital ups will actually "do" anything for them—an expectation I hope to challenge and ask them to reconsider on a collective scale.

When I began this project, there were no digital platforms—or print for that matter—that connected graff grrlz worldwide. Today any dedicated graffiti lover can easily and quickly find graff grrlz through their various digital signatures. Feminism done/performed *in* the network is also feminism doing/performing *a* network, working the connections enabled. The effects of grrlz "working" the network are obvious in hindsight; over the past twelve years feminist sensibilities, affects, and energies have circulated through various digital platforms and have irreversibly altered the sociocultural landscape for graffiti grrlz. In the introduction to their special issue on feminism and media practices, "Doing Feminism: Event, Archive, Techné," Rentschler and Thrift define their conceptualization of "feminist activist techné" as "the technical practices and practical knowledge feminists come to embody as they do feminism with media. Feminists build technological, affective and cultural infrastructures through which they produce, disseminate and share resources, ideals and knowledge."[49] Posting, sharing, liking, and commenting in a graffiti grrl network has become habitual for connected graff grrlz and their soon-to-be connected friends and peers. A visit to any one of the active platforms discussed here will illustrate how habitual, indeed expected, it has become to get up and then get online. The feminist activist techné that has developed over the past decade has and will continue to manifest in how graff grrlz perform feminism in everyday life—their sensibilities reverberating throughout the nondigital world and manifesting in actions like all-grrl painting jams (see chapter 5).[50]

Granted, not all graffiti grrlz participate in these various digital forms in the same ways: some because of an understandable desire for anonymity, others because they do not have access, and still others because of their distaste for social media. Also, many of the creators of these spaces experience what we might call digital feminist burnout—running out of the money to pay your web host or the leisure time and energy required to sustain continuous online activity. Each digital iteration of the graff grrl network performs feminism differently, and each comes to its own kind of "end" unique to the realm of the digital (abandoned, discontinued, relocated, but always "saved"), but the resistant sensibility deeply rooted in the experience of being a grrl in a sexist male-dominated subculture keeps the network alive.

The transnational digital network they have created, and continued to cultivate, sprouts ever-new possibilities for making connections in the present but also for reaching back into the past to discover what might have been lost to graffiti's subcultural story. The frequency with which pages go offline speaks to the conditions of ephemerality inherent to graffiti writing and digital spaces. But the trend to connect online persists because the graff grrl digital network is not limited by mainstream (hetero)normative chronology nor is it a topically linear endeavor. It is rhizomatic. One digital feminist act sprouts another, not necessarily in succession, but sometimes simultaneously from different parts of the world: overlapping, running parallel or perpendicular, intertwining organically, rooting here and there spatially, and moving forward and backward in time *at the same time*—allowing us to affectively map "the paths, resting places, dead ends, and detours" in graffiti grrlz herstory off- and online.[51]

4

Re-Membering Herstory and the
Transephemeral Performative

Graffiti is a means of expression. It is a way to externalize
whatever your feelings are. From the beginning that was the
purpose—to express and make it last, to tell the history of
your times.
—Mugre (Colombia)

An active writer from 2004 to 2008, the Brazilian graffitera Z drew her
inspiration from insects such as butterflies, moths, beetles, and bees
because they are "very little, beautiful and people are afraid of them!!"[1]
Somewhere between a throw-up and a piece, her insects were magnified
in scale, symmetrical, one-dimensional, with solid tertiary colors and
defined by thick clean black outlines finished with wispy, equally spaced
lines projecting from the outline—creating the illusion of movement
and the potential for flight. She transformed concrete urban spaces with
nature's creations, images that communicate incremental change in their
very visuality. Z utilized the stories associated with these creatures to
record her experience, to inspire her fellow urban residents to make the
most of their potential for personal, social, and political change—to
express her desire to see that change happen. Like the other members
of Rio de Janeiro's first all-grrl, explicitly feminist crew—Transgressão
Para Mulheres (Transgression for Women, or Tint for Me)—Z signified
her status as a Brazilian graffitera by tagging her pieces with a pixação-
styled symbol that invokes the iconic fist of resistance and solidarity
with a feminist twist. Painting the feminist fist, with a handstyle that is
unique to Brazil's southeastern cities of São Paulo and Rio de Janeiro,
indicated their geographic specificity and their solidarity with the feminist objective of grrlz' empowerment.

   Graffiti is a form of writing, and as such (according to Jacques Derrida) it is "a powerful means of communication," that can extend "very
far, if not infinitely, the field of oral or gestural communication."[2] As

Figure 4.1. TPM Fotolog page screengrab.

an oft-criminalized and disparaged kind of writing, however, graffiti's life cycle has led to a common understanding that the art form is ephemeral—that it is "something which has a transitory existence."[3] Graffiti's founding aesthetic of proliferation (get up as much as possible) is shaped in part by various kinds of negation. Graffiti marks disappear due to the natural breakdown of surfaces and the fading of paint due to various natural elements, but it also "disappears" at the hands of other writers and nonwriters. It is common for writers to "line" (paint a line through) the tags and pieces painted by those they consider toys, or rivals. Writers also commonly "go over" or "line" each other's work by replacing a peer's graffiti with their own often to reclaim a spot coveted (because of high visibility or level of difficulty) by other local writers. And for their part, authorities at various levels of government and civilian life, hoping to eliminate any evidence of the subculture to maintain social order and a certain "quality of life," regularly buff (paint over or erase with chemicals) the graffiti writing— and thus the "vandal"—from public space.[4] Implicitly, then, graffiti art is simultaneously characterized by the potential for infinite communication but also by ephemerality—something "in existence, power, favour, popularity, etc. for a short time only; short-lived; transitory"— something that disappears.[5]

However, no matter the condition in which they remained on the wall, Z's butterflies—arguably the creatures most often cited as metaphor for both transformation and ephemerality—reappeared in 2009 when I clicked my way from her GraffGirlz.com artist page to her crew's public Fotolog page (www.fotolog.com/tpmcrew/mosaic/). Photographed and uploaded to GraffGirlz.com, the butterflies that Z painted on a wall in 2004 under Rio's hot sun did not simply fade away. To tell her story and "make it last," Z chose to put her graffiti writing online. In doing so, she contributed to the graffiti grrl digital network, began to self-archive, and utilized the capacity of the digital to extend the communication of her message "very far." Her butterflies were saved, uploaded, and transmitted into digital space, and now they exist in multiple times and places beyond their "life" on the wall.[6]

Defying the expectation that graffiti marks will disappear, Z's butterflies remained present, active, and performative. Z's digital performance of presence led me to believe that TPM was an active crew. Overjoyed with the thought that I had located Brazil's first all-grrl graffiti crew, I eagerly analyzed the most recent Fotolog posts and began translating the comments under those posts, slowly devising a plan to meet them and see them in action firsthand. As I mentioned in chapter 2, prior to my research in Brazil and Chile I did not think all-grrl crews existed, so you can imagine my excitement and anticipation. I only learned that the grrlz had retired in 2010 when I was sitting face-to-face with founders Prima Donna and Om in Rio de Janeiro.

Because their graffiti continues to perform their presence as it circulates online, I was able to follow their digital footprint and ultimately document their oral herstory. The disorientation in time that I experienced following Z's butterflies to TPM's Fotolog offered an opportunity to conceptualize the dynamic between proliferation/negation, here/ there, and past/present that characterizes graffiti writing as it exists online. In what follows, I offer a neologism for conceptualizing ephemera in the realm of the digital—"*trans*ephemera"—by examining how graffiti writing performs presence off- and online through a recounting of TPM's herstory.[7] I enter this abstract theoretical terrain to highlight the transformative effects of a digital presence for graffiti grrlz' place in subcultural history and memory.

TPM's Herstory

Usually adorned with jewelry resembling ankhs or the astrological symbol for Venus, Brazilian graffitera Prima Donna's indigenous goddess characters consistently invoke and celebrate the relationship between the earth and the power of the "eternal feminine."[8] Unlike any other writer I have met, Prima, an eco-feminist activist, came to graffiti culture "from the woman's movement" and as a twenty-three-year-old adult.[9] Looking to expand her pedagogical toolkit as a public-school teacher, in 2001 she

Figure 4.2. TPM Fotolog page screengrab.

attended a Hip Hop workshop on using rap as a site for discussing racial prejudice and sexism. The facilitator of that workshop invited her to join a graffiti art class he was teaching and in that class Prima met other women invested in Hip Hop. Wasting no time activating the women in the class, she approached the other grrlz about working together and in no time they formed the Hip Hop collective Quilombola. The name of their collective called upon their Afro-Brazilian ancestry; *quilombola* is the word for someone who lives in a *quilombo*, a community created by "the descendants of slaves who fled Brazil's cotton plantations in the nineteenth century."[10] Quilombola boasted a membership of between twenty and thirty girls who would meet regularly on weekends to celebrate their arts practice. In the beginning, Prima was the only graffiti grrl in the collective; the others were b-girls and rappers.

Noting the gender disparity in Rio de Janeiro's Hip Hop community in general, and in graffiti specifically, she began searching for other graffiteras throughout Brazil. Meanwhile, Quilombola organized a Hip Hop party in Lapa—the central neighborhood in Rio, known for Friday-night parties that shut down the traffic on surrounding streets. Unlike other parties where women were admitted entry for free—presumably to attract more men, the same way that clubs and bars offer women drinks for free—everyone was charged admission. The handful of graffiteras in attendance casually considered forming their own crew, but nothing materialized that evening.

Prima was two years into her research efforts, collecting the names and contact information for graffiteras throughout Brazil. Wanting to put that research to good use, Prima and the grrlz from the workshop organized the first all-grrl graffiti meeting in Brazil in 2004 in São Paulo. At the event, after painting, the writers participated in panels and spoke with each other and the spectators about grrlz' place in Brazil's graffiti culture. Prima's feminist activist agenda was the motivating force behind integrating their conversations about subcultural and social inequities related to gender with a celebration of art and Hip Hop aesthetics. According to Prima, that event marked TPM's "official" creation—Z, Om, Nessa, and Ira were the original members.

Prima's activist efforts flourished between 2004 and 2007, gaining momentum at every stage: a casual group became a crew with notoriety; research borne from one person's curiosity became an activist phone tree connecting graffiteras throughout Brazil; the phone tree became an email listserv, and the listserv became a yahoo group called GraffiterasBR (functioning simultaneously but separately than the network rooted in GraffGirlz.com, mentioned in chapter 3). Prima recounted with pride the fulfillment she experienced each time GraffiterasBR organized a meeting, often in São Paulo. She also noted how their collective art making gained value in the larger community, proven by multiple invitations to paint murals for various Hip Hop events. The experience of participating in a network of passionate, artistic graffiteras validated and fortified Prima's commitment to feminist activism through Hip Hop.

In an effort to empower the other girls in the crew, and give them the opportunity to decide what sorts of activities TPM would participate in and produce, Prima "resigned" from her leadership role in 2007. The shift in structure—from a kind of hierarchy to a collective—ultimately led to TPM's dissolution. Although Prima did not state this outright, my observation is that the nonhierarchical collective structure made organizing unmanageable, given the differences in intent and purpose among the crew members. Within her graffiti community, Prima was accused of being a feminist killjoy; her radical feminist politics made it hard for her to get along with the writers who "just wanted to paint without politics." The other grrlz wanted the group to be centered on the art form they shared, and as the killjoy, Prima was "the one who [got] in the way of an organic solidarity."[11] Painting with a specifically feminist political agenda was not why the grrlz had joined TPM; the political focus was Prima's passion, not the group's. In her words, "TPM lost something" when her feminist vision was no longer guiding the crew's activities. Paradoxically, the something that was "lost" is precisely the something that I found online—an all-grrl crew actively performing feminist purpose through subcultural expression. Their graffiti writing continued the work of communicating their presence (feminist fists and all), even though they had stopped painting anything new.

Digital ups complicate notions of ephemerality because they are not always or "wholly" disappeared, nor are they always or "wholly" remaining. Graffiti art online actuates a different kind of ephemera, one that transgresses normative understandings of presence and materiality, time, and space. These transgressions matter because they enact a change in the status quo when it comes to the gender bias in graffiti subculture's history. Therefore, we must account for those changes to acknowledge and elevate the performative work of ephemera online. Introducing the "Trans-" edition of *Women's Studies Quarterly* (*WSQ*), Susan Stryker, Paisley Currah, and Lisa Jean Moore provoke readers to think seriously about how scholars might begin "to critically trans- our world."[12] Issue contributors set a precedent for the various ways in which "trans-" can complicate and elucidate nonnormative subjectivities and subcultural acts. They share an investment in "bursting 'transgender' wide open, and linking the questions of space and movement that the term implies to other critical crossings of categorical territories."[13] Taking my cue from contributors to this *WSQ* volume in an effort to cross the categorical terrains of graffiti art as an ephemeral art form, and the ephemeral as that which does not remain, I offer the term "transephemera." With this term, I invoke "trans" as a performative prefix that has a transformative effect on conceptualizations of ephemerality bounded by conventional understandings of temporality, spatiality, and materiality. Or, in performance studies parlance: a prefix that *does* something.

Affixing "trans" to ephemera destabilizes static notions of ephemerality that do not adequately describe the performance of cultural products online. As mentioned above, it is a common and expected occurrence that a writer's tag will be buffed (scrubbed from the surface with chemicals), lined (written over by another writer), or fade (under the sun's ultraviolet light). But it is important to recognize that buffing, lining, and fading are *generative* acts of negation; they provoke the writer to get up in that same spot once more.[14] Before painting one of her goddess characters in a new spot, for example, Prima would anticipate the necessity of painting another one in that same spot at some point in the (near or distant) future—holding your spot against the odds of erasure is one of the main imperatives for writers out to claim place. Utilizing "trans" as a prefix emphasizes the generative potential in acts of negation and highlights the coproductive aesthetics of ephemerality and proliferation foundational to graffiti art subculture. These aesthetics are compounded exponentially with the use of the Internet. Graffiti offline may be ephemeral, but graffiti online is transephemeral.

Transephemeral objects are what Benjamin might call "mechanical reproductions" of material performances (images of graffiti) that are made into digital files, which are then activated and circulated in cyberspace.[15] The performative work of the transephemeral object (aka the transephemeral performative) is to propel the graffiti performance's presence and meaning not only outward from the beginning performance event or forward into indefinite times and spaces, but also backward as the memory of a mark that materialized in the past yet simultaneously exists in the now. Digital ups not only support "two of writing's key elements—technical virtuosity and its publicity-generating function"—but also exaggerate those elements.[16] For graff grrlz, the "political promise of the performative" in their online performances is that in meaning more, saying more, and doing more they are able to revalue graffiti culture's gender-biased conventions; getting up and getting over return to graffiti culture modified by their presence online, slowly but surely reversing the effects of a canon constructed without them.[17]

In *Brazilian Hip Hoppers*, Derek Pardue asserts: "Young women have been part of hip hop culture in Brazil since the beginning; however this participation has not translated into even basic terms of reference."[18] Catching digital ups reconfigures how writers are able to "translate" graff grrlz' participation into more than basic "terms of reference." The case of TPM demonstrates that through the performative effects of transephemeral objects, graff grrlz can re-member (as in memorialize and as in put back together) the stories of their predecessors and reconstitute themselves in graffiti history. With the understanding that "there is no political power without control of the archive, if not of memory," it is important that we understand how catching digital ups enables grrlz to participate and have (some) control over the ways in which their graffiti art is re-membered, a strategy for visibility that also reconstructs *her*story in a subculture definitively shaped by *his*story.[19]

Graffiti Performs Presence

Graffiti writing is always acting, always live, always communicating through performance beyond graffiti writers' physical presence, beyond their initial bodily performance (beyond the moment of getting up). Graffiti is a performance executed often under the cover of night, hidden from an immediate or attentive audience. The graffiti signature (tag, throw-up, character, or piece) performs without and beyond the actor's physical presence for an implied audience that may or may not be present at the time of the event but is always considered as part of the act. While the principles guiding writers' primary aesthetic choices and responses to legal implications depend on locale, there is one unchanging guiding principle throughout the Hip Hop diaspora specific to graffiti: be prolific. The incentive behind repetitively and relentlessly getting up on as many spots as possible ("burnin' " the competition) is to be visible enough so that you can successfully communicate your existence and your abilities: it is to be present. The ontological imperative of graffiti writing as performance is that the initial mark must then perform the presence of the writer. To validate the performance of presence the graffiti must be seen "acting" by the graffiti community; the community affirms the subject's belonging and subcultural identity. The subcultural mandate is to perform your presence for an audience that will appear later: an audience that is not meant to witness the graffiti's creation. Spray painted "in order to communicate something to those who are absent," Prima's goddesses and Z's insects perform their presence in their absence.[20] As is evident in the case of TPM, graffiti communicates presence even when the subject herself is radically absent, even when she has disappeared from the scene. The graffiti grrl lives through her graffiti image: the representation of her performance *is* the performance. Digital ups allow the repetitious performance of presence in another realm.

Conceptualizing graffiti writing as the performance of presence challenges the prioritization of liveness (and, in fact, how liveness itself is theorized) and the body in definitions of performance—an ever-present consideration within the field of performance studies (reanimated recently by discussions of "re-performance" mostly in the visual arts).[21] In *Unmarked: The Politics of Performance*—a touchstone on this topic— Peggy Phelan claimed that the life of a performance exists only in the present that "cannot be saved, recorded, documented, or otherwise participate in the circulation of representations of representations."[22] In her approach, performance exists only in a normative present, a "now" confined to the limits of the uncomplicated material. The other modes of representation for that performance (video, photograph) are not considered a performance in her frame because of how she theorizes "now," the "present," and "live." For Phelan, these modes of representation are no longer performance but become something else entirely. Through this framework, Prima Donna's performance of feminism is only "performance" in the moment of its happening—her goddess characters and letters only perform feminism as the paint coats the wall. But, as was made clear when I became an audience member, a spectator, through my use of the Internet, those goddesses continue to perform Prima's ecofeminism beyond the live moment of painting, fulfilling their purpose as "the written." "For the written to be the written," Derrida asserts, "it must continue to 'act' and to be legible even if what is called the author of the writing no longer answers for what [she] has written . . . whether [she] is provisionally absent," or, as is the case for members of TPM, if she has simply stopped producing new writing.[23] Phelan's frame as is cannot account for the way that graffiti art performs presence—on- or offline. Within graffiti culture's principles and intentions, the thing that remains when the body making the mark disappears is precisely what enables the performance and activates the performativity, the "representations of representations"—the photographs, now digitized.

Rebecca Schneider discusses the historical implications of understanding disappearance and ephemerality as part of performance in her article "Archives: Performance Remains." "If we consider performance as 'of' disappearance, if we think of ephemerality as 'vanishment,' and if we think of performance as the antithesis of 'saving,' " she provokes, "do we limit ourselves to an understanding of performance predetermined by a cultural habituation to the patrilineal, West-identified (arguably white-cultural) logic of the Archive?"[24] Challenging the privileging of disappearance in Phelan's conception of performance and her dependence on the "logic of the archive" in considering performance as "that which does not remain," Schneider asks if we in fact "ignore other ways of knowing, other modes of remembering, that might be situated precisely in the ways in which performance remains, but remains differently."[25] When graffiti writing is witnessed online, the bodily performance is unavailable past the normative present, past the "now" in which it was happening in the physical world, but it is actively communicating presence through a different representational mode—the photos TPM crew members archived on Fotolog. What remains after the bodily performance of graffiti writing is purposeful. In order to reimagine the temporal and spatial boundaries of performance in relation to graffiti art in the digital realm, we have to pay attention to what remains and how (and why) those remains are left to be found.

Presence Remains, Remaining Present

Graffiteras spend minutes or hours painting their tags, throw-ups, and pieces with the full awareness that the images will not survive in the form in which they were originally created. Knowing this, the writers' primary concern is how their graffiti will circulate, how it will be engaged, and how their presence will be recognized and actualized. Lady Pink explains this aspect of graffiti art in a short film by Jane Teeling, *Kiss It Goodbye: Lady Pink Paints New York City*: "It is nearly impossible to try to preserve something for the sake of art. And when we painted subway trains, perhaps we learned that lesson the hardest of all. You paint your train [*blows a kiss*], kiss it goodbye—you might never see it again. Maybe someone won't even take a photo of it, and it will just be a memory." Graffiti art provides a gritty, unexpected, and relentless public commentary on the politics of ownership and the question of public space under settler colonialism, imperialism, and capitalism. It is a subculture that uses the power of words to communicate—even when the image is but an illegible name proclaiming presence, even when the writer knows she must kiss her creation goodbye. Writers have an intimate understanding of the relentless undulation between creation (appearance) and erasure (disappearance), but just as appearance does not promise "total" visibility, erasure is not a deterrent or an endpoint. Rather than succeeding in discouraging or defeating the writer, erasure is a productive provocation, a dare: do better; be bolder; take more space; write again!

With a letter combination that resonates sonically as it registers visually, the sparsely embellished letters O and M vibrate off of the wall—inverted and graffiti-styled, Om's version of the Sanskrit symbol signifies the sacred philosophy by which she lives. Om is a practicing Hare Krishna and wanted her tag name to represent that part of her identity. "Om is a meditation. Om is a mantra, a universal sound, so when you think, you are meditating."[26] Om believes that her graffiti should be more than an individual gesture or action: "it is a message. Om is a peaceful sound." Om also paints mandalas, either freehand or stenciled, augmenting her message of peace, balance, interconnectedness, and spirituality with a gesture toward the Buddhist philosophy that nothing in the universe is permanent. She punctuates the message with the pixação-styled fist of feminist resistance that signals she is a member of TPM.

Years before acting on her inclination to paint, Om was inspired as a teenager by the 1996 film *Basquiat*; in 2000 she became the first woman in Nation Crew. Before joining TPM, Om recounted, "It was difficult because there was a lot of resistance with women doing graffiti." Giving examples, she noted several incidents where she was literally denied space on the wall and access to ostensibly shared paint or particular colors (with the implication that if she used them, the paint would be "wasted"). After joining TPM she felt "more assertive and strong" because she had the opportunity to articulate her experiences of being oppressed in the larger graffiti community with a group of grrlz who could commiserate. Om made a point to note TPM's historical significance and sociopolitical importance as a feminist group: "Today women can graffiti without the same kind of issues, and TPM is of great importance in that respect because TPM cracked the prejudice and paved a way for the other women."

Om was not exaggerating their impact. When I went to Rio, the many grrlz I spoke with consistently named TPM as their predecessor. TPM's performance of feminism through graffiti art does not have the capacity to "pave the way" because it was present at one time, but because it is actively present now in the form of a digital reproduction that circulates and engages an online public. Ivor Miller's assertion that "aerosol art testifies to a will to live and a refusal to submit" is another way of describing the ontology of graffiti art performance accentuated once the art is made digital: TPM's presence remains despite the disappearance of the writers; their performance remains despite the fading of the paint on the wall.[27] The reproductions of Om's mandalas and letters, stored and shared online, remain beyond the local or national, beyond the logic of the archive, and beyond a single event—queering the strictures of temporality, spatiality, and materiality. Therein lies the "how" of the upsurge in the number of graff grrlz and their increased visibility, enabled by digital media. The trace (*of* the performance and *as* the performance) left behind on the wall after the writer has made herself scarce now habitually circulates on the Internet in a different ephemeral ontological condition and becomes part of an ever-growing digital archive, a point in an infinite network transforming the subculture aesthetically, socially, and politically.

Subcultural Memory and the Archive

Before the Internet became a dominant location for posting yourself/your graffiti to the virtual public, documentation of tags, throw-ups, and pieces lived primarily in blackbooks (sketchbooks) and printed photographs. Collectors and aficionados made decisions about what was saved and how it was valued in their private archives. Access to materials (photos/sketches) depended on one's immediate network—what kinds of writers one knew, what kinds of writers one valued, and what kinds of writers one devalued, labeled "other," and/or purposefully ignored. Scholars, journalists, or the writers themselves then mined those personal archives for various kinds of publications (coffee-table books, scholarly manuscripts, magazine articles) that then became the histories and commenced the historiography. The problematics of this for graffiti grrlz in a hetero/sexist male-dominated subculture should be obvious: What is remembered? What is saved? Who decides the value of what is saved? What are the factors that go into these decisions? Archiving is not a politically neutral activity (and nor are the results of those archives); it happens in the context of a subcultural value economy; the project of remembering graffiti history (like any history, really) is always already laden with gendered, racialized, sexualized, classed ideologies. Prima's research project on graffiti grrlz in Brazil was at least in part informed by this realization: being remembered matters. It is no wonder, then, that her efforts to remember Brazilian graffiteras quickly turned digital; the digital is a tool for self-archiving that challenges the hetero/sexist power dynamics of the archive—these grrlz are not waiting "to be saved." They save themselves.

Interrogating the social and political potential of a digital existence for those who have literally been written out of history requires that we queer conceptions of time (the digital revels in nonlinear temporality) and notions of ephemerality in relation to the archive's constitution and interpretation. While Schneider considers the remains of performance as immaterial, José E. Muñoz interrogates the conditions of materiality itself in "Ephemera as Evidence: Introductory Notes to Queer Acts." Muñoz considers how queer works of art do not leave the kind of trace that would be easily accessed by those with punitive, disciplinary gazes and often violent intentions. Instead, the trace is by necessity a kind of "invisible evidence" recognized by those in the know.[28] "Queer ephemera," as he deems it, challenges the static relationship between the archive and materiality while emphasizing the importance of memory and/to performance. For him, queer ephemera is "firmly anchored within the social" and "includes traces of lived experience" maintaining "experiential politics and urgencies" beneath, betwixt, and between the layers of visibility. For Muñoz queer ephemera is an indication of what has occurred, but "certainly not the thing itself."[29]

The notion of queer ephemera constructively unpacks how TPM's online existence modifies notions of materiality—that what is considered "material" remaining evidence does not have to be composed of matter (the performer's body in "real" time), but may be made of affect, of memory, and of code (os and 1s). But the implications of invisibility and continual erasure at the hands of others are of paramount importance for graff grrlz whose main imperative is to be visible, to be recorded, to be recognized for their participation. If there is no perceptible evidence for even those "in the know" (other writers), then the performance cannot be performative—TPM's feminist graffiti art cannot inspire, provoke, change history, or pave the way for future generations of writers if there is no visible evidence. Graffiti online queers notions of ephemerality and materiality in such a way that there *is* evidence to be saved. Wrestling with the boundaries of the archive (what is present or absent and why), Jack Halberstam asserts that "we need to theorize the concept of the archive, and consider new modes of queer memory and queer history capable of recording and tracing subterranean spaces."[30] For graff grrlz the Internet is one such archive, one subterranean space where their performances are kept, validated, and circulated as live memories performing presence. As images of marginalized histories, these digital representations are produced and shared out of a desire—indeed a political necessity—for participation in the construction of subcultural memory.

In *How Societies Remember*, Paul Connerton argues that "images of the past" are and must be acknowledged as, remembered, transferred, and sustained through a recognition of their traces, of what remains in whatever form it remains in.[31] The images of TPM in the past remain, leaving evidence of their subcultural acts that the Internet and its users are capable of saving. The spectacle of the TPM crew in action, for example, is unavailable past the normative present. And yet the knowledge that TPM was there—defiantly and joyfully wielding spray paint to write their names on a wall—remains. The Internet saves the evidence of the provocation fulfilled, of the performance realized and allows it to be performed again and again—just as it is meant to.

Connerton argues that memory must be understood as a social entity transmitted by and through, primarily, ritual and habitual performances. He emphasizes the importance of some kind of trace that connects the way we experience "now" with the ways we experienced "then." Indicating the significance of embodied and nontraditional sociocultural memory-making processes, he posits that "for some time now a generation of mainly socialist historians have seen in the practice of oral history the possibility of rescuing from silence the history and culture of subordinate groups. Oral histories seek to give voice to what would otherwise remain voiceless even if not traceless, by reconstituting the life histories of individuals."[32] Knowing that the gender bias that informs the graffiti studies archive also informs the transmission of oral history, graffiti grrlz are "rescuing" themselves from silence and reconstituting themselves despite various kinds of erasure by making their graffiti work public and digital. What I would like to suggest is that the act of posting one's graffiti art to the Internet is a new mode of transfer happening within an affective digital network. Not only are grrlz "rescuing" their silenced histories and building them into Hip Hop graffiti subculture's history through the work of the transephemeral performative, but by doing so they are also enriching the Hip Hop diaspora in such a way that includes (if not centers) their work.

In the oft-quoted but endlessly instructive text *Imagined Communities*, Benedict Anderson reminds us that "all communities larger than primordial villages of face-to-face contact (and perhaps even these) are imagined. Communities are to be distinguished, not by their falsity/genuineness, but by the style in which they are imagined."[33] In graffiti subculture, the style is decidedly and paradoxically counterpublic; a graffiti "writer's meaningful and unique artistic practices were developed [in the United States] on the trains, illegally, performatively, and noncommercially."[34] The fact that graffiti is a criminalized subculture affects questions of accessibility and approachability; putting oneself online makes the inaccessible stories, evidence, and existence of graffiti grrlz accessible—able to be remembered. In "E-scaping Boundaries," Emily

Noelle Ignacio explores the ways that gender, race, and culture figure into building a nation when the "images of a nation" can be articulated by anyone through accessible technological advances, as opposed to the authoritative power structures traditionally in charge of nation building. "Because the Internet is a transnational space where people from all over the world can converge, [scholars] can better examine how this kind of technology affects the construction of national, racial, ethnic, and gendered identities and can help create new coalitions apart from, rather than through the maintenance of, these socially constructed boundaries."[35] Creating and maintaining a digital presence allows these countercultural "deviants" to control their image and manage the representations circulating about them (to an extent). Further, a larger audience can witness their performances of place and belonging, can witness their digital ups and imagine them as cultural producers—as relevant participants in Hip Hop graffiti subculture across the diaspora. While they may not command the conventional historical accounts of graffiti subculture, these grrlz are setting the tone of the narrative for the future.

How societies remember depends on what they save and how they do so. We can save conversations and interactions that happen online, download an image, take a screen shot, and in these ways extend the work of memory making, archiving countercultural practices, and constructing minoritarian histories. A thoroughly reproductive performance that deviates from conventional acts and processes as related to gender roles, the logic of the archive, and modes of visibility, the transephemeral performativity of graffiti imagery has the capacity to shape history, memory, and thus the boundaries of community—generating a radical shift for marginalized subcultural participants. The Internet, specifically digital communication software and social media apps and sites, has given rise to this form of performance; transephemerality is specific to digital media.

Due to their infinite iterability, transephemeral objects construct and reconstruct the particularities and politics of queer acts in time, space, memory, and consequently history. The transephemeral performative mark presents an opportunity to think the relationship between materiality and memory outside of the logic of the archive that currently informs the development of the graffiti canon. The same logic that informs conceptualizations of the archive informs what is "worthy" of being saved, printed, and published. Prior to the availability and relative accessibility of the Internet, being minority subjects within a counterpublic subculture, the TPM crew's place-making presence was doubly removed from the construction of history, from the field of vision—the canon—influenced by patriarchal sociopolitical hierarchies of power. The opportunity to participate in the transmission of history, the making of memory, and the allocation of cultural value in the digital world is of critical political importance when your position in the analog world is hindered by your social demographic.

TPM as a feminist crew doing feminist events is no faint memory lost to history, but, as represented online, is an active transephemeral object existing both in the time/space of the photo capture and in the time/space of the Internet user's now. Fotolog provides one means for TPM to claim power as agents of the way that the memory of their work exists in, and matters to, the constitution of Rio's graffiti history. The threat of losing something to the past, to a displaced history as time marches "forward," is diminished when what could be lost lives online. In *Illuminations* Walter Benjamin writes that "memory creates the chain of tradition which passes a happening on from generation to generation."[36] The Internet is a site where happenings are continuously passed, where "acts of transfer" happen, and where "social knowledge, memory, and a sense of identity [are] reiterated" moment to moment through the bodily acts of posting, clicking, saving, interacting, and sharing.[37] Transephemeral performatives are mediated acts of transfer; instead of person to person, these performances are person to technology to person. Digital places like Fotolog provide unique time/space opportunities for anyone with access to the Internet, a digital camera, image-uploading software, a scanner, or a smartphone to become a producer or consumer of an alternative recording of history by participating in the chain of memory transfer. The transephemerality activated by their digital artistic act re-members TPM, despite their "disappearance."

Re-Membering TPM's Herstory

> GRAFFGIRLZ: According to you, being a woman in graffiti, which is a mainly masculine world, is it an asset or a difficulty? How are you perceived by the male writers?

Z: Being a woman in this world is a difficulty, like being a woman in the world, but nothing that discourages me. Sometimes people don't expect good graffiti work from a woman. When we make something good they say that we paint like men!?? What?!! Sometimes we are not invited to paint some walls.[38]

When asked by the editors of GraffGirlz.com why she loved graffiti, Z responded, "I love graffiti because it's a social art, available to everyone." Sociality is a crucial component of the production, consumption, and reproduction of graffiti culture—it is made for those who are part of the graffiti community proper and for the general public (although surely, it means something different to each audience). Those places on the Internet that specifically invite participation from "everyone" function as sites of memory, or, as Pierre Nora would call them, "lieux de memoire."[39] The memory of the creative labor taken to produce Z's graffiti is located in and secreting from these sites. Because we can never be sure what exactly happens to those images once an Internet user interacts with them, the history made through this site of memory is certainly fraught with uncertainty. Websites go up and down and walls get painted over, but countercultural rhythms, queer rhythms, leave traces on the surface and online—and in the memories of individuals and collectives.[40] When Nora considers the difference between memory and history, he notes that "memory is life. . . . It remains in permanent evolution, open to the dialectic of remembering and forgetting, unconscious of its successive deformations, vulnerable to manipulation and appropriation, susceptible to being long dormant and periodically revived. History, on the other hand, is the reconstruction, always problematic and incomplete, of what is no longer. Memory is a perpetually actual phenomenon, a bond tying us to the eternal present; history is a representation of the past."[41] The memories of Z's work, once they drift away from her purpose and performance and exist mainly online, enter into an open and vulnerable process of being altered and understood to mean differently than originally intended. As performatives, Judith Butler reminds us, TPM's signatures are excitable, they are "uncontrollable," excessive, communicating more and differently than intended and not only in "a momentary happening."[42] Even before writers put digitized images of their work online, they performed a purposefully and necessarily precarious representation always in process, always circulating, always disappearing and reappearing. Z's butterflies drift, but they also land, attaching to sites that "anchor, condense, and express" excitable memories in service of a constantly restabilizing history.[43] The comment function and the tag function allow the poster to contextualize the images if she so chooses and thus grounds the memory even as it travels through the digital world as a reproduction susceptible to alterations. The susceptibility to alteration for a digital file, another facet of graffiti's aesthetic of negation, further demonstrates the transephemerality of graffiti as it exists online. However, susceptibility to change, risk of loss, and potential for erasure are valued as powerful aesthetic components, not weaknesses, in graffiti culture. In a 2012 article for the *Village Voice*, the Hip Hop historian Jeff Chang states "what makes graffiti an art form is the ability to dangle itself over the abyss—and occasionally fall in."[44] Writers know that their images, their performances of self via representation, can and will get "lost" in the ever-growing space of the Internet; they will "go down" (fall in) with the site that hosts them. But for writers, the ups are always worth the risk of the fall.

Being in the midst of the digital era of graffiti subculture, we cannot know the long-term effects of contemporary graffiti writers "taking" cyberspace. However, we can and must account for the role that moving from the brick wall to the digital wall plays in the history of the art form, in the evolving aesthetics of the genre, and in the social dynamics of its participants. In the digital era, social media spaces are the spaces of social ritual, vehicles for affecting the way TPM's message is dispersed and transformed. Without their images and words living now online, this all-grrl, feminist crew might be forgotten. Now it is made available to a wider public capable of re-membering and of actively including TPM in the transference of memory and the creation of history. The Internet opens the labor of memory making to a global public—or at least those with Internet access—expanding out from the local and connecting to the social realm of the digital diaspora. Z's graffiti continues to perform her purpose, which was to communicate "directly, free and public . . . for ordinary people." Transephemeral performatives archive outside of the traditional systems that are generally used to exclude those same people whom graffiti writers are trying to reach—the public, the disenfranchised and the marginalized, those who have historically been left out of deciding what society (or subculture) remembers.

At the very end of our three-and-a-half-hour interview, Prima noted that it does not matter who was the first graffitera in Rio, "the important thing is who keeps painting." Marking their presence in subcultural memory by remaining present digitally allows TPM to secure their place in history and to ensure women's participation in the chain of tradition, which carries their legacy from generation to generation. Anarkia Boladona attests to the fact that her organization Rede Nami is a direct descendant of TPM (see chapter 2). Rio's first all-grrl crew does not disappear; their feminist actions and their role in the foundation of Brazil's graffiti subculture do not fade into the background. Quite the contrary. The transephemeral performativity of graffiti subculture online demonstrates the political potentiality in a spatiotemporal, digital, and analog presence, one that re-members that, despite their seeming or actual absence, the graffiteras of TPM are present and continue to act, to inspire, and to transgress boundaries. TPM remains to be found, and found again—a reminder of the cultural work Brazil's first all-grrl crew accomplished when they decided to claim digital space.

Coda

In the early years of my research, in an effort to develop an oral history specific to graffiti grrlz I made it a point to ask each grrl to tell me what she knew about graffiti grrl history. The kinds of responses I received depended on many factors: age (the older grrlz knew a bit more); connections (the grrlz who were the only women in their crew repeated an androcentric history); and location (writers tend to be more familiar with their local history and the "classic" New York City stories from '80s films and texts). It soon became clear that I would get the same stories about Lady Pink repeatedly, with a bit of variation depending on the country (for example, Spice is a legend in Australia, Mad C in Europe). My inability to collect the stories through oral history or an examination of every secondary source available made my original project, then titled "Burnin' Up the Graffiti Canon," a seemingly impossible task, which only became more impossible as the project transformed from a hemispheric examination of graffiti grrlz in the Americas into a transnational ethnography. Consequently, I reached a point when I simply stopped asking the grrlz what they knew about women in graffiti history and committed to including as much backstory as possible in my book. I decided to focus on the context—the story that would explain why it is so hard to locate and assemble graffiti grrl herstory to begin with.

In this chapter on the transformative potential in transephemeral objects to give minoritarian subjects the power to historicize themselves, I claim that graffiti grrlz are not waiting for their stories to be rescued—they are, and have been since they went online, doing the work of self-archiving as best they can. I discovered the most recent example one morning in March 2017 while scrolling through my Instagram feed. I came upon an image of Charmin 65 of the infamous ExVandals crew painting in Brooklyn, posted on the "@GraffitiHerstory" user feed (www.instagram.com/graffitiherstory). The caption to the 2016 photo read "Can't start this off right without giving respect where respect is due! The first #Graffiti female #lady to cross over to the #subway-train yards in the 1970s #Queen #Goddess #Charmin65 #ExVandals" (www.instagram.com/p/BDuE1GdLOD6/). Charmin 65 is one of the graffiti grrlz whose name is repeated in canonical texts such as *Getting Up* and *Aerosol Kingdom*, but her story remains untold.

The "@GraffitiHerstory" project is worthy of our attention because there are still only a few places where graffiti grrl history is available—including the digital spaces and published accounts I have discussed in previous chapters (refer to the introduction for a discussion of the canonical texts). While the sites I mentioned in this chapter and in chapter 3 certainly contribute to the project of historicizing graffiti grrlz and making their presence known, most of the sites are no longer online and the ones that are provide more images than stories, more quotes and captions than descriptions. The oldest example, as far as I know, is the "Female Writers" page on the website *@149st: The CyberBench: Documenting New York City Graffiti*, which claims a copyright of 2001 (www.at149st.com/women.html). Visitors to this page are treated to information about grrlz painting in New York City's boroughs in the "early 1970s," "mid to late 1970s," "1980s," and "1990s–present day," but each section has only a few sentences with very few hyperlinks. In other words, the sparse information that does exist is scattered, never presented in a collection.

Addressing the gap left in graffiti history when grrlz' stories go untold is the mission of the "@GraffitiHerstory" project. Considering how contemporary graffiti grrlz across the diaspora utilize their affective digital network to organize all-grrl graffiti painting jams (the subject of the next chapter), I was not surprised to discover that "@GraffitiHerstory" is the social media presence of the annual all-grrl paint jam series *Her Story*. *Her Story* was launched in May 2016 at a legal Inwood wall in the Bronx.[45] The first jam included Lady K Fever (originally from Vancouver where she started bombing in the '90s), Meli, Rocky 184, Charmin 65, Miss Boombox, Gem13, and Neks. Lady K Fever, the series organizer, interdisciplinary artist, curator, and community educator, explained to Lois Stavsky of StreetArtNYC.org that "women are underrepresented in the graffiti world. The mission of *Her Story* is to provide us female writers with a supportive environment to tell our stories while sharing our skills with others." Because "@GraffitiHerstory" is a new project, the scope and impact (largely dependent on peer support) are still unknown, but the impetus and the effort of taking on a project that would collect graffiti grrl histories are not to be ignored or taken for granted by people invested in graffiti studies. Because graffiti writers have an online presence that makes the subculture's past and present more accessible than it has ever been, contemporary graffiti studies scholars have a unique opportunity to advance the field; I hope it is not wasted. As the growing number of all-grrl crews and the visibility of all-grrl painting jams attests, herstory is not something that only exists in the past, it "is still being written."[46]

5

Transforming Precarity at International All-Grrl Jams

Let's be a group . . . like a movement. Let's not female bash—
there's enough of that, why should we contribute to it? Let's
make this massive army of "femme fatales."
—JesOne (USA)

The performativity of gender is thus bound up with the
differential ways in which subjects become eligible for
recognition. . . . The desire for recognition can never be
fulfilled—yes, that is true. But to be a subject at all requires
first complying with certain norms that govern recognition—
that make a person recognizable. . . . We think of subjects as
the kind of beings who ask for recognition in the law or in
political life; but perhaps the more important issue is how the
terms of recognition—and here we can include a number of
gender and sexual norms—condition in advance who will
count as a subject, and who will not.
—Judith Butler, "Performativity, Precarity and Sexual Politics," iv

Hailing from Queens, New York, an Italian American graff grrl named
JesOne explained that she designed her *ToughLove* T-shirts to fashion an "army of femme fatales," a movement of graff grrlz working to
strengthen one another, rather than reproduce the hetero/sexism prevalent in the subculture.[1] Referencing the all-too-familiar hypersexual
archetype of films and novels—the "femme fatale"—JesOne's intention
was to draw on the uninhibited utilization of a particularly feminine
gender performance to gain power within a social situation. Many of
the grrlz in this study have expressed their desire for a space that would
foster peer recognition, an alternative to always being discounted, or not
counted at all within the subculture, or Hip Hop culture, because of their
gender presentation or gender identity. Recall Lady Pink's sentiment that

"if you're too feminine you're not successful" (from chapter 1). Graffiti grrlz, and the girls and women involved with other elements in Hip Hop culture throughout the diaspora, routinely take matters into their own hands in an effort to eliminate this dynamic.[2] They create various kinds of spaces—digital spaces (see chapters 3 and 4), spaces in their cities (and beyond those borders) for all-grrl crews (see chapter 2), and event spaces to celebrate their artistry. The latter is the focus of this chapter.

dream hampton, a renowned Hip Hop journalist, reminded onlookers of this fact at a June 2012 debate called "Hip-Hop on Trial: Hip-Hop Doesn't Enhance Society, It Degrades It," hosted by the Barbican Centre in London: "even as we are faced with misogyny, women in Hip Hop have [always] created spaces to be confrontational about that sexism and misogyny."[3] Despite the persistence of these women in Hip Hop, time and again their efforts go unnoticed or unremarked upon; in that same debate on whether Hip Hop "degrades or enhances society," not one of the nineteen speakers (seventeen men, two other women) engaged hampton on her point—essentially discarding what could have been a productive alternative direction for discussion. Instead, the panelists and moderators repeatedly circled the question of language in rap music: the internalized racism of the "n" word, and the misogyny of the "b" and the "h" words. Stuck in the same cyclical concerns about Hip Hop music, what Tricia Rose calls the "Hip Hop Wars," the panelists missed an important opportunity to illuminate those alternative spaces that hampton attempted to bring to the center of the debate. Here I acknowledge the importance of hampton's provocation, and rethink the terms of the debate on Hip Hop's beneficial or detrimental effects on society, by looking to the creation of spaces that are not only alternative, but also unexpected, perhaps even counterintuitive.

Two annual, international all-grrl events, Ladie Killerz (Australia) and Femme Fierce (United Kingdom), afford opportunities for graff grrlz to publicly perform as "femmes" or "ladiez" within a transnational subculture where the performance of hetero/sexist male masculinity is the convention that determines who gets counted as a subject of Hip Hop culture. Otherwise experiencing tremendous precarity because of the politics of gender difference, events such as these reimagine the value and worth of graff grrlz to the subculture. Different in focus from, though certainly tied to, theorizations of precarity that centralize precarious life in terms of nations or material concerns (food, shelter, health), here precarity is theorized on a subcultural register—in terms of the social relations between subcultural actors participating in annual events that hope to transform a male-dominated hetero/sexist environment. Graffiti subculture thrives on social relation; in this economy, aesthetics and peer recognition have value, but who gets to spend or accrue this value through their artistic labor differs based on gender conventions. Graff grrlz are vulnerable within this economy because their aesthetics *and* their bodies (thus their peer recognition) are valued differently—often, their artistic contributions do not "count" and their bodies have a value based in sexualization and objectification. Within their own subcultural society, hetero/sexist patriarchal structures of difference result in a gendered precariousness that actively undervalues graff grrlz' presence. Of course, all graff grrlz do not experience the exact same kind, or depth, of precarity—the process of precaritization depends wildly on who you are (ethnicity, class, sexuality), where you are (geopolitically), and what you are doing (immediate context).[4]

"Belonging" is always a precarious enterprise: without being too dualistic, whenever there is an "in" there will be an "out." However, the way these grrlz battle for their "in" to the culture through these events is counterintuitive. They do so as "ladies," "ladiez," "girls," "women," "femmes," and so on. They come together strategically under a discourse of seemingly untroubled femininity in a subculture dominated by, dependent upon, reproductive of, and marked by masculinity. The performance of femininity is not valued within graffiti subculture unless it is tied to sexuality, so when the subjects conventionally associated with femininity (cisgender women) perform an identity that is of no "use" to graffiti subculture, "the assertion in their very social organization, of principles of equality in the midst of precarity" transforms not only the boundaries of belonging, but also the gendered conventions that inform those boundaries.[5] Subjects assumed to be inherently and only ever feminine, performing feminist masculinity en masse, force a shift in those boundaries if only temporarily. Through the strategic (à la Gayatri Spivak in 1993) public performance of an undervalued gender identity (woman), these "ladiez" and "femmes" claim their subcultural ownership, transform their precarious social belongings, and activate the social and political power of feminist collectivity.

Ladie Killerz

When you break it down, we're a bunch of ladies who kill
spots with graffiti.
—Joske (Australia)

The Australian annual event Ladie Killerz was created by skater/graff
grrl Joske (FLW, COCKTAILS crews). Joske, who like many of her graff
grrl peers spent her teens skateboarding, can be easily described as an
arts entrepreneur in her forties, who identifies as a "Caucasian, atheist,
minimum-wage earner who enjoys and partakes in sexual activities with
both men and women."[6] A close friend (Ratsko, also a skater girl) introduced her to graffiti subculture and taught her some of the mechanics
of the form in 1998. During a self-imposed "maternity leave" from 2000
to 2004, Joske began networking with other graff grrlz in Australia and
documenting their work. Continued exposure to the culture reignited
her passion and she soon picked up the marker and paint can and began
tagging again. Wanting her pieces to be read from afar, she bombs in
classic New York City public style, making sure to grab a new spot
whenever possible: "I fucking love taking spots before anyone else. It's
a game that I'm rather good at." She enjoys painting legal walls with
friends and compares it to a leisurely summer day complete with food,
beer, and other indulgences. But she favors "destroying public property"
like walls, trains, and track sides because "it is a far more superior feeling
of satisfaction." Painting graffiti is an energy release—both creative and
destructive—but it is also a way for her to "reclaim the night" and leave
an intensely gratifying mark.

With almost a decade of experience writing and connecting with
other Australian graff grrlz, including Ivey (from chapter 1) who introduced us over email, Joske organized the first Ladie Killerz event in 2008
(www.facebook.com/ladiekillerzgraffjam). I have been following Ladie
Killerz on Facebook for years, lamenting the difficulty of traveling to
Australia and being so grateful for their digital presence. Ladie Killerz'
annual and mostly clandestine assembly mimics the ephemerality of
the art form, a precarious ontological condition rehabilitated into a strategy for claiming the (sub)cultural, social, and institutional privilege of

place, of belonging, and of survival. Originally an opportunity for Joske and her girls to get together and jam, it developed into something more.

> Ladie Killerz began in 2008 with an all-girl crew (Helen Keller Crew) going on a rap spray holiday. ISHK, METHO, ISIS, SEAR and myself JOSKE, descended upon Adelaide, South Australia for a weekend of partying and painting. A year passed and we decided to do it again but opened up the invites to other females within our immediate network, so in 2009, POISE, METHO, LOTUS, THORN, ISHK, ISIS, SEAR, SAKIE, FLEUR and myself traveled to Brisbane, Queensland for a weekend of painting and debauchery. 2010 rolled around and the core HKC crew members decided to make Ladie Killerz an annual event and opened it up to an even larger network of graff grrlz. We laid down a few basic rules → graffiti wall jam (no paste ups or street art, just straight up graffiti letters. Sure we've had a few character painters and large format stencil artists in the past, but mostly the focus is on the art of writing letters). → art exhibition (for the other dope female "street artists" to get their shine on). → after party (for obvious reasons!) We pass the LK baton onto our ladies who are experienced in event management in other capital cities throughout Australia, and keep the proverbial ball rolling.

Going strong, brought to life each year by new and returning graff grrlz in a different capital city, the Ladie Killerz jam for 2015 was held in Adelaide. Joske passed the baton for on-site organization, but retains the power to decide location and uses her coordination skills to organize the participants and keep the social media presence of the event alive. Her continued involvement also ensures that the goals and structure originally set for the event are maintained. Ladie Killerz jams are grass-roots events with no commercial sponsorship or corporate interests by design (funded instead through donations from participating artists and "homies") that act as nurturing social spaces for graff grrlz; they "make it happen because [they] want it to happen." They also make it happen somewhat clandestinely—though friends and family join them while they paint, they keep the location somewhat private so as not to attract a general public audience. The numerical "they" depends on many factors, ranging from five to thirty-three "ladiez." Joske related that the ladiez come "from all different walks of life: mothers, daughters, sisters, young, old, teenagers, hip hop heads, punks, anarchists, hippies, lovers, haters, large, small, skinny, tall, all skin tones, [and] all skill levels" to paint—any standing personal differences are set aside and friendships are formed where before there were none. According to Joske, "the sheer joy on the faces of the new girls when they meet other female writers for the first time" is obvious and infectious.

Sometimes the jam has a theme, such as in 2012 when Ladie Killerz had a "Prom Party." The rules of the jam were simple: "wear a prom dress, pick a random tag, smash out a chromie" (a chromie is a piece filled with one metallic color, generally silver, but could be gold). As expected not all of the grrlz followed the rules. In a short video filmed and produced by Joske, we see the mostly white/light-skinned tattooed arms of "prom queens" donning evening gowns with ruched shoulders and tea-length dresses with lace-bodice ruffles of sky blue, periwinkle, black, cyan, and violet paired with brooches and ruffled tea gloves.[7] These queens are also wearing baseball caps backward; rocking hot-pink tights; sporting pearls, hair bows, and sneakers while drinking bottles of beer; climbing through windows; and carrying backpacks full of paint around what looks like a bombed-out, abandoned brick building. The queens at this prom take pleasure playing with gender presentation, expectations, and assumptions in a half-serious, half-mocking, and totally snarky manner. Everything viewers need to know about the interplay between the performance of femininity and masculinity is illustrated in a close-up of one of the grrlz' hands: one freshly manicured in a pale glittery pink and the other covered in silver spray paint.

The performative feminist cultural work of Ladie Killerz lays crucially in the participants' refusal to be fully legible or knowable under the palimpsestic sign they appropriate—"ladies" in prom dresses become ladiez who resist their marginalization and erasure together. "By understanding girls' resistance as an affective act of deregulated play that works within, yet simultaneously against, the dominant scripts" we are better able to understand how graff grrlz' precarious belongings are transformed during these jams.[8] They revel in a kind of gender nonconformity specific to cisgender women. Similar to Halberstam's assertion in *Female Masculinity* that "heterosexual female masculinity menaces gender conformity in its own way," so, too, do cisgender women's performances of feminist masculinity within the context of graffiti sub-culture.[9] Menacing gender conventions does not come without a cost.

Whenever those subjects who are normally disempowered within a particular social/cultural/political space are empowered by taking that space, there is bound to be criticism and backlash.

> Usually the only negative comments we receive come from a small hand-ful of unimportant male graffiti toys with damaged egos, and it's generally over some bullshit attitude of "why do you need a women's only event" and "why can't I just wear a dress and paint the wall." For our last jam in Melbourne, I secured an awesome space by gaining permission from the three male crew granddaddies who take ownership of that particu-lar wall. I arranged a power supply from the neighboring business and pulled a few favours in regards to buff paint and spraying the wall with the buff. I chose to buff the entire wall space, whether we needed it or not, so as to provide a clean slate. My reasoning to buff out the entire wall was respectful and sensitive of the graffiti politics but regardless of this, it came under scrutiny from some (albeit male) writers, because they believed their pieces were "gone over" unnecessarily. I found this attitude extremely immature, especially as the opportunity now existed for them to re-paint their space. Boys will be toys!

The ways that the politics of gender influence the politics of wall owner-ship are made crystal clear in this example. Taking space is part of the graffiti game; being buffed is a reality that provokes a re-claiming of the space on the wall (see chapter 4 on generative acts of negation). Thus, it is clear that the backlash Joske experienced is meant to secure (and reposition) the gendered status quo against an event that effectively dis-rupts it.

Critiques such as these, especially in reference to an event purpose-fully organized to address the effects of gender difference, do particu-larly noxious work. The toxic masculinity performed by those slinging criticisms is powered by Western gender conventions, but also—and more alarming in this context—the language of postfeminism. Asking the postfeminist question "why do you need a women's only event?" implies that we are beyond needing spaces and events just for women because this is not the "old days" and women are equal now, duh.

Wondering why one "can't just wear a dress and paint the wall" is an indication that the ways that sex and gender affect social position or access to space and power in graffiti subculture have not been considered (indeed, the time it takes to understand such dynamics is likely also considered *not worth it*). Even the slightest gesture of empathy and consideration would bring one to the realization that understanding graff grrlz's social position of sexualization, tokenization, and marginalization within the subculture requires much more than wearing a dress while painting. Patronizing assumptions such as these disregard that the event is designed for people who—whether in skirts or pants—live a life where their "feminine" gender informs their social precarity *daily*, not just one time and not just as a disingenuous self-serving performance. For cisgender and transgendered women, the performance of femininity within hetero/sexist, white supremacist, capitalist patriarchal societies has consequences—that vary in kind and severity, of course—related to autonomy, safety, and belonging. So, no, you cannot "just wear a dress" and paint. Gender is performed, but the effects of that performance have specific material consequences that should and need to be respected.

Whatever form the rationalizations for these kinds of critiques and questions may take, the effect is further subjugation—a reassertion of wall ownership based on gender—even when the donning of a dress is an effort to participate as a gesture of solidarity. The dismissal of events like Ladie Killerz exemplifies the discourse that led Nancy Macdonald to argue that the male masculine social dynamics of graffiti culture are meant to act as a safeguard against feminist advancement. But as I argued in chapter 1, there is not only *one* kind of masculinity being enacted in graffiti subculture. The graff grrlz are performing a masculinity that is not about safeguarding graffiti culture from feminism, but rather one that is shaped by participation in graff culture and a feminist sensibility and proclivity for collectivity, solidarity, empowerment, and support. Joske explained that feminism can be identified through empowering activities that demonstrate "the importance of women" as producers of more than "tiny humans." By participating in Ladie Killerz, these grrlz transform their precarious belongings by performing their femininity while they assert their feminist masculinity—"smashing out" those chromies, ruffled tea gloves and all.

Fierce Feminist Takeovers

Some people go to the gym, some people do needlepoint, I
guess. This is what I do, which is not very common I would
say for a thirty-eight-year-old woman to still be doing.
But I hang out in dirty tunnels and I like it.
—Itsa

On International Women's Day 2014, for the first time in history, more
than 100 Hip Hop graffiti and street artists assembled for the Femme
Fierce: Leake Street All-Girl Takeover paint jam under the London
Waterloo Station in Lambeth.[10] A year later (also on International
Women's Day), I was standing at the Leake Street entry staring into
a cornflower blue tunnel packed with bodies obfuscating the exit—
watching, documenting, playing, smoking, drinking, talking, laughing,
dancing, and, of course, painting. The dizzying aerosol aroma coming
from the cans of over 150 graffiti and street artists permeated the infamous "Banksy Tunnel."

Femme Fierce was imagined and then realized by the British writer
Chock, an original member of the United Kingdom's first all-grrl crew
Girls on Top (www.facebook.com/GirlsOnTopCrew), and the curator,
dealer, and street art aficionada Ayaan Bulale. Chock was exposed to
graffiti at seventeen while traveling with her then-boyfriend during the
mid-'90s.[11] During that trip, overcome with the beauty and grit of the
art form, she decided to drop the skateboard ("I was a rubbish skater")
and focus her energies on graffiti writing. Almost twenty years later,
Chock's graffiti style is a cross between public and wild; her pieces take
a moment to decipher even for the trained eye because her lines are as
bold as her colors. Amid the already complex composition of lines and
colors there is often also a character added to the mix (her favorite is a
panda). Her artwork reflects both the unruly and the deliberate compo-
nents of the Hip Hop culture she loves—sometimes it is silly and sometimes serious. In 2000, Chock and her friend Ned were tired and "bored
of being the only girls" painting and felt that "most of the male writers
[they had] met [were] not gentlemen." Soon thereafter they formed Girls
on Top, naming their crew in such a way as to signal their desired place
for grrlz in the subcultural hierarchy.[12]

Writing graffiti "rebuilt" Chock's sense of self: it "allowed me to sur-round myself with people who inspire me, not drag me down." Wanting to extend the space GOT made within the subculture to other grrlz and give them a chance to be more than "a token girl painting in a crew of boys" and a place where they could surround themselves with support-ive writers, Chock began organizing all-grrl painting jams. In one of my earliest email exchanges with Chock, she identified herself as a "white female jedi. Straight. Loads of people think we are lesbians haha."[13] The "we" in this case refers to her crew GOT, whose deviant gender per-formance translates into perceived homosexuality: they paint with all grrlz, they act masculine, and therefore they are presumed to be gay. Sometimes the grrlz manage the sentiment with laughter, sometimes with an indifferent shrug, and sometimes with a direct response, but the assumptions they face and the individual negotiations they make do not detract from the critical cultural work of building one another up by painting together. The 2014 inaugural Femme Fierce—a moniker chosen to convey a gathering of "females with attitude"—was a natural extension of Chock's work.

> Femme Fierce is dedicated to unearthing and highlighting the best of the burgeoning female artists on the street art scene in the UK and beyond. Coinciding with International Women's Week, Femme Fierce is a celebra-tion of women that create art in studios, lurk in dark alleyways, scale roof tops, enter abandoned buildings and add colour to the concrete walls that make up our cityscape for the love of the covert and oft-maligned world of street art and graffiti.

The news about Femme Fierce spread by word of mouth and social media (www.facebook.com/FemmeFierceEvents). Various reports—both formal and informal—from the first event claim that grrlz from the Middle East, Africa, South America, and Europe answered the call for participation by funding their own travel and accommodations; they were trying to beat a Guinness Book of World Records for the largest street art event.

Witnessing Chock's work with graff grrlz in the United Kingdom manifest in a second iteration of Femme Fierce (organized by Bulale in Chock's absence) was nothing short of exhilarating—despite the fact that out of the approximately 150 artists painting on that cold and damp Sunday afternoon, there were only eleven Hip Hop graffiti writers: Steffi Bow, Throne, Cyber, Akit, Mish, Itsa, Evay, Baek, Pixie, Mons, and Weardoe. Wondering if they, too, felt "the buzz," I asked each writer I interviewed for her reaction to the event and without fail they used words like "liberating," "alive," and "open." We joked that perhaps the buzz was due to the fumes. Beyond the emotional response, it was a quantifiable success: with so many "fierce femmes" present, their skills and rightful place in the subculture could not be denied.

After the overwhelming and involuntary sense of "arrival" subsided, I could not help but wonder: could this energy last? What good would the event really do for graff grrlz who were in the extreme minority, even at an event geared toward them? What would be the impact of this performance on their precarious position within graffiti subculture, within mainstream society? Femme Fierce is a highly advertised event held in a public space frequented by street artists. But it is not solely about painting together, or painting to gain subcultural capital; it is also about raising money for charity and winning mainstream society's validation—getting press recognition and attracting corporate funding sources. In 2014 the tunnel went pink for the organization Breast Cancer Care (www.breastcancercare.org.uk), and in 2015 the tunnel was painted blue for the "Because I Am a Girl" rights campaign by PlanUK (www.plan-uk.org/because-i-am-a-girl).[14] Femme Fierce is exactly the kind of sanctioned artistic deviance that one might expect to find in a "creative city" where the precarity limiting deviant subjects' lives/lifestyles is (seemingly) temporarily suspended to allow for "the embrace of creativity as an economic and cultural salve for the postindustrial city."[15]

Writing about Sydney, Australia, Cameron McAuliffe observes that writers in "creative cities" like Sydney and London must negotiate multiple subjectivities produced by the moral geographies governing urban spaces whereby street art is good, creative, and productive in contrast to graffiti, which is bad, destructive, and unproductive (read: unprofitable). Femme Fierce made the dual moral geographies (subcultural and mainstream) governing this event quite visible. In contrast to the "bad" art illegally placed on various surfaces of the cityscape by "bad" citizens, Femme Fierce was an opportunity "for graffiti writers and street artists to produce 'good work'" as good citizens with an active role in civic participation.[16]

Femme Fierce is "authorized" by the neoliberal language of the "creative city," which requires those at the edge of deviance to perform their edge for profit (the city's profit, not theirs) in exchange for tolerance and sanctioned spaces to paint.[17] In most cities in the Global North, graffiti of the unauthorized variety is still classified as urban blight, and writers—as artists who are subject to the juridical-political institutions that frame their modes of expression as deviant—are still considered criminals. Managing the "front" of this neoliberal rhetoric in contrast to the reality of having "too much edge" is the ground that all writers who paint illegally and legally share.[18] For graff grrlz, the multiple subjectivities negotiated in the legitimized public space of the Banksy Tunnel—the vandal and the good citizen—are weighted with the threat of losing subcultural capital ("real" writers do not paint legal walls) and the threat of being connected to your illegal transgressions by painting openly in public. Despite the weight of these threats, the eleven graff grrlz in attendance consciously refused to be dissuaded from participating precisely because of their precarious position as graffiti writers who are also women.

In "Performativity, Precarity and Sexual Politics," Judith Butler suggests that "how performativity links with precarity might be summed up in these questions: How does the unspeakable population speak and make its claims? What kind of disruption is this within the field of power? And how can such populations lay claim to what they require?"[19] Like Ladie Killerz, Femme Fierce welcomed graff grrlz not as tokens, not as sexualized objects, not as second-class artists, but as comrades galvanized by an undervalued gender signifier: femme. One of the primary and crucial effects of the collective performance at Femme Fierce is that the graff grrlz made and staked a claim, designating their lives as recognizable, readable, and valuable to the subculture, publicly and blatantly.[20] In response to their precarious social (and physical) position, the grrlz at Femme Fierce collectively claimed the subcultural recognition and place that they require. In doing so, they temporarily disrupted the "field of power" spatially by changing the affective experience of the tunnel, socially by expanding the consuming public with new media, politically by subverting subcultural conventions, and aesthetically by choosing to paint letters instead of characters.

Writers get up under the cover of night—in a tunnel, under a bridge, down an alleyway. A "good spot" is one that is visible to passersby, but also allows the writer to be hidden. Most good spots require the writer to first go through those deep, dark places and shortcuts that most people do not frequent—especially at night, at least not on purpose, and certainly not alone. Graffiti grrlz act exactly the opposite of how individuals with bodies assigned female are socialized to act in order to keep themselves safe when in public spaces at night: they wear dark clothes to blend in (rather than bright ones to stand out); they avoid streetlights (rather than go out of the way to walk under them); they are quiet (rather than on the phone or shaking keys); they do not do anything that would make their presence known. Because the art they make is criminalized, they hide. In protecting themselves from the police, they become more vulnerable to other dangers. And they know this. Painting collectively in a public space changes the affective environment of the "fields" in which they paint.

"I have never seen so many women in this tunnel," a nineteen-year-old French writer, Mons, shared. "Usually when I come, I am alone."[21] Mons lives in London and frequents the Leake Street tunnel; her tag name is short for monsters. When we spoke, I was shocked to learn that she had only been writing for a year. She is a textile design artist and illustrator/graffiti writer who taught herself by "paying attention" to London's graffiti scene. Femme Fierce was the first time she had ever painted at a public event: "I usually come here, a few days a week at least, and I've never done this in front of people. It's usually pretty empty." Standing idly pretty early in the day, she had obviously executed her impressive piece quickly (for a new writer) and it was on par with some of the more experienced writers painting in the tunnel that day. Her piece was on a wall near the tunnel exit; standing about seven feet tall, the crisp letters were half-bubble half-block-style, colored with shades of aqua and grape, and finished with a classic shadow effect for depth. I asked Mons if she feels safe when she comes to the tunnel alone. She replied that she is always hyperaware of her surroundings and sticks to the edges of the tunnel—closer to the exits.

While I do not want to overgeneralize or speak for those who feel otherwise, in my experience the gender dynamics in graffiti subculture generate an extremely visceral affective response to space for those who identify and present differently than the hypermasculine cisgender men that dominate the room/street/alley. As a feminine-presenting

Figure 5.1. Mons, Femme Fierce, London, 2015.

individual, whenever I go to events for graffiti writers—even if I have been explicitly invited, know the people, or it is *my* event—my body reacts to the environment. It reacts to being outnumbered. "If [Femme Fierce] was a [typical] graffiti jam," a Scottish writer, Evay, explained, "it would be *all* guys and one girl." In *The Promise of Happiness*, Sara Ahmed unpacks the relationship between space and affect: "we may walk into the room and feel the atmosphere, but what we may feel depends on the angle of our arrival."[22] Graffiti grrlz come into the space of graffiti subculture from a gendered, racialized, and sexualized angle and all that this intersection of subjectivities entails in regards to sexual violence. Our bodies not only feel that angle of arrival—they anticipate it. Grrlz who paint on the street are fully aware of the dynamics they are stepping into when they step out. The tension or anxiety of anticipation was neutralized and replaced with a general (if temporary) sense of calm and security that day.

"It feels really positive," an Australian expat, Itsa, enthused. "It feels like an energetic, happy vibe. . . . It doesn't feel competitive. . . . I don't know why that is and I don't want to say [that it is] because there are no men painting."[23] The atmospheric difference that she does not want to attribute to a lack of a male presence may very well be a lack of a certain *kind* of male presence: the kind that takes all of the space in a room, on the train, or on the wall; the kind fueled by cismale privilege; the kind that is disempowering; the kind that sexualizes and marginalizes; the kind that makes certain spaces feel unsafe.

I went back to the tunnel the day after Femme Fierce to experience the space one more time before traveling back to the states; the sense of optimism that I had had not twenty-four hours earlier faded almost immediately. One of the street artists, Annatomix, had painted a monochromatic geometric jaguar. By no means was her piece outrightly "feminist," political, sexual, or "girl powery." It was about form, line, and composition. Nevertheless, someone had painted penises all over it, including one suggestively positioned next to the mouth.[24] Visual gender violence such as this happens all too frequently. In general, graffiti or street art that is being dissed by another writer is usually demeaned through some form of sexualization and/or feminization. Annatomix knew her piece was vulnerable; when we spoke, she mentioned that it would happen to most if not all of the pieces in the tunnel because the mostly male local graffiti scene was angry about the event. What better way to get back at a bunch of women for taking up "claimed" wall space than visually reasserting your hypermasculinity? None of the grrlz I spoke to about Annatomix's piece seemed surprised in the slightest bit; they expected the backlash.

Some of the grrlz expressed feeling some social anxiety while they were painting because they were not used to having an audience, having their face associated with their work, or allowing the two to be associated and shared on social media. Part of the "totally buzzin' " feeling of (relative) safety, liberation, and solidarity, as Evay described it, was also due to the sense of being seen not only by an immediate audience but also by the cameras, phones, and microphones capturing the event and transmitting the happenings throughout the world.[25] Hundreds of people walked through the tunnel, passersby and journalists of various sorts, documenting everything and extending the audience in a way that is incalculable through digital communication. From the beginning, the organizers and participants of Femme Fierce used the power of social media to advertise and harness support, to raise funds via Kickstarter, to attract graff grrlz from all over to come and paint together, *and* to gather an audience. There is a "Femme Fierce Artist Info" secret page on Facebook, with (at last count) 149 members; a public Facebook community page, Femme Fierce: Leake Street All Girl Takeover with 5,128 likes/followers (www.facebook.com/FemmeFierceEvents); a website (www.femmefierce.com); a YouTube channel with 25 subscribers (www.youtube.com/user/FemmeFierce); an Instagram account with 1,221 followers (instagram.com/FemmeFierce); and a Twitter account with 696 followers (twitter.com/FemmeFierceUK).[26] I was not even in attendance in 2014, but because of the "social storytelling" platform Storify (storify.com), I was able to collect digital documentation from various sources and put them together in one narrative available online (storify.com/4JustJessP/femme-fierce-storified). Painting at Femme Fierce generated a feeling of importance (look at all the people who came to see us paint), of safety (no need to look over my shoulder here), of pleasure (it was fun!), and of solidarity (we are doing this together, not in isolation) that—though fleeting in real time—is now archived online.

Painting legally and quasi-commercially goes against the fundamental rules and conventions of the Hip Hop graffiti writers' subculture. But for these writers, because the event was a fundraiser on International Women's Day, with a theme and a purpose that spoke to their political devotions, those rules and conventions were outweighed by the goals and the promise of a particular kind of environment that they knew would strengthen their visibility as a group and foster a sense of belonging. The graff grrlz at Femme Fierce may have subverted subcultural conventions about anonymity, but they were sure to uphold the convention around letters: painting letters is paramount; it is what separates the writers from the street artists. Negotiating those parameters, some chose to paint with a name they do not bomb with, others did not.

Toward the end of the event, and on the less busy side of the tunnel toward York Street, I caught up with a writer from Yorkshire, Throne79 (UKS, TnT).[27] Her slime green and eggplant purple piece was in all capital letters. The "caps lock" of her personal font is the part of her aesthetic that does not vary (www.flickr.com/photos/85075188@N06). What varies are the bodies of the letters themselves: sometimes they are bulbous with minimal enhancements (basic 3D, basic shadows/light), and other times the letters look like dancing body parts reminiscent of an LA2/Keith Haring collaboration. A relatively new writer, she settled into her tag name based on her favorite Hip Hop album: Jay-Z and Kanye West's 2011 *Watch the Throne*. Throne painted not only "because it [was] International Women's Day," but also because there are "not many female writers" or many opportunities for her "to write with [other] female writers."

Standing in front of her piece, comprising floral bubble letters situated on a bed of grass green leaves and complemented by tulips and daisies, Evay shared that she had been writing as one of a two-person all-grrl "crew" for about a year. She took a ten-hour bus ride to London for the one-day event, and she hopped right back on that same bus the very next day. She said that she had been bombing for six years and does not usually paint legal walls, and yet she went out of her way to attend Femme Fierce. "I couldn't believe there was going to be 150 female artists. There's only two of us [in Edinburgh]!" Like Throne, she could not resist the experience Femme Fierce offered of meeting and painting with other graff grrlz. Knowing they would be vastly outnumbered by street artists, as they were the year before, these grrlz took it upon themselves to "represent" graffiti writers generally, and graff grrlz specifically.

Figure 5.2. Itsa sketching out her piece, Femme Fierce, London, 2015.

Itsa, the Australian ex-pat who appreciated the "energetic happy vibe" of the event, is a thirty-eight-year-old heterosexual cisgender woman of mixed heritage. She uses "itsa" when she paints legal walls. It is "short for itsadisorder" but also flexible in terms of application—"itsa Sunny Day, Itsa shame, Itsa good day for a paint" (@itsadisorder; facebook.com/pages/Itsa-Disorder). Itsa painted her piece in one of the more visible, well-lit areas of the tunnel. Her obsession with New York–style graffiti is obvious: her funky forest- and grass green–filled letters were outlined with highlighter yellow, embellished with arrows, a halo, and starbursts of light (white paint); her letters were surrounded with tags and shout-outs, and also had signature bubble doodads floating inside them. Easy to read and a pleasure to look at, Itsa's graffiti certainly represented her aesthetic affinities. She explained, "There is a lot of street art here so I wanted to represent old school graff. I am doing this event to raise the profile of the charity and to make sure that graff is represented in an increasingly homogenized world of street art and commercialism."[28] When you have painted for as long as Itsa has, you witness the transformation of the culture. At fourteen in 1990, she was "obsessed with the New York graffiti and hip hop scene." She created a small all-grrl crew (HGB) and

> rivaled the boys in street bombing around my city. There were no legal walls back then, but occasionally we got permission to paint pieces. . . . There was no such thing as graffiti paint back then so we used what we could get our hands on, including car paint, mixing ink for homemade pens using shoe polish containers. I had friends in the United States sending me NYFATS [spray-paint caps], which didn't fit my paint tins, and had to adapt things a little.

Being a part of Femme Fierce was important for Evay, Itsa, and Throne, not only because it was International Women's Day and for a good cause, but also because they wanted to represent grrlz as *writers*, painting letters.

In Hip Hop culture, reppin'—representing one's affiliations—is paramount. Power, be it social, political, or economic, comes from community and, as I mentioned in chapter 3, that power can be tapped by reppin' one's cultural and/or geographic community.[29] Reppin' can also do the work itself—as a representative you make your people visible, you give *them* power. To have a sense of why representing graff grrlz at Femme Fierce would be important, it is essential to note that despite being mostly U.K.-based, most of these writers did not know one another. Mons and Itsa are a great example. For this newcomer and veteran, with an approximately twenty-year age difference, there was surely the opportunity for an in-person transmission of history, knowledge, skills, and support that otherwise only exists online. And yet, prior to my interviews with them, they did not know the other existed. Mons and Itsa's missed connection was a missed opportunity for apprenticeship and camaraderie (if not friendship). The fact that they did not know their contemporaries—who were painting in the same tunnel, on the same day, in the same city—is due to a lack of visibility and representation within the subculture. The general lack of knowledge graff grrlz have about other graff grrlz is a by-product of a host of issues, most coming down to the gendered construction of representation itself: grrlz are marginalized in historical works, neglected (or invisibilized because of their tag names) on most graffiti websites, and thus erased from the social imaginary. In chapter 4 I argued that having a digital presence can and does shift this reality for grrlz, but there is a long way to go before their stories circulate to the extent that they become naturalized historical accounts of the subculture.

When I asked Throne how she learned to write letters, she said it was from watching her older brother and his friends. Evay learned from an ex-boyfriend: "if it wasn't for him, I would never have tried to do letters." We spoke about the kind of art being made in the tunnel (mostly characters) in relation to how one learns (mostly from a mentor). "If [my ex] hadn't showed me how to do it," Evay explained, "I probably wouldn't be painting actually. Because it was too scary. When I was seventeen, eighteen, walking past [writers] it was very intimidating." Generally speaking, if a graff grrl does not have a mentor, she paints alone; she may prefer that to dealing with the drama and bigotry of hetero/sexist male-dominated spaces. However, painting in isolation has consequences. One such consequence is the drop-out rate. My experience as a researcher (and as a former teenage girl surrounded by boys who wrote graffiti) suggests that it is more common than we might think for a girl to pick up a spray can and give it a shot. The experiences that come afterward are what matter. Girls have to develop a handstyle and can control (same as all writers), but far too often they do so without advice, encouragement, or community. Add to this the experiences they may have because of their gender that male writers do not have to worry about (sexualized rumors, for example, or familial restrictions), and it becomes really clear why some girls lose confidence and give up. And when they do give up, the reasoning is couched in essentialized gender (girls are not tough enough), when clearly context is everything. Live painting subverts the idea that grrlz cannot write or should not try to because they will not be as good, or because it is too hard; reppin' themselves as writers in front of a sea of other "femmes" they demonstrate the fallacy of those ideas and offer an example of success for up-and-coming graff grrlz.

Mons and Itsa may have missed an opportunity to connect at Femme Fierce, but the potential is there for new connections between graff grrlz and apprentice or mentor relationships. Femme Fierce is a "safe" space for street artists and graffiti writers to learn from one another. Perhaps an artist who has limited herself to characters or a paintbrush will find the courage to pick up a can and sketch out some letters. And vice versa: a writer who internalizes the rules and conventions for graffiti art might let herself explore a character or a stencil on a legal wall without fear of losing her subcultural place for "selling out." As Chock noted, Femme Fierce "was different from the GOT [jams] in that it brought graffiti and street artists together. Something that is generally frowned upon or straight out dissed within the UK graffiti scene quite frequently." Besides creating relationships among writers and street artists, Femme Fierce not only lets the world in to a subcultural mode of expression that has traditionally excluded the public from live performance, but also exposes them to women artists, challenging gendered assumptions about graffiti writing and street art. The sheer number of women in the group belies the commonsense notion that graffiti art is a man's world, a place to exercise male masculinity where women artists are a rarity. Painting as graff grrlz under a banner of "femme"-ness exposes and transforms their precarious subcultural belongings.

While it is clearly an event meant to empower women, Femme Fierce is not unilaterally considered a feminist event by all of its participants.

Chock considers herself a feminist and Femme Fierce a feminist event because "it is a celebration of female artists; especially in graffiti, we are still in the minority and have had to fight for recognition." Itsa, who considers herself a feminist by virtue of her actions but does not like the narrow ways the term "feminist" is understood, thought the title of the event emphasized those narrow perceptions of feminism: "the title unfortunately has a lot of sort of 'feminazi' kind of something to it that puts a lot of people off." According to this "feminazi" perception of feminism, a feminist event would necessarily be a separatist event—no men allowed or in sight. For Evay, who does not identify as a feminist, Femme Fierce was not a feminist event for the very reason that it *did not* exclude men: "There [were] guys everywhere. There [were] two guys painting in lipstick and wigs. What are they doing here? It's not feminist. Guys were invited to come and watch." Like Evay, Mons did not see Femme Fierce as a feminist event . . . at first:

> Not really. Of course it is for International Women's Day and everything. It is feminist in a way—we are showing how strong we can be. We are women and we are showing you, but I don't how to explain. It is feminist in some way but that's not my reason for coming. It's not because it is just for girls. That's not one of the reasons that made me want to come. It's actually one of the things that I was like *ehhhh.*

Balancing the parameters and purpose of the event with her perception of feminism (which she admitted to not thinking about at all prior to our conversation), Throne said, "In a way, yes, this is a feminist event. No [I am not a feminist], it is a masculine hobby in a way so it's good that girls are doing it." In all of their responses, there was a great deal of tension between conceptualizations and definitions of "feminism" and how the participants felt about the purpose and experience of the event in reality. At Femme Fierce, as at other graff grrlz events, feminism is a practice, not a theory. Feminism emerges through performance, through affect, through aesthetic, through commitment, and through intention. Feminism's emergence transformed the grrlz' sense of place and community; if only for that day the possibility of the transformation was felt and lived, generating a sense of hope for the future.

Undoing the "Undoing of Feminism"

We do not claim that every transgression of conventional femininity constitutes de facto feminism. Pushing against the boundaries of what constitutes acceptable femininity does not necessarily mean that gendered power inequities are being challenged, let alone transformed. Political agency arises when people, interacting in groups, identify an issue or structure of inequality that becomes the conscious object of their resistance through collective action to redress institutionalized privilege.
—Currie, Kelly, and Pomerantz, "Skater Girlhood," 303

JesOne's imaginary utopian "massive army" of femme fatales materialized in Femme Fierce and Ladie Killerz. The graff grrlz in these voluntary, ad hoc "armies" are empowered subjects, making themselves visible both within the graffiti subculture and to the general public by claiming and subverting various femininities in tandem with performing feminist masculinity. Their sociopolitical subordination, their status as numerical minorities even within their own subculture, and their biopolitical vulnerability in everyday life as cisgender women become the "conscious object of their resistance." These armies assemble and disassemble—coming together in a fashion that mimics the ephemerality of their chosen arts practice—to claim the (sub)cultural, social, and institutional privilege of place, of belonging, throughout the Hip Hop diaspora.

Angela McRobbie argues that "something quite unexpected has happened" in popular culture, mass media, and various institutions (be they educational, political, or social): liberal feminism has been "taken into account . . . to suggest that equality is achieved," and to suggest that feminism "is a spent force."[30] Critiques of all-grrl jams such as Ladie Killerz and Femme Fierce take feminism "into account" similarly. They disparagingly answered Chock's question "What's wrong with a girls' day out?" with the notion that such events are old-fashioned and unnecessary. However, as bell hooks reminds, "Abandoning the idea of sisterhood as an expression of political solidarity weakens and diminishes feminist movement. Solidarity strengthens resistance struggle."[31]

The idea that "a girls' day out," an event specifically focused on bringing grrlz together in solidarity (not necessarily as "sisters," but as comrades) is no longer necessary is feminism taken into account, which is how feminism is undone. The truth of the matter is that if there was not a rather hostile environment for graff grrlz, events like these would be no big deal, humdrum even. But if we judge by the participants' reactions and experiences, they were anything but. If graffiti grrlz let those who scoff at their all-grrl events convince them that the collective gatherings are unnecessary, they themselves will participate in feminism's undoing. The cultural work of Femme Fierce and Ladie Killerz demonstrates the urgency, the need for these events contra critiques that "undo" feminist urgencies. Knowing that, collectively, they are oppressed, these grrlz perform femininity in a feminist masculine gesture of rebellion and awareness.

The very gender difference that normally marginalizes and isolates the grrlz is what empowers them as they paint in solidarity. If we know anything about belonging to community, especially community based on identity, we know that the privilege of belonging has everything to do with being of the majority. Of not being *different than*. Of being in the right body for the performance of the subject position galvanizing the community. At Femme Fierce where a "femme" gender identity is a given, or at Ladie Killerz where one's subjectivity as a "ladie" is a given, the strategic umbrella term holds them together in solidarity as it allows them space to be individuals valued equally; difference does not disqualify. They claim space together and in doing so make room for the differences and complexities hidden beneath umbrella terms like street artist, graffiti writer, woman, femme, ladie. The difference in participants' subjectivities, their sense of self and identity, do not have to be hidden or elided in order to perform this feminist act of community. The call is to come as you are, donate what you can, paint the best you are able, and have a good time. Because the differences are acknowledged, the empowerment these graff grrlz feel is that much more sustainable and, well, powerful.

The all-grrl jams considered here perform a feminism that undoes the undoing of feminism. By claiming space for an "all-grrl" jam and then performing gender and grrl-hood in ways that oppose subcultural conventions and mainstream pop-culture provocations, these graff grrlz demonstrate the performative potential of painting collectively. If postfeminism, as a product of neoliberalism, disarticulates and hollows out the institution-shifting desires of radical feminist endeavors, as McRobbie contends, then events like Femme Fierce and Ladie Killerz rearticulate a radical feminist ideology concerned with solidarity and support through the art of graffiti writing.

We should, however, be careful and critical of how these events might participate in feminisms' undoing when they become popularized/mainstream because they are dismissed as evidence of women's "equality." While Ladie Killerz upholds the subcultural rules and regulations around corporate sponsors and commercialism (and even around having a public), Femme Fierce does not. One consequence of such a move, in terms of long-term effects, is that by the second year, Femme Fierce was already turning into the kind of event that most graffiti writers avoid. Increasingly geared toward the mainstream, for reasons related to funding according to Bulale, Femme Fierce will probably always be more populated by street artists, or gallery artists who occasionally paint on walls.

In the summer of 2015, Chock and Pixie (both from the Girls on Top crew) stepped away from Femme Fierce. Rather than being an annual jam/get-together, in their opinions it was becoming a commercial entity—even being courted by *ELLE* magazine for a "girl power" campaign using the slogan "One woman's success makes EVERY WOMAN STRONGER" (with the corresponding hashtags #morewomen and #ELLEfeminism). The event and some artists were featured in an article in the online version of *ELLE* (www.elleuk.com/now-trending/more-women-girl-squads#image=22), and the November 2015 print version featured a group photo of those "fierce femmes" willing to participate. While graff grrlz' position within graffiti subculture is precarious because of their gender, it seems their belonging within events that are supposed to address that precarity (such as Femme Fierce) has become similarly vulnerable. At an event where an act otherwise considered a crime is legitimized through the discourse of a creative city, not only is feminism instrumentalized and used for postfeminist gain, but the "edge" of graffiti subculture is as well. The "vandal" is taken into account—the edge is softened at a family-friendly event brought to you by corporations like *ELLE*, for example. In this move, the anti-establishment ideology of writing graffiti is undone as is the radical potential of feminism. One of the participants on the Femme Fierce Facebook page commented, in response to a call for artists to post a photo of themselves pledging their solidarity with *ELLE*'s slogan, "If Elle magazine gave a damn about feminism it wouldn't be full of adverts and articles which make women feel inadequate about their bodies." She also shared with me, via instant message, something she had seen online: an image of a new nail polish called "Off the Wall" that when used supposedly leaves the effect of spray paint on your fingernails. She joked that the ad for this nail polish would probably run alongside the story and images for the #morewomen campaign in *ELLE*. The (subtle?) message here is that consumers can purchase the look of rebellion without doing the work of the "rebel," without risking the social, economic, and political consequences of deviance—this is postfeminism.

Ladie Killerz, a grassroots event funded by participating writers and their friends, is seven years strong, but remains very small in terms of the number of participants and visibility, and thus perhaps has less of an impact on the world of graffiti. Femme Fierce is, at the time of this writing, moving into its fourth year, with an ever-growing public face. Thinking about precarity and ephemerality through these two similar yet different events leads us to more questions than answers: What is the cost of corporate sponsorship? Is there something we can salvage when/if our well-intentioned all-grrl jams are co-opted? What is the cost of representation and how does that balance with the opportunities afforded by visibility?

What if we, instead of lamenting the way that these events are co-opted by neoliberal postfeminist capitalism, choose to focus on the affective moments during Femme Fierce—when we felt alive, and liberated, and in solidarity? Is it fair to expect stability—for events, and the organizers, to remain fixed in a certain way of being or doing—when the art form that the events are organized around is itself mobile, fleeting, kinetic, always becoming? Capitalism cannot capitalize or exploit those moments where the radical potential of all-grrl jams becomes a felt experience, when they transform into a collective affect. In the ephemerality of those fleeting moments, we see and feel together how strategically performing as a group of individuals in solidarity with one another, boldly, publicly, and without fear makes a difference in a hetero/sexist male—masculine subculture . . . if only temporarily.

Conclusion

Connecting One Graffiti Grrl to Another

Under the partial cover of umbrellas, hoodies, and brightly colored ponchos acquired at the closest bodega, AbbyTC5, Neks, Queen Andrea, Erotica67, Miss163, Pixie, and Chock braved the ceaseless sneaker-soaking drizzle while they each painted their interpretation of the theme "My Thuggy Pony."[1] With wildly distinct styles (and levels of experience) the grrlz executed their pieces, accessorizing the letters with "sexy" ponies, "gangsta" ponies, ponies with laser eyes, royal ponies, ponies with "bling," tattooed ponies, and ponies wielding spray paint. Refashioning the image of the "little pony" with their feminist masculine graff grrl attitudes, theirs were stylistically different from the ponies we associate with the "My Little Pony: Friendship Is Magic" franchise.

Weeks before, knowing Pixie and Chock (both from the Girls on Top crew) would be in Manhattan for the opening of their first New York gallery show (I was the curator), I asked Miss163 and Erotica67 to help me find a wall for an all-grrl jam bringing together two of the United Kingdom's first all-grrl crew members with local grrlz. They came through with a wall on Boone Avenue in the Bronx and on the rainiest gray day one can imagine, these grrlz collectively took to writing their names on a bubble-gum pink background with bright-white clouds dripping from the moisture. As I watched each grrl style her piece, get feedback from the others, dance to the music playing in her earbuds, stand back to measure proportions, problem-solve the wet surface, and take breaks in Abby's minivan, I was struck (as I always am) by the way they work together while working individually, and by the ease with which they related to one another. Working on a common theme brings them together in a way not much else would. Together they altered the surface of that wall by reimagining what "little ponies" might be capable of doing, being, becoming. Friendship is magic, indeed.

Figure C.1. Pixie, "My Thuggy Pony," Bronx, NY, 2013.

I hope that *Graffiti Grrlz* has created the space for graff grrlz' stories to emerge and demonstrate how they negotiate their belonging to, and visibility in, a hetero/sexist male-dominated subculture embedded in a patriarchal world. Graff grrlz make a practice of cultivating the spaces between aesthetic, social, and geopolitical binaries by being in and on public space; assertive; aggressive; risk takers; confident; daring; dominant but not oppressive; playful; hardworking; resistant to convention; prone to deviation; and invested in both independence and collective activity. They deconstruct conventional understandings of femininity and masculinity by enacting a kind of gender performance painted outside the lines of socially imposed heteronormative gender binaries. They transcend the limitations of the material world by utilizing the boundless capabilities of the digital to archive themselves and each other, to circulate their digitized images, and to foster transnational communication between grrlz and beyond national borders. They form all-grrl crews and do the feminist work of peer mentorship, sexual empowerment, and consciousness raising—collectively imagining something different, something more, something better.

Graffiti allows these grrlz to experience empowerment, pleasure, belonging, and connection not because their graffiti personas represent their "real" identities, but rather because the representation is realized through an artistic practice that performs a precarious and defiant presence: defying the bounds of time and space, defying the bounds of gender conventions, and defying the comfort of stability and knowability. What Patricia Hill Collins, a Black feminist scholar, deems the "matrix of domination," Brian Massumi calls a grid—an abstract structure upon which subjects are positioned and, once visible on this grid, can then be located and represented.[2] The grid defines constructed subject positions and enables the reproduction of those positions *within its own parameters* (which he deems "prescripted possibilities"). Massumi's critique of standpoint epistemology theory (whereby acknowledging one's position on the matrix of domination assists in examining the path toward liberation) is that it neglects a crucial point: in order to serve its purpose, the matrix (re)situates subjects on the grid—even revolutionary, politically conscious subjects. Tracing critiques of representation politics back to feminist thinkers who valued standpoint epistemologies such as Audre Lorde—who argued in the early 1980s that the master's tools will never dismantle the master's house—we know that "grids happen," that "social and cultural determinations [e.g., race, gender, and sexuality] feed back into the process from which they arose."[3] According to the logic informing Massumi's critique, however, if graff grrlz position/represent themselves as gendered subjects, the possibilities and limitations are prescribed—they become knowable subjects because they have stabilized their identities.[4] In a way, this is one of the great fears of making one's gender identity known: that if they know you are a girl, they will treat you like a girl. But what these grrlz do reject is that knowing should then equal to being treated less than. The sheer visibility of graff grrlz, the networks they built, the group awareness they fostered, the events and crews they galvanized—these are all direct results of their conscious self-positioning as gendered subjects on the grid—the only determinant they allow to be visible ("knowable") on- and offline.

The politics of their positionality are slippery; even as they represent themselves collectively as "grrlz," their individual performances as "graffiti writers" dislocate them on the grid of normative knowability: place, time, gender, race, sexuality, and so forth. The possibilities that graffiti subculture offers for the transformation of gendered social dynamics are better understood as what Massumi calls "unprescribed potentials": "Possibility is a variation *implicit in* what a thing can be said to be when it is on target. Potential is the *immanence* of a thing to its still indeterminate variation, under way."[5] Because graffiti art is an artistic practice predominantly dependent on circulation without signifying an identified body or "fully" located subject, it exists in the realm of unprescribed potentiality (Massumi's "virtual"). When I use "identified" here, I mean that more often than not graffiti art lacks evidence of sociopolitical classifications like race, sexuality, and gender—the lines of intersecting identities are purposefully hidden behind tag names. And even when the writer does mark her tag name, modifying "Reds" with "Miss" for example or by using gender signifiers like flowers or hearts in the tag or piece, she upsets the normative, prescribed possibilities of the subject position "graffiti writer"—the things we *think* we know about the performing body in terms of gender, race, class, and sexuality in the subculture.[6]

The representation performed in graffiti writing is complicated and challenges the ethos informing traditional modes of representation under liberal democracy: if subjects are made visible, social and political power follows, and their "voice" is guaranteed. Representing oneself through a graffiti tag name situates a writer while performing alterity, anonymity, and difference—this is a different kind of representation that does not rely on the grid for power. Graffiti grrlz perform a different kind of standpoint epistemology, one structured less by knowing and claiming a location on the grid and more by doing something that feels revolutionary. The politics of their participation in graffiti subculture have shifted precisely *because* graffiti grrlz are locating themselves, representing themselves, making their subject positions as grrlz visible in such a way that deconstructs that very position: collectively, as a group of individuals affectively connected.

Graffiti Grrlz covers a lot of ground in terms of the writers and the changes they have ushered into the culture, but a lot of work remains to be done. There are countless graffiti grrlz whose names I still do not know, histories that are forgotten (or will be), all-grrl jams that exist only in memory, all-grrl crews that existed before the Internet and social media, *and grrlz who were known as kings but will never be known as women*—forever hidden despite the work they put in. Each time I connect with a scholar interested in graffiti they ask me the same question: how did you find the grrlz? The simple answer is that I never stopped looking. I have communicated with *many* graffiti grrlz over the years, many more than I could feature at length in this book, but all of their stories matter. If *Graffiti Grrlz* has proven anything it is that we must look beyond what we think we know. If you see the tag name "Utah" on a wall, for example, you might not think that she was one of the most notorious writers from the United States now living abroad to avoid more jailtime.[7] Scholarship on contemporary graffiti subculture should make including women and queer folk priorities from the start. If I can find them, you can too. There are so many more resources available today than there were in 2002 for finding writers; there are no more excuses. Similarly, there are no more excuses (if ever there were) for bolstering the hetero/sexist ideologies prevalent in graffiti subculture (and Hip Hop culture) transnationally. Imagine a subcultural environment that is not tied to hetero/sexism and then manifest that change by shining more light on, and offering more resources to, Hip Hop heads that have a message true to the form, one that nurtures community uplift, creativity, collectivity, and inclusion. Demand the same from those avowed feminists who claim to have our back, but then do nothing to actually get it.

Passing the Mic

In 2004, I organized my very first all-grrl jam with Miss17, Dona, Claw-Money, and Lady Pink in Tucson, Arizona, to complete my master's thesis project, "Women Bomb: Burnin' Up the Graffiti Canon." I wanted to create a space where the grrlz could work together, be witnessed painting, and interact with the local community. I wanted to use my resources to effect change, to make a small difference in how graffiti grrlz were respected, treated, and appreciated—not only by their male peers, but also by one another. While they painted, local writers sat and watched—sometimes for hours on end—in hopes that one of the grrlz would tag their blackbook (which they did). The production was originally to be titled "Girls Unchained," but as they painted that changed to

"Bitches 'n' Stitches." Originally working in the usual fashion where each writer has her own spot on the wall with space in between to demarcate, they chose to connect their works by modifying them into patchwork pieces "stitched" together, making one quilt. They wanted to pay homage to quilting as a form of women's undervalued artwork, and the potential in that work for subverting oppression and making connections between women.

My intention has always been to use whatever power and privilege I may wield as an academic and author to pass the mic to the grrlz—to give them the opportunity to connect to one another on an affective, inspiring, even revolutionary register. As *Graffiti Grrlz* demonstrates, these women are already deeply engaged in network building off- and online. Nevertheless, while individually they may receive accolades, their presence as a group of "grrlz" has yet to be valued equitably—no matter how much they get up and get over. My hope has been to facilitate ever more and ever deeper connections between graffiti grrlz by offering a careful and sincere analysis that deconstructs the hetero/patriarchal conventions buried within a subcultural narrative (featuring grrlz as tokens but never protagonists) and a subcultural practice that

Figure C.2. "Bitches 'n' Stitches" detail, Access Tucson, Tucson, AZ, 2004.

breeds beef for fame (encouraging grrlz to protect that "special" status at the cost of solidarity and sisterhood). I hope that my intervention creates a conceptual and practical space for these girls to experience the kind of connection that is felt deep in the belly: the kind that is transformative when shared and validated by a group. By offering my analysis of how graff grrlz have made substantial, quantifiable, qualitative changes in the subculture on a transnational scale, I have offered a new way of looking at graffiti subculture. Recalling that AbbyTC5 did not know that her participation mattered to the development of Hip Hop culture (one of the greatest artistic/social/political movements in human history), my hope in connecting the grrlz' disparate performances of feminism across the diaspora is that they will no longer doubt that they matter, and further that they will not hesitate to cast doubt on those who try to make them feel otherwise.

To honor the time we spent together, and the opinions, experiences, and observations they entrusted to me, I asked as many grrlz as I could if they had a message for aspiring graffiti grrlz. They responded with a range of messages that are empowering, invigorating, humorous, and challenging. The collection of quotes below may seem unnecessary to readers familiar with the subculture because they are accustomed to grrlz having *less* space—be it on a wall, in a book, a magazine, or a film. But if *Graffiti Grrlz* was meant to accomplish anything, it was to amplify these grrlz—their words, their graffiti writing, their presence, and their importance. Thus, by sharing their messages at length here, they make the last intervention.

ABBY (USA): If you want to bomb on a mass scale, knock yourself out, but don't publish your recent exploits online because chances are, some cop somewhere is looking for your ass. They can and will track you down.

AILA (BRAZIL): If you want to paint graffiti, paint graffiti!

ALMA (CHILE): Just go for it. Like throwing yourself in a pool even if you can't swim. I have made many twists and turns before I started. But after I dedicated myself to it, it was monumental. There is no bad in it, just go for it. Motivate yourself and paint. To do it is to learn. If you can paint with graffiti with another woman that's ideal because then you can share ideas and styles. You can learn how to do it together.

ANA (BRAZIL): It feels good making pixação: never stop.

ANTISA (CHILE): I think that for anyone who wants to do graffiti, don't think "oh, I am a woman or, oh, I am a man." Do it because you like it. You have to have a passion for it, to do it over time. Be patient with learning, have goals. And do it! If you like painting characters, paint them. If you like painting letters, paint them.

ARE2 (USA): Never use your body to get ahead. It's the cheapest way to fame, and you'll lose respect.

BISY (CHILE): I think the first step is the hardest thing for a woman who wants to start painting—you must overcome prejudice, stigma, and fear, but once you do your whole life changes. I think it's a great tool. You need to know to take advantage . . . focus on self-improvement through the creativity and expression the form allows. Painting your voice in the street becomes an act of courage and perseverance, without realizing it you transform the city, along with transforming yourself; transform everything around you.

CHOCK (AUSTRALIA): Paint for the love and paint from your soul.

CLAWMONEY (USA): If I can do it, anyone can.

DANAPINK (CHILE): Vo' dale!

DONA (USA): Always stay unexpected.

EGR (CANADA): Paint because it's how you communicate with the world. Paint because you need to. Don't let the bastards get you down!

ENEY (CHILE): May your painting fly free as a bird! Graffiti is my life and I always need a good quality of life.

EROTICA67 (USA): Know your "HER" Story. The female struggle was not a bloody battle but rarely documented from the get-go so often times overlooked. Do we know who was the first female writer? Do we know the female pioneers? Give respect for the females who paved roads. That is why seeing pictures of bombs from Eva 62 and Barbara 62 or tags of Janet or Lady Bug or pieces by Abby . . . they are so endearing because that is part of our "HER" Story.

EVAY (SCOTLAND): Don't be scared. Keep painting.

FREE (BRAZIL): It's to get your freedom, to be independent. And you must be patient to do whatever you want to do, and then you have to do it.

GIGI (CHILE): Girls, do not be afraid to go out to the street with colors. Intervene, remember that you are social beings, expressing voice and dreams in a world seemingly hopeless. The first impulse is the most important; once you have started you can't stop. The biggest motivation is the work within yourself: you see how it evolves and how you achieve self-improvement. You do not need validation from the rest, because painting in the streets is the challenge in itself, independently of gender.

HOPS (USA): Don't ever bring attention to the fact that you are female. This is about equality, and part of that means putting yourself on the same plane as everyone else in order to receive the same respect and acknowledgment. You are a graffiti writer, plain and simple.

INJAH (BRAZIL): When you do something that you really love, that is how you grow beautiful and bigger every day.

ITSA (UK): Keep going. Do the hard work. Don't expect it to be easy. It takes work to get respect. Get up every weekend. Get your paint and put in the work. The results pay off, you'll get there. You don't just press the nozzle and art comes out—you need to do the work. Don't let anyone put you down. Accept criticism and learn from it.

IVEY (AUSTRALIA): If it's what you love, then that's all the motivation you need.

JERK (USA): Always strive to do better and never settle or assume you're any good at what you do.

JOSKE (AUSTRALIA): Do graffiti for you!

KIF (MEXICO): Always be honest with what you do, with what you say and what you live. Keep yourself real, you and your graffiti!

LA KYD (NICARAGUA): If you like to do graffiti, do what's in your heart without thinking about the negative comments of others; never give up, there doesn't have to be an obstacle that may prevent you from achieving everything you want.

MEME (USA): Put in work, push yourself as hard as you can! Take yourself seriously and others will, too. The best way to be in life is to treat others how you would want it in return. Really . . . just go bombing!

MICKEY (NETHERLANDS): Paint because you want to paint. Paint because you need to paint. Make your art and always support each other.

MISS163 (PERU/USA): Be fearless when you're scared, and if you are scared you are doing something right!

MISS17 (USA): Paint! Be loyal. Be uncompromising. But, mostly, be dedicated. Get up or shut up!

MONS (UK/FRANCE): Learn your graff history, respect the elders, and forget about legal walls—there's a world of wicked walls and spots out there!

MOTEL7 (SOUTH AFRICA): Always do it for yourself, ignore the negative noise, and always wear gloves!

MRS (USA): If you want to do graffiti make sure you are doing it for yourself and not anyone else. Don't do it because other people are doing it because once the negative aspects of graffiti start rolling in (and they eventually will . . . in one way or another) you'll want to feel like it was worth it and you'll want to have as little regrets as possible, if any. Go big or go home.

MUGRE (COLOMBIA): I feel that they should do it for themselves because they love to do it, not only during the time the boyfriend teaches her because the truth remains that although being a woman inside the graffiti scene has its advantages, to win the respect and excel you have to have a lot of discipline and consistency and a lot of love for what you have done.

NASKA (CHILE): Don't be scared! Don't stop! There is a period in your life that you have to try to rise above; just do it! Also, it is important to know other graffiteras for inspiration, ideas, and support! To learn your own style.

NISHCASH (AUSTRALIA): If life gives you lemons—paint that shit gold!

NUNGI (USA): If you want a space or recognition in this culture, you have to get out there and fight for it, and be very verbal and self-promotional.

OM (BRAZIL): Peace.

PAU (GERMANY): Never let anybody tell you that something is not possible. Never let fear guide you in making your precious decisions. We have the great privilege to read our environment from a very particular perspective and to be connected by a passion that makes us partners in crime before we even met. Our passion to express ourselves and to fight for it makes us stronger than we sometimes are conscious about. We are creating power in one of the biggest art movements in history ever—so what vision are you gonna show at your next wall?

PIXIE (UK): Paint to express your own unique style—nobody else in this world is going to be able to do that for you.

QUEEN ANDREA (USA): Practice so much, practice a lot. Become an expert at what you do. Work really hard every day; be convinced that you're the best. Just work hard. Really work hard and try to be the best, really, in a nutshell. But if you don't put in the work and if you don't do it yourself from your own inspiration, then you don't really have much. And people will notice over time, they'll see your dedication and see how devoted you are to your craft. But you have to put in the time. And then it's also important to find mentors—people who can take you under your wing. And I'm lucky to have had people to pass wisdom on to me and to teach me things and to point out things that I didn't see and to make me better. But really my advice is to go hard and to not stop—to go hard and to not stop because if you're really dedicated to it you won't stop. And after a while you're going to make an impact and that's important. It's important for the culture but it's more important for yourself and to feel your accomplishment and your dedication. It's like the illest thing you could do.

RENONE (USA): If you love it, do what it takes, put in work, and be about it. Respect others and you will gain respect. Take the time to learn, and there's a fine line between arrogant, cocky, and confident. Also . . . I would paint in giant platform heels and dresses if the mood struck me. I always had a krylon mini in my mini backpack (don't hate—those were big back then); don't make excuses, just get up.

SANY (CZECH REPUBLIC): Girls are coming up and we are stronger than ever. We are doing what we want and we represent freedom, so let's come together!

SAX (SPAIN): Do what you feel with graffiti and enjoy being a vandal.

SHAPE (CHILE): Don't stop. In the face of any obstacle—paint the same. If you know how to find the pleasure in painting, it will work as an antidote to whatever life brings.

SHIRO (JAPAN): Keep doing what you believe. Do yourself, original style. Don't imitate somebody else. The path is not in your front, the path is in your back. Express yourself in your own way.

Sɪ (Bʀᴀᴢɪʟ): Be happy and be what you are. Never go with the mind of the other people.

Sɪɴᴀᴇ (Gᴇʀᴍᴀɴʏ): Be true, stay true to yourself as a woman; don't try to be like a dude to get respected. Just stay who you are. I don't compete with no one. I hope we all gonna make it!!!

Sᴏʟɪᴛᴀs (Cʜɪʟᴇ): If you want to, you can! There are many difficulties in life. I can say, "Oh, I have problems with this and that and I don't have time and I don't have money," but if you really want to do something then make it happen. Nothing else matters. Try to be happy. Try to be happy without money, without work, without Nikes.

TᴀsʜRᴏᴄᴋ (Aᴜsᴛʀᴀʟɪᴀ): Just keep going and don't be afraid to be wack at first. We all started out awful and if you keep at it, you will get good! Remember to respect your elders and pay your dues bombing and mastering the art of the tag and throw-ups. And yo, for the love of the art, don't just do characters coz real graffiti is all about the letters baby! And, lastly, do it for yourself and not just because you think it's cool or because you happen to be dating a writer or want to flash your hot body all over Instagram. The girls in this book will hate you for it!!!!

ACKNOWLEDGMENTS

Upon learning that I had been working on *Graffiti Grrlz* since 2002, my editor, Ilene Kalish, asked if I would be willing to hand over the manuscript. I told her not to worry. I would be more than happy to let the manuscript go when it was ready. She nodded kindly, but I suspect she knew how difficult it would be for me to *actually* hand it over. A great deal has happened personally and professionally over these last fifteen years. I have moved (back and forth across the country), married, divorced, earned a PhD, lost several (animal and human) loved ones, married again, moved overseas for a postdoc, secured a tenure-track position, and birthed a son—these are just the highlights. As I navigated these life happenings, I was also negotiating my belonging as an outsider within academia (a first-generation, working-class queer Latina) and as an outsider to the subculture I was studying. Throughout it all, the research was the constant; the project acted as a kind of grounding purpose. No matter the situation, the work of centering graff grrlz' voices and highlighting how they have shifted their subculture has always been paramount. I feel a tremendous ethical responsibility toward the grrlz who gave me their time, entrusted me with their stories, welcome me into their homes and at their dinner tables, offered me their couches, chaperoned me around their cities, connected me with friends, invited me to participate in events, and cared enough to challenge my conclusions.

The constant was not just "the work," but the communities I built while doing it. I look back and I see the people who were there—the ones who saw the power and the purpose in the project and believed (and reminded me) that I was capable of completing it. Researching women who write graffiti within a society that demonized and criminalized writers and a subculture that sexualized and marginalized women: there seemed to be a roadblock at every turn—especially in the beginning. While at the University of Arizona, I benefited tremendously from the wisdom of Jules Balén, Harmony Hammond, Miranda Joseph, Kari

McBride, and Sandra Soto, and I am especially grateful for the methodological guidance offered by Elizabeth Lapovsky Kennedy and the real talk I received from Monique Wittig (RIP). Thank you to Laura Briggs for being such a motivating force in my life; first as an advisor and then as a mentor, colleague, fierce advocate, and friend. I am particularly thankful for her willingness to step up when José (my PhD advisor) passed away and I found myself without his guiding light at a crucial juncture in my career. I look forward (sort of?) to our next 4:00 AM chat while everyone else is sleeping and we are writing. Shout-outs to my University of Arizona cohort kat sabine, April Huff, Keisha King, Carolyn Hovendon, Anne Bonds, and Agatha Beins—may we "bust up and break down systems of oppression" forever, and may we bump into each other sooner than later.

Much love to those who made the department of performance studies at New York University feel like home: Laura Fortes, Noel Rodriguez, Shanté Paradigm Smalls, Imani Kai Johnson, James Reed Ball, Alex Pittman, Brandon Masterman, Barrak Alzaid, Yassi Jahanmir, Li Cornfeld, Kestryl Cael Lowrey, Natalia Duoung, Sandra Ruiz, Leon Hilton, Gelsey Bell, Marisol LeBrón, Claudia Sofía Garriga-López, Krista Miranda (ever my writing buddy and comrade in feminist killjoying), Marcos Steuernagel, Beth Stinson, and our beloved Stefanos (who left us too soon). Now I can "take it easy" for at least a little bit, Stefanos, I promise. Thank you to my committee members for sharing your wisdom and guiding me through the project: Tavia Nyong'o, Diana Taylor, Cristina Beltrán, and especially to my late advisor, José E. Muñoz. From your otherworldly vantage point, José, I hope that you can see that I did, eventually, stop interviewing people. A million hugs and kisses for Mariellen Sandford who gave me a chance at TDR and taught me how to edit, which taught me how to write, and eventually helped me locate an authorial voice that feels true to who I am and the scholarly work I want to accomplish.

Thank you to my mentee from the State University of New York at Stony Brook, Eileen Quaranto, who worked diligently transcribing interviews. Thanks to the generous financial support of the American Association for University Women, I was able to continue writing motivated by the knowledge that the feminist academic community believed in the project. I am indebted to Debra Levine for alerting me to an opportunity at NYU Abu Dhabi that afforded me the time, space, finances, and intellectual support to further develop the geographical scope of my fieldwork as a postdoctoral fellow. And though I was only there for a year, I would be remiss to forget my Abu Dhabi crew: Maya Allison, Mark Swislocki, Elsa Periera, Kevin Coffey, Diane Chester, Lauren Seaman, and Marion Wrenn.

I have been extremely fortunate to find immediate community in my first tenure-track position. Thank you to my Women's, Gender, and Sexuality Studies colleague-friends Kathleen Dowley, Meg Devlin O'Sullivan, Heather Hewett, Edith Kuiper, Concetta Chandler, Karl Bryant, and Annee Roschelle for making me feel welcome and encouraging my work at every turn. Thank you to my colleague-friends in other departments at the State University of New York at New Paltz: Sharina Maillo-Pozo, Rachel Somerstein, Kiersten Greene, Andrea Gatzke, Cris Livecchi, and Melissa Rock. Thank you to all of my #academicmom sisters, providing support and feedback through the digital wonders of social media: Savannah Shange, Nik Cesare-Schotzko, Leticia Moreno, Jennifer Stoever, and Jennifer L. Nye. Anyone who knows me, knows that I am one of those people who relies on social media (probably too much). Thank you to my digital community on Facebook for making the writing process a little less isolating and for being ever available for crowdsourcing, reassurances, and resources.

Beyond my academic community, I have an immense support system in *mi familia*—through blood and through bonds. Thank you to my Dorchester crew for always making sure I keep it real even (and especially) when I became "Dr. Jessy." Thank you for sticking with me even after I left Boston, keeping in touch, and making sure I knew I always had a home with all of you; HSK for life! A special thank you to my besties Elizabeth Hanley-Grande, Shauna Robinson, and Marisa Lacey: the "New View" always knows what to say to make you feel like a rock star. Thank you, Holly Popielarz, for being an inspirational friend during my journey into the world of visual art and artmaking when we were undergraduates at the University of Massachusetts Dartmouth, and especially for being willing to wrap my body in plaster at multiple points in our friendship. Thank you to my mother, Maria Colón Alvarado, who raised my sister and me by herself under less-than-ideal circumstances. Mighty and fierce, she taught us how to survive and gave us the freedom to thrive as individuals. Thank you to my father, el salsero Edwin Pabón, for his smiles and positivity even in the hardest of circumstances. Thank you especially for reminding me, Tito, and Lisandra that our happiness is what matters most. Special shout-out to my brother Tito for sharing that Pabón "#getupandgrind with a smile" work ethic with me; your passion to succeed motivates mine. My "little" sister Krystal Weisberg is the real wordsmith of the family. Here are "ten words" for you: I hope to see your poems in print one day. Thank you to all my aunts and uncles who have shown nothing but unconditional love, especially my *tío* Amado Colón (RIP) and my *titi* Norma, whose "no me joda" attitude I inherited and carry on with pride and grace (I hope). *Gracias* to my *abuela* Nydia for raising me over the summers and teaching me the joy in cooking for others. Every single day, I wake up grateful to have the unequivocal support of a true partner in Scott Barfield. Thank you for putting your photography career on hold, uprooting your life, and moving across an ocean so that I could further my dreams. Thank you for defying gender roles with me (best "house husband" ever!) and for doing everything when I had the energy to do nothing. Thank you for inspiring me to choose motherhood; if it were not for the light and joy I see in you and your approach to the world, I would never have known the transformative experience of becoming Matéo's *mamí*. And though you are too young to read these words now, thank you, Matéo, for nursing quietly while I typed, sleeping on my chest while I read, and tugging at my shirt when it was time to take a break and play! Your smiles are grounding, your laughter is transcendent.

Some of the professional relationships I initiated with the grrlz featured in this book turned personal as we aged together (and in some cases experienced simultaneous life milestones). Because in more ways than one, this was a collective process, there are grrlz in particular who deserve special shout-outs for their solidarity in uplifting grrlz in the game, devotion to the project, and willingness to let me into their world: AbbyTC5, Anarkia Boladona, Are2, Chock, ClawMoney, Ivey, Kif, Meme, Miss17, Motel7, Miss163, Pau, Pixie, RenOne, Sany, Shape, Sinae, and Tash. Letting go is hard, but if publishing a book can be likened to getting up on a wall based on taking the risk of exposure for all to see— then I have to follow their lead one last time and get up or shut up.

APPENDIX

Blackbook

Tape recorder, microphone, batteries, camera, and my red canvas black-book. When packing for a research trip, though I dutifully remembered to bring these essentials—I was often without the most important object: markers. Lucky for me, the grrlz are accustomed to using what is at hand to make their mark: Meme took a grape purple spray can to the width of two pages while we spoke in humid Miami (it took days to dry well enough to close and years later the pages are sticky); Motel7 made the most of the pen and baby blue highlighter I dug out of my backpack in Cape Town; Injah glued a full-page sticker of a bare-breasted woman with heart-shaped nipples onto the front page (launching a conversation for us about the value of stickers versus tags or pieces when you mark public space with sexualized imagery); and Jups stenciled an orange butterfly complemented with a black Sharpie tag. Though I never remembered to buy a proper set of markers for my blackbook adventures, I eventually learned to keep a plain old black Sharpie on hand—even on days I did not plan to do fieldwork.

Graffiti writers are collectors: they "collect" public space when they tag it, they collect photographs of favorite pieces (theirs and others), they collect out-of-stock paint colors, they collect tagged-up subway maps, they collect each other's stickers, and, most importantly, they collect one another's signatures. After marking my book—if it had not already come up in conversation—the grrlz would ask, "Are *you* a writer?" The question is not unexpected. After all, the conventional behavior with blackbooks is to exchange them: a tag for a tag. The black-book is a record of the writer's interactions with others; it is usually a mutual exchange, but sometimes a toy will ask a king for her signature to collect it in the way a fan might ask a pop-culture celebrity for an autograph. My experience was more akin to the latter. I think of my "grrlz only" blackbook as an archival object, a sacred object where I did some collecting of my own.

Offering your blackbook is a sign of respect, which explains why some male writers were offended when I passed over them to ask the grrl sitting beside them for her tag. My explanation that my blackbook only had grrlz in it pleased the grrlz, but satisfied only some of the boys—the rest tagged it anyway. Rather than make a fuss in the moment, I simply ripped them out and saved them elsewhere. Like all archival practices, what I saved in my blackbook was guided by my political commitments and overall research project to create more spaces for graffiti grrlz to occupy.

I had different ideas about what I might do with the blackbook once I was done with the research: perhaps use the pages as a kind of collage for the inside covers of my book, or maybe put the images on a digital map with related info about the grrlz. And then I realized the blackbook really belongs with the manuscript because each signature tells a story of a meeting, of time spent, of connections and memories made. While we were sitting on her bed debriefing about our week conducting interviews in Rio de Janeiro, for example, Kia (Anarkia Boladona) pulled out her own markers to draw a "KIA" in hot pink perpendicular to the two pages she had chosen. When AbbyTC5 and I could not find time during our trip to North Carolina, I did the unthinkable and sent it home with her; it felt like a holiday morning when she mailed it back with not one but two beautifully executed pieces (one read Bitch106 and the other reads Abby). And though I had it with me when she visited New York City, Are2 and I were so engrossed in our conversation we forgot about my blackbook entirely; a week later she mailed me a tagged-up brown paper bag and some priority-mail stickers (in classic fashion) with instructions to put them in my book however I wanted. The style, content, and detail of the autographs I collected vary: What supplies do we have? How much time do we have? How much room is there and which pages are available? (Writers are always looking for the most space in the best spot—surface does not matter.) Sometimes they would write a message ("Hi Jess!"), sometimes they would add the place (London!"), sometimes they would add the date, and other times they would do none of those things—but the mark itself reminds me of the encounter.

The best part of handing off your blackbook (which also involves some trust) is that you can watch the writer flip through, recognize names, ask about tags, and share stories of this and that (e.g., "what is she like?"). In other words, by asking a graffiti grrl for her signature, I invited her into the story of my research and into the larger dialogue about women who write graffiti across the diaspora. Though I could not include all the images from my blackbook, offering readers a peek of my collection is an invitation to join the conversations, experiences, and interactions I had while completing *Graffiti Grrlz* through the communication style the grrlz prefer: visual.

Figure A.1. Shiro.

Figure A.2. Shape.

Figure A.3. Queen Andrea.

Figure A.4. Prima Donna.

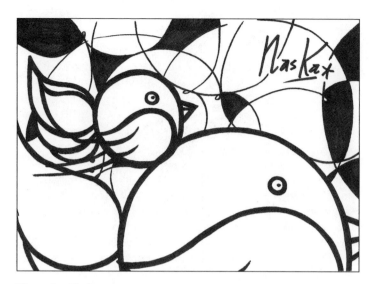

Figure A.5. Naska.

Figure A.6. Motel7.

Figure A.7. Miss163.

Figure A.8. Merlot.

Figure A.9. JesOne.

Figure A.10. Itsa.

Figure A.11. Hops.

Figure A.12. Girls on Top.

Figure A.13. Evay.

Figure A.14. Erotica67.

Figure A.15. Dona Lady, Pink, Miss17, and Claw.

Figure A.16. AbbyTC5.

NOTES

INTRODUCTION

1   I am aware of the convention for visualizing graffiti writers' tag names by capital-izing them; I chose not to follow this form. Also, mindful of the various forms that "Hip Hop" takes, depending on where it appears (hip-hop, hiphop, Hip hop), I take my cue from Daniel Banks and capitalize both the Hip and the Hop to refer to the culture as a proper noun. "Hip Hop is a global culture," he explains, "and for many heads, including myself, it is also a nation, one that transcends the ge-ography of birth and embodies its own utopic ideal. I therefore consider Hip Hop to be a proper noun." In addition to his instructive reasoning, not capitalizing Hip Hop would follow a convention for referring to musical genres, which would reproduce the common slippage whereby rap music is used to mean Hip Hop and vice versa. The music is only one piece of Hip Hop culture. Banks, *Say Word!*, 1.

2   In addition to our conversation at Davidson College, I conducted three interviews with Abby over email (in November 2011, October 2012, and August 2013); all quotes from Abby are from these interviews. As with the rest of the interviews throughout the text, individual interviews are listed in the references.

3   See Gastman and Neelon, *History of American Graffiti*; and Masi308, *Corn Bread*.

4   I oscillate between "graffiti subculture" and "graffiti culture" to indicate that graf-fiti art is a subcultural practice, but it is also part of popular culture. The differ-ences between using "artists," "writers," and "vandals" should be made evident, depending on context: scholars, including myself, tend to refer to these subcul-tural actors as "artists"; the "artists" refer to one another as "writers" because that is the form their artwork takes; and the "writers" are deemed "vandals" because they are writing on surfaces without permission.

5   Powers, *Art of Getting Over*; Miller, *Aerosol Kingdom*. Wildstyle is the genre of graffiti art most readily associated with Hip Hop; it is illegible to most and is char-acterized by a simultaneous deconstruction and reconstruction of letters—"wild" letters. Writers have always had to develop strategies for keeping their identities confidential while simultaneously putting their identities out for the world to see; wildstyle, one method used in this regard, exemplifies the ongoing anxieties of producing a public art form that values privacy.

6   For my remarks on the similarities and differences between Hip Hop graffiti art and other forms of street art, see Pabón, "Ways of Being Seen."

7   The word "character" is used in graffiti vernacular to refer to nonletter compo-nents, such as animals, people, and cartoons.

8 See Chesney-Lind and Hagedorn, *Female Gangs in America*; Currie, Kelly, and Pomerantz, *"Girl Power"*; Gaunt, *Games Black Girls Play*; Mazzarella, *Girl Wide Web 2.0*.

9 In December 2013, the Hip Hop and Punk Feminisms working group at the University of Illinois, Urbana-Champaign, hosted the "Hip Hop and Punk Feminisms: Theory, Genealogy, Performance" conference. The call for proposals stated that the

> conference will bring together artists, activists and academics to stage
> new conversations about women of color and women of color feminisms
> across cultural forms too often perceived to be wholly distinct—hip hop and
> punk. Both hip hop and punk have received significant scholarly attention
> since the 1970s, but despite their near-simultaneous emergence in global
> cities wrought anew through multiple, devastating wars and global economic
> restructuring, rarely are the two brought into conversation with each other.

See hiphopandpunkfeminisms.weebly.com. For more on girls and punk, see Leblanc, *Pretty in Punk*.

10 Kelley, *Yo' Mama's Disfunktional!*, 54.

11 Chalfant and Silver, *Style Wars*.

12 The panel discussion was "Martin Wong: Exploration in Race and Masculinity in Graffiti Culture." For more on the founders of Hip Hop graffiti art, see Chalfant and Prigoff, *Spraycan Art*; Cooper and Chalfant, *Subway Art*; and Ahearn, *Wild Style*.

13 Murray and Murray, *Broken Windows*, n.p.

14 Austin, *Taking the Train*.

15 Kelling and Wilson, "Broken Windows."

16 In 2014, I published an interview with Abby about her work, and her 2013 show *HomeGirls*. See Pabón, "Interview with AbbyTC5."

17 For gangs, see Phillips, *Wallbangin'*; Grody, *Graffiti L.A.* For urban decay, see Castleman, *Getting Up*; Ferrell, *Crimes of Style*. For fine art, see R. Jones, *Inside the Graffiti Subculture*; M. Thompson, *American Graffiti*.

18 For diasporic aesthetics, see Miller, *Aerosol Kingdom*. For its lost potential, see Murray and Murray, *Broken Windows*. For youth culture, see Ganz, *Graffiti Women*; Naar, *Birth of Graffiti*. For history, see Martinez and Nato, *Graffiti NYC*; Felisbret and Felisbret, *Graffiti New York*; Gastman and Neelon, *History of American Graffiti*; McCormick et al., *City as Canvas*; Chalfant and Jenkins, *Training Days*; H. Love, *Miami Graffiti Art*. For curriculum development, see Rahn, *Painting without Permission*. For male masculinity, see Macdonald, *Graffiti Subculture*. For design training, see Snyder, *Graffiti Lives*.

19 Miller, *Aerosol Kingdom*, 16.

20 Walsh, *Graffito*, 10–11.

21 Ibid., 30.

22 McRobbie and Garber, "Girls and Subcultures," 12. Originally published in Hall and Jefferson, *Resistance through Rituals*.

23 McRobbie and Garber, "Girls and Subcultures," 14.

24 Castleman, *Getting Up*, 81.

25 Cooper and Chalfant, *Subway Art*, 41.

26 Powers, *Art of Getting Over*, 14.

27 See TEDx Talks, *Feminism on the Wall*.

28 Jackson Jr., *Real Black*, 176. In places where graffiti is illegal, "realness" is attributed to writers who strictly paint illegally using aerosol to write letters in appropriate styles (wild, public, block, etc.), in other words, "bombers." The designation "real" can certainly apply to writers who are not strictly bombers, especially once removed from contexts where graffiti making is criminalized, but the implication in all cases is that realness is rooted in the risk and danger of strictly illegal activity.

29 Cedric Douglas, personal Facebook message to author, February 5, 2013.

30 In February 2013 I conducted three interviews with RenOne over email; all quotes are from these interviews. After we connected, RenOne contacted her local community art center—Mother Brooks Arts and Community Center—and secured a job teaching graffiti to preteens and teens each summer; she also curated a show, *Out of the Everywhere: Evolution of the Graffiti Artist*, in 2014.

31 Handstyle refers to the handwriting style of the writer.

32 RenOne, instant message with author, May 15, 2017.

33 Ibid.

34 Nochlin, "Why Have There Been No Great Women Artists?," 158.

35 Butler, *Bodies That Matter*.

36 In *Queer Latinidad*, Juana Maria Rodríguez frames her negotiation of disciplinary boundaries by stating, "Traditional disciplinary boundaries become inadequate containers for subjects whose lives and utterances traverse the categories meant to contain them. . . . [T]he very disciplines that divide Latin American from North American, music from literature, politics from performance, or queer studies from Latino studies have been based on paradigms constituted through our marginalization" (30). See also Reinharz, *Feminist Methods in Social Research*, 51.

37 Scott, "Evidence of Experience," 777.

38 Regarding "disembodied" objectivity, in contrast, Donna Haraway offers "feminist objectivity" as that which "is about limited location and situated knowledge, not about transcendence and splitting of subject and object. It allows us to become answerable for what we learn how to see." Haraway, "Situated Knowledges," 583. "Hiphopography" was conceptualized in the late '80s and early '90s by James G. Spady and introduced in the 1991 text *Nation Conscious Rap: The Hip Hop Vision*. Spady argued that scholars interested in studying Hip Hop culture needed to approach it in a Hip Hop manner: divisions between the scholar and the subject have to be put to the way side, communities and individuals have to be engaged on their own terms, and the researcher should come to the project with an understanding of the history, the value structures, and the jargon used. See also H. Samy Alim's description of hiphopography as a combination of ethnography, biography, and oral history that emphasizes a giving back to the community

studied, in Alim and Hi-Tek, " 'Natti Ain't No Punk City.' " For queer feminist ethnography, see Lapovsky Kennedy and Davis, "Constructing an Ethnohistory of the Buffalo Lesbian Community"; Lewin and Leap, *Out in the Field*; Newton, "My Best Informants Dress."

39 From 2012 to 2014 I curated shows for writers, including for Anarkia Boladona, AbbyTC5, Shiro, Miss163, Girls on Top Crew, Mrs, Erotica67, Queen Andrea, and ClawMoney at the bOb Gallery and Bar in Manhattan. In 2013, as mentioned earlier in the introduction, I invited Abby to Davidson for a live interview. In 2016 as part of the Liberal Arts and Sciences "Without Limits" series, I commissioned Pau to paint a large outdoor canvas, titled *Kra: The Moon,* at the State University of New York at New Paltz.

40 When possible, I offered the grrlz the opportunity to read what I had written about them and provided feedback as a mutually respectful way to be transparent and allow for disagreements.

41 Ahmed, *Promise of Happiness.*

42 Gastman and Neelon, *History of American Graffiti,* 25, 28.

43 "In 1981, [Henry] Chalfant organized ["Graffiti Rock,"] a performance of rap and breakdance with an aerosol painting as a backdrop at the Common Ground performance space in Soho, downtown Manhattan. This was among the first events that brought the forms together in unprecedented ways." See Miller, *Aerosol Kingdom,* 151. One of the first articles about Hip Hop available to a national audience appeared on April 22, 1981, in the *Village Voice.* In "Physical Graffiti: Breaking Is Hard to Do," Sally Banes enters the b-boying world of the Bronx and Harlem to report on the "cool, swift, and intricate" dance style that shifts "aggression into art." She describes b-boying as a dance of "masculine vitality," one that is "a celebration of the flexibility and budding sexuality of the gangly male adolescent body," developed in contrast to what it is not—female. She ends by noting that "part of the macho quality of breaking comes from the physical risk involved. It's not only the bruises, scratches, cuts, and scrapes . . . part of it is impressing the girls." In this brief but renowned article, heterosexual desire and a "boys will be boys" physicality are conflated and collapsed onto the bodies of her interviewees. Naming the then-new dance form "physical graffiti"—a term used later by PopMaster Fabel Pabón in his 1999 essay "Physical Graffiti: The History of Hip-Hop Dance"—Banes effectively tied the two art forms together via social and aesthetic characteristics. See Banes, "Physical Graffiti," 9, 8, 11. See also Miller, *Aerosol Kingdom,* 149.

44 Castleman, *Getting Up,* 131, 40. On funk music and Hip Hop, see Vincent, *Funk.* See R. Thompson, "Hip Hop 101"; Keyes, *Rap Music and Street Consciousness;* and Schloss, *Making Beats.*

45 Miller, *Aerosol Kingdom,* 146, 152.

46 See Steven Hager's "Afrika Bambaataa's Hip-Hop" in Cepeda, *And It Don't Stop,* 12–26.

47 Martha Cooper explained that "hip-hop was packaged, and in a sense we packaged it." Miller, *Aerosol Kingdom,* 152.

48 Rose, *Black Noise*; Chang, *Total Chaos*; Murray Forman, *'Hood Comes First*; Perry, *Prophets of the Hood*; Dimitriadis, *Performing Identity/Performing Culture*.

49 Derrida, "Signature, Event, Context."

50 Jackson Jr., *Real Black*, 182.

51 In addition to Rose's *Black Noise*, I found the following texts invaluable: Pough, *Check It While I Wreck It*; Pough et al., *Home Girls Make Some Noise!*; and Morgan, *When Chickenheads Come Home to Roost*.

52 In 2001, this post appeared:

> Graffgirl wants . . .

> Do you know any ILL chicks that get up? paint? We do and that's why we started graffgirl.com, a directory of female graffiti artists. GRAFFGIRL still needs your help . . . We want GIRLS who can represent! PASS THE WORD. PHOTOS appreciated!!! bixel-photos: bixel_soa@yahoo.com

I was not able to verify if this was a separate or related endeavor to what became GraffGirlz.com. Similarly, though also unrelated to GraffGirlz.com, TashRock [aka Queen MCTash] posted

> Female writers only!

> Women that Rock

> Check out my profiles on some of the best writers 'round the world—who just happen to be female. . . . www.oneeightthree.com/html/tashfriends. html I'd love to hear from you and if you're good, spotlight your work on my "women that rock" site. tashrock@hotmail.com

53 Invested in attending to alternative ways of being and doing previously unaccounted for, [Judith] Jack Halberstam introduces the concepts of "queer space" and "queer time" to provide "new understandings of space enabled by the production of queer counterpublics" and analyzes "those specific models of temporality that emerge within postmodernism once one leaves the temporal frames of bourgeois reproduction and family, longevity, risk/safety, and inheritance." I conceptualize graffiti subculture through paradigms such as queer time and queer space in chapter 4. Halberstam, *In a Queer Time and Place*, 6.

54 "The Queerness of Hip Hop/The Hip Hop of Queerness" was a one-day symposium at Harvard where I first presented my ideas on feminist masculinity (see chapter 1). See Snorton, "As Queer as Hip Hop."

55 Kozinets, *Netnography*.

56 Hine, *Virtual Ethnography*; Kozinets, *Netnography*.

57 In her article "Globalizing Intimacy: The Role of Information and Communication Technologies in Maintaining and Creating Relationships," Gill Valentine expands the general assumption that intimacy requires physical proximity and asks her readers to consider how the Internet alters the boundaries of intimacy (367).

58 Fielding, Lee, and Blank, *SAGE Handbook of Online Research Methods*.

59 She thanks "Aetoy, Angel, Arsef, Bule, Claw, Camo, Dona, EGR, Faie, Jolie, June, Kyf, Kweenz Destroyz, Lady K, Piwa, Rosy, Style, [and] Toofly for their articles and opinions." Foxy Lady, "CatFight: Female Graff Update Issue 5," 16.

60 I have tried to locate the creator of GraffGirlz.com since 2008. I assumed it was Foxy Lady (because of the connection to *Catfight* I discuss in chapter 3) until she clarified. Mickey and Queen MCTash generously offered to help me find the truth, but even with our combined efforts we were unable to pinpoint a specific grrl.

61 GraffGirlz.com was saved 136 times between December 12, 2005, and August 1, 2015, on the Wayback Machine. The menu bar offered users the choice to navigate directly to one of the 180 "GraffGirlz" listed or click through twenty-six options where writers were organized "By Country": Australia: Civah, Egoh, Glimps, Heir, Igasm, Spice, Tash; Austria: Fatcat, Soma; Brazil: Anarkia, Deninja, Jana Joana, Pan, Tikka, Z; Canada: Egr, Ekos; Chile: Acb (RIP), Anis, DanaPink, Fusa, Inger; China: Fice, Redy; Czech Republic: Goro; France: Camo, CandyBule, Dyva, Elfik, Eli, Elir, Else, Ester, Joly, Jonis, June, Kawet, Kensa, Kita, Klor, Lady k, Lenie, Malice, Mamzel, Many, Moloko, Presk, Rakli, Safir, Shay, Shove, Sista, Thia, Toner2, Venus, Ynoe, Youpiyeah, YZ; Germany: Azem, Diva, Fany, Jolie, Junek, Lazy, Mauz, Sear, Sheron, Sinae; Hungary: RenyBrown; Italy: Aetoy, Angel, Arka, Faie, Fire, Fransy, Kyra, Maria, Nemo, Soul, SuperB2, This; Japan: Gazel, Sekty, Shiro, Vol; Mexico: Akira, Gripa, Nalah, Pides, Traumas; Netherlands: Asia, Duna, Flady, Fren, MsX; New Zealand: Diva NZ, Ouch; Peru: Snire; Poland: Amyck, Foxy; Portugal: Bela, Dikra, H2oney, Queen, Sphiza, Suave, Xuma; Puerto Rico: Bles, Yami, Zori4; Russia: Alsik, Byrn, Okada, Quel; South Africa: Faith47; South Africa/Switzerland: Smirk; Spain: Aishu, Ansia, Aserf, Chikita, Clöe, Crayne, Den, Dona, Dune, Dusie, Emit, Flor, Fly, Full, Gash, Gata, Hydra, Inma, Julieta, Kaperucita, Kira, Kyo, Laia, Luna, Mae, Malicia, Mias, Mizy, Nabi, Neya, Nisha, Numi, Oink, Only, Ovni, Piwa, Pola, Rasta, Ruby, Savage girl, Sax, Seora, Soda, Sora, Stil, Vonda, Yubia; USA: Acet, Are2, Claw, Ema, Erotica67, Gates, Gloe, Indie, Kuta, Lady K Fever, Mezkal, Miss17, Mora, Phem9, Pink, Scarlet, Secret, Sherm, Shiva, Siloette, Somer, Toofly; Ukraine: Mayya; United Kingdom: Chock, Fauna, Lyns, Waleska.

62 At the time of this writing there were two documentaries featuring only graff grrlz in the fundraising and production phases: *All She Wrote* by Idalina Leandro (www.indiegogo.com) and *Street Heroines* by Alexandra Henry (streetheroines. tumblr.com). Both films take an international approach and highlight graffiti grrlz from multiple countries; the latter also includes street artists. You can view trailer teasers at vimeo.com/68883290 and vimeo.com/channels/streetheroines. *Girl Power* showcases writers from the Czech Republic, Germany, Hungary, France, Switzerland, Spain, Slovakia, Slovenia, Italy, Poland, Austria, the Netherlands, South Africa, and the United States. See Bogner, "Let Us Spray."

63 Sany, interview with the author, November 2, 2012.

64 Sany, instant message with the author, October 29, 2015.

65 Warner, "Publics and Counterpublics."

66 See West and Kalamka, " 'It's All One.' "

67 Tiongson Jr. characterizes the debate on rap as hinging "on whether or not hip-hop constitutes an African American expressive form but also the extent to which

hip-hop signifies blackness even as it has evolved into a global expressive form."
Tiongson Jr., *Filipinos Represent*, 2. On the globalization of Hip Hop culture,
see Condry, *Hip-Hop Japan*; Osumare, *Africanist Aesthetic in Global Hip-Hop*;
Fernandes, *Close to the Edge*; Mitchell, *Global Noise*; Basu and Lemelle, *Vinyl Ain't
Final*.

68 On the commercialization of radical black aesthetics and the content of rap lyrics,
see Cepeda, *And It Don't Stop*; Jeffries, *Thug Life*; Neal and Forman, *That's the
Joint!*; Perkins, *Droppin' Science*. On the consumption by white Hip Hop music
lovers, see Harrison, *Hip Hop Underground*; Kitwana, *Why White Kids Love Hip
Hop*; Baldwin, "Black Empires, White Desires." Aisha Durham makes a similar
observation about gender difference in her recent book, *Home with Hip Hop
Feminism*: "Research continues to be devoted to black boys and men who use
cultural tools honed in hip hop to make sense of our postmodern world in the
face of deindustrialization, police brutality, underemployment, and gang violence.
That said, it has been the gender analysis of hip hop feminism that has pushed our
understanding of masculinity and its intersection with sexuality, class, and race in
the field" (11). See also Guevara, "Women Writin' Rappin' Breakin'," 49.

69 Sharpley-Whiting, *Pimps Up, Ho's Down*, xvi.

70 Pabón and Smalls, "Critical Intimacies."

71 Tiongson Jr., *Filipinos Represent*, 91.

72 In "The African Americanization of Hip-Hop," Tiongson Jr. provides a literature
review of early accounts and demonstrates how they established a "close as-
sociation between hip-hop and African Americanness." Tiongson Jr., *Filipinos
Represent*, 6. Also, on gender and nation specifically, see Kaplan, Alarcon, and
Moallem, *Between Woman and Nation*; Collins, *From Black Power to Hip Hop*;
Puar, *Terrorist Assemblages*.

73 In an interview for VH1's Hip Hop Honors event celebrating women in Hip Hop,
ClawMoney mentions that girls should look up to rappers like Queen Latifah and
Missy Elliot. See www.vh1.com.

74 Following Patricia Hill Collins and Raquel Z. Rivera, I capitalize the B in Black
when it refers to African Americans specifically, and I lowercase the b when it
refers to Afro-diasporic subjects.

   In *Black Sexual Politics*, Collins explains the usage of a capital B to refer to
African Americans: "I capitalize the term Black when it serves to name a racial
population group with an identifiable history in United States. For African
Americans, the term Black is simultaneously a racial identity assigned to people
of African descent by the state, a political identity for petitioning that same state,
and a self-defined ethnic identity" (17).

   Rivera explains her intentional usage of the lowercase b and capitalized B
similarly in *New York Ricans from the Hip Hop Zone*, noting, "Given the varied meanings that blackness can have—in some cases referring only to African
Americans and in other cases to all Afro-diasporic people—I will be using 'black'
and 'Black' as two distinct concepts: 'black' as the racial or sociocultural category

that refers to people of the African Diaspora and 'Black' as the U.S.-based ethno-racial category that refers specifically to African Americans" (9).

75 There is antiblack, white supremacist thought (especially in the United States) backing the erasure of white bodies in Hip Hop, perpetuating criminalization and the corresponding visual narrative. One instance of the visual narrative about graffiti writers, though modified in an interesting way, appeared on the Fox Network's show *King of the Hill* in 2002. "Bad Girls, Bad Girls, Whatcha Gonna Do" opens with the usual cast of characters standing on their corner aghast at what they have found: a "Q-Bag" throw-up, which appeared on their fence overnight. The vandal turns out to be a teenage girl named Tid Pao, Connie's cousin who is visiting from Los Angeles. As the story unfolds, we learn that Tid Pao is not just "visiting," but rather hiding from her gang because of a drug deal gone bad. Her character is by no means a subtle representation of the "graffiti vandal." She is a gang member sporting Hip Hop fashion that marks her as an inner-city girl of color. Her gender and ethnicity, though counter to the stereotypical portrayal of Asian girls, were necessary components for the plot: by way of her exotic "feminine wiles" she convinces Bobby to help her cook crystal meth, pretending she is interested in him romantically. Heterosexualized almost as quickly as she is racialized and classed, Tid Pao uses her adolescent sexuality to get what she wants from Bobby and Bobby attempts to be the bad boy "cool" kid he thinks she wants him to be. As he tags "poo" on the fence, he says, "Check it out girl, I'm representin'!"

While a dated *King of the Hill* episode may be a rather unexpected example for how the image of the "graffiti vandal" is produced and consumed through media, it is an apt one. In a span of thirty minutes the audience has a number of problematic stereotypes affirmed: the otherwise good, and geeky, suburban white kid falls into the trouble-making trappings of a big-city girl who "coincidentally" happens to be a graffiti writer/gang member/drug dealer. In an interesting take on the implications of his study, Miller "wondered if the emphasis on the Caribbean/Latin American nature of a culture created in New York City did not become a way for politicians to blame it on immigrants, as if it were not a response to regional and national tensions." The progressive view that the economic gains produced by Hip Hop culture belong to the Afro-Caribbean community that created it, and the antiblack conservative view that the Afro-Caribbean community created Hip Hop and is thus solely responsible for the deterioration of society (celebrating violence, perpetuating a culture of poverty, and oppressing women) have one thing in common, albeit for different reasons: the removal of the white numerical minority from Hip Hop. The (continued) silence around the involvement of white people plays into the racialization of criminality so tied to Hip Hop practitioners: rappers and graffiti writers are consistently represented as violent gang bangers. While it is true that part of the social unrest and financial crises in New York City that produced Hip Hop also generated a great deal of gang activity, painting graffiti was actually a way for kids to avoid gang membership, or at least have a different nonviolent role in a gang (Chang, *Can't Stop Won't Stop*).

In her study on the difference between gang graffiti and Hip Hop graffiti art, *Wallbangin': Graffiti and Gangs in L.A.*, the anthropologist Susan Phillips argues that "people write hip-hop graffiti to represent themselves within an arena of hip-hop graffiti writers [. . . ;] they work to establish a name and a position within that arena for reasons that are additive and positive. Hip-hop graffiti is about creation, not destruction." She is right in her contention that the act is done to establish a self, even if her distinction between violent gangs and nonviolent graffiti crews is a bit too neat. Miller, *Aerosol Kingdom*, 16, 17; Phillips, *Wallbangin'*, 310–311; Boowhan and Kyounghee, "Bad Girls, Bad Girls, Whatcha Gonna Do."

76 Fluro shared,

> For me personally, Hip Hop is a big part of my graffiti and has had a huge influence on it, from the music I listen to, the style of letters or characters I draw, the colours I use etc. I also got into graffiti through my Bboy friends, and I've always been around a lot of the other elements of Hip Hop. In general I don't think graffiti is confined to Hip Hop at all nowadays, it's really its own culture. It is often linked back to Hip Hop in a lot of ways, and graffiti style is prominent in the other elements of Hip Hop—clothing etc, but it has gone so many other different ways, so many people that write graffiti are into so many different things.

Unless otherwise noted, all quotes from Fluro are from an email exchange in October 2009.

77 Snyder, *Graffiti Lives*, 2–3.

78 In *New York Ricans from the Hip Hop Zone*, Raquel Z. Rivera describes how the marginalization of Latinxs from Hip Hop's origin story and contemporary profile is an effect of limited conceptualization of blackness and diaspora. "Whether mass-mediated or academic, accounts of hip hop's history tend to explore it either as an exclusively African American phenomenon or to mention Puerto Rican and/or Latino participation in passing but still end up focusing their analysis on African Americans. Puerto Rican stories and specificities are marginalized from these narratives because the cultural similarities and intersections between both groups are not sufficiently understood. African heritage or "blackness" in the United States is understood primarily through the African American experience. Therefore, although Puerto Rican culture is part of the African diaspora in the Americas, it is not usually imagined as being black." Rivera, *New York Ricans from the Hip Hop Zone*, 20. Similarly, situating his Chican@ subjects within Hip Hop in *The Chican@ Hip Hop Nation*, Pancho McFarland makes a crucial point about the relationship between diaspora and origins: "Hip-hop is most certainly a creation of the African Diaspora, even if its origins are *more complex and polycultural* than most think." McFarland, *Chican@ Hip Hop Nation*, 18; emphasis mine.

79 See Ziff and Rao, *Borrowed Power*.

80 In the foreword to *The Vinyl Ain't Final*, Robin D. G. Kelley reminds readers that the founders of Hip Hop were children of immigrant parents displaced by globalization, and he argues that Hip Hop must be contextualized as transnational from

the start. He states, "While the economy has been global for a very long time—at least since the days of the transatlantic slave trade—we have witnessed a marked difference in scale and degree of concentration since the 1970s." Kelley, "Foreword," xi.

81 Gilroy, *Black Atlantic*.

82 On blackness and appropriation through performance, see Johnson, *Appropriating Blackness*.

83 Here again, Ivor Miller's scholarship grounding Hip Hop graffiti and Hip Hop culture in the Afro-Caribbean diaspora is indispensable. He discusses Cuban Santeria, Brazilian Candomblé, Southern Creole, Cajun cooking, and Salsa music as characterized by the diasporic aesthetic of "section and fusion." His analysis gestures toward ways of thinking through the distribution of practices by people not conventionally understood as "belonging" to the traditions they have selected and fused. Miller, *Aerosol Kingdom*, 34.

84 Since images of Hip Hop masculinity began to circulate commercially in the 1980s (Kurtis Blow selling Sprite in 1986, for example) they have become increasingly static, especially as "gangsta rap" rose in popularity and profitability in the '90s. "Despite hip-hop's historical ethnoracial hybridity, the innumerable contributions of female practitioners and fans, and the discursive contestation between the sexes embedded in hip-hop texts, most commercially successful American hip-hop has had a black male face, body, and voice." See Noz, "50 Greatest Rap Commercials"; Jeffries, *Thug Life*, 9.

85 Sharma, *Hip Hop Desis,* 215.

86 Ibid., 216.

87 A similar perspective was taken by Susan Phillips in her assessment of the criminality associated with graffiti art making: "the fact that the chosen medium is marginal and illegal often correlates to the types of people who produce graffiti—people who are themselves marginalized, even *if only through the manner they choose to express themselves.*" Phillips, *Wallbangin'*, 23.

88 Tiongson Jr., *Filipinos Represent*, 8.

89 Pinto, *Difficult Diasporas*, 5, 16–17.

90 Ibid., 7.

91 Sharpley-Whiting, *Pimps Up, Ho's Down,* 27.

92 In 2012, I curated a solo show for Shiro at bOb bar on the Lower East Side, which she titled *Eternally Mimi*. See shiro.bj46.com.

93 Dona, instant message with author, January 4, 2016.

94 In her 2000 text *Feminism Is for Everybody*, bell hooks does not use articles (definite or indefinite) when referring to "feminist movement." I understand, and employ, this subtle move as a linguistic strategy for signifying action. Feminist movement is a verb, something one does.

95 While I unpack the effects of neoliberalism and capitalistic discourses about global girl power on graff grrlz (see chapter 1), my focus differs from transnational feminist work that focuses on subjects' relationships to nation-states, the

global economy, and NGOs. I refer to this book as transnational feminist work to accurately describe the ways that the performance of feminism crosses national geopolitical borders, and to situate my visual and cultural studies project in relation to studies of globalization. See Briggs, "Transnationalism"; Grewal and Kaplan, *Scattered Hegemonies*; Moghadam, *Globalizing Women*; Reilly and Nochlin, *Global Feminisms*.

96 Lorde, "I Am Your Sister," 295.

CHAPTER 1. PERFORMING FEMINIST MASCULINITY IN A POSTFEMINIST ERA

1 Cisgender is in parentheses here because Macdonald does not distinguish between transgender men and cisgender men. Macdonald, *Graffiti Subculture*.

2 Halberstam, *Female Masculinity*, 6.

3 The queer feminist scholar [Judith] Jack Halberstam reminds us that masculinity is about "embodiment, identification, social privilege, racial and class formation, and desire," not simply an effect brought about by having a cisgender male body. Halberstam, "The Good, the Bad, and the Ugly," 355.

4 In *Pimps Up, Ho's Down*, Sharpley-Whiting discusses expressions of a "swaggering" masculinity in young black females "where mimicry (of the worst of male behavior)" grounded in sexism and misogyny masquerades as liberation. Sharpley-Whiting, *Pimps Up, Ho's Down*, 144, 147.

5 Macdonald, *Graffiti Subculture*, 97, 130–131. In *Prophets of the Hood: Politics and Poetics in Hip Hop*, Imani Perry argues that, "as a masculinist form with masculinist aesthetics, Hip Hop, and the art form's masculinist ideals of excellence and competitiveness, have often forced women to occupy roles gendered male" (156). Similar to Macdonald's usage of infiltration, and Perry's description of women being "forced" to act masculine, we see a similar perspective in Castleman's exchange with Wicked Gary about the grrlz in the Ex-Vandals Squad crew. Wicked Gary explained that "our girls were basically good looking 'cause they were into themselves . . . they weren't about fighting, they didn't have to be like hard rocks and they could still be girls and have something about them, like shape and jiggle." Grrlz in their crew "could still be girls" (read: feminine) who "didn't have to be" masculine like the boys. Castleman, *Getting Up*, 103. Suggesting that women, as "infiltrators" in Hip Hop, are "forced" to "occupy" masculinity (here defined by attributes like "excellence" and "competitiveness") implies a lack of agency, and positions women as temporary consumers of a masculinity not rightfully theirs.

6 Theories such as Macdonald's betray graff grrlz' experiences and undo the work of gender performance theory that clarifies that we are all acting "as if," regardless of whichever particular performance we choose to enact, because, as Judith Butler contends, "there is no 'proper' gender, a gender proper to one sex than another, which is in some sense that sex's cultural property." Butler, *Bodies That Matter*, 312.

7 The conflation of heterosexuality with cisgender male masculinity in the iconic figure of the graffiti writer is troubled when we look to figures such as Earsnot, a gay Black man who started writing in Manhattan in the '90s. In a 2012 video posted by Land of Chrome, titled "Earsnot Interview—Graffiti Artist," Earsnot discusses how his sexuality was always a point of discussion—often hearing "he's a faggot." A quick look at the video's comment thread demonstrates the malicious white supremacist heterosexist attacks that he endures as an out, Black writer. He explains that graffiti helps him express himself because mainstream representations of Black people and gay people not only fail to account for his realities, but also deny him the subject position of "man" as a racialized and sexualized Other. "I love graffiti," he adds, "it helps me maintain the idea that I'm a man."

8 For exceptions to the rule, see Clay, "'I Used to Be Scared of the Dick'"; McCune, "'Out' in the Club"; Smalls, "'Rain Comes Down'"; and Sharma, *Hip Hop Desis*. The performance of masculinity in women is also a topic that some scholars of reggaeton have considered: see Rivera-Rideau, *Remixing Reggaetón*; and Rivera, Marshall, and Pacini Hernandez, *Reggaeton*. Fifteen years ago, in *Female Masculinity*, Halberstam made the following observation: "despite at least two decades of sustained feminist and queer attacks on the notion of natural gender, we still believe that masculinity in girls and women is abhorrent and pathological" (268).

9 McFarland, *Chican@ Hip Hop Nation*, 174.

10 Guevara states, "Women elaborate styles and subjects of their own that are often very different from those of the men." Guevara, "Women Writin' Rappin' Breakin'," 58.

11 In "'It's All One:' A Conversation between Juba Kalamka and Tim'm West," founders of the now-defunct queer crew Deep Dickollective (and pioneers of the Homohop movement) discuss Hip Hop historiography. Questioning the construction of the authentic Hip Hop body, Juba asks, "Who's 'real'? Are straight Black men who sample records by white women 'real' b-boys?" To which Tim'm asserts, "The conversation is not just about the reclamation of hip-hop by Queers . . . but a reexamination of how we've imagined hip-hop in ways that have de-emphasized and discounted Queer presence." Tim'm and Juba are not only concerned with the reformative work of the Homohop movement; they are also restoring the history of queer visibility into Hip Hop's cultural memory, opening "conversations about homophobia as an extension of sexism and misogyny" and attending to "the erasure of inappropriate faggotry" in Hip Hop culture. Throughout their conversation they cite Hip Hop's queer influences (club music, disco, lofting, voguing, Basquiat) and expose the heteronormative misogynistic mythology of the straight, urban, poor, Black male "authentic Hip Hop body" as grossly inaccurate. The privileging of hetero/sexist male masculine authenticity at the center of Hip Hop silences anything "other than," anything "inappropriate," and it subsequently erases women and queer practitioners in historical accounts and contemporary representations. West and Kalamka, "'It's All One,'" 200, 203.

12 Racking refers to stealing cans of spray paint. Miller, *Aerosol Kingdom*, 31–32.

13 In her article of the same name, Joan Morgan coined the phrase and declared herself a "Hip Hop feminist," stating that she needs "a feminism brave enough to fuck with the grays" at work when she enjoys shaking her booty to "bling-ass-make-money-biaatch" music. A crucial call to feminists who love Hip Hop and Hip Hop heads who believe in equality, Morgan's article called for a feminism that "samples and layers many voices, injects its sensibilities into the old and flips it into something new, provocative, and powerful." Morgan, "Hip-Hop Feminist," 280, 281. Whitney A. Peoples investigates the terms of engagement for "hip-hop feminists" in her must-read article " 'Under Construction.' " She is explicitly concerned with building a mutually beneficial bridge over generational divides informing the difficult relationship that Hip Hop participants have to feminism and vice versa. In addition to the Hip Hop feminist texts already cited, see Kwakye and Brown, *Wish to Live*.

14 hooks, *Feminism Is for Everybody*.

15 On girl power produced by what Andi Zeisler terms "marketplace feminism," see *We Were Feminists Once*. On postfeminism and girl power, see Gill, "Culture and Subjectivity in Neoliberal and Postfeminist Times"; Currie, Kelly, and Pomerantz, *"Girl Power"*; and Gill and Scharff, *New Femininities*.

16 In *Girls, Cultural Productions, and Resistance*, Michelle S. Bae and Olga Ivashkevich reimagine what resistance and agency mean in relation to girls. For them, "girls' resistance is not found in the neoliberal, capitalist idea of a free-willed girl subject who exercises both feminine and masculine qualities under the popular banner of 'girl power' . . . that creates an unproblematic and highly hedonistic view of the girl subject, whose fantasy and desire are fulfilled via her choices, and never struggles with the popular representations and narratives she encounters" (56).

17 hooks, *Feminism Is for Everybody*, 70.

18 Are2, email interview with author, February 18, 2013.

19 All quotes from Are2 are from an email exchange in 2009 unless otherwise noted.

20 See Bourland, "Graffiti's Discursive Spaces"; Bowen, "Graffiti Art"; Austin, *Taking the Train*; Fisher, "How the Tate Got Streetwise"; McCormick et al., *City as Canvas*; and Wacławek, *Graffiti and Street Art*.

21 Writing about Asia One's b-girl crew No Easy Props, Imani Kai Johnson explains that the crew is "named after an admonishment of giving 'easy props' or unearned respect to b-girls for simply being present rather than for being good." Johnson, "From Blues Women to B-Girls," 25.

22 McRobbie, "Top Girls?," 732.

23 Ibid., 733. For the patriarchal bargain, see Kandiyoti, "Bargaining with Patriarchy."

24 Miss17 became the first graffiti grrl featured on the cover of *The Infamous* magazine for issue #2 in 2010; the cover read "Miss17 Out for World Domination." Issue 7 featured Few and Far. See shop.theinfamousmag.com/.

25 All quotes from Miss17 are from interviews conducted over email in 2009 unless otherwise noted.

26 Hoch, "Toward a Hip-Hop Aesthetic."

27 *Oxford English Dictionary*, "braggadocio, n. and adj.," *Oxford English Dictionary* online, Oxford University Press, www.oed.com (accessed August 8, 2012); *Oxford English Dictionary*, " 'arrogance, N.' " *Oxford English Dictionary* online, Oxford University Press, www.oed.com (accessed August 8, 2012).

28 In April and May 2009, the McCaig-Welles Gallery in Brooklyn, New York, exhibited a show called *Queens Arrive: International All Female Graffiti Artists*, featuring graffiti grrlz ClawMoney (NYC), Indie184 (NYC), Abby (NYC), Mickey (Amsterdam), Hera (Germany), Fafi (Paris), Nina (Brazil), Silo-ette (San Fran), Acet (New Jersey), Zori4 (Puerto Rico), Spice (Australia), Egr (Canada), Koralie (NYC/France), Klor (Canada), Femme9 (Kansas), and Sherm (Los Angeles). On the exhibition card "queens" was spelled "queenz." See "Girl Graffiti."

29 To watch my video *Following Carmen Sandiego . . . er Miss17 around Athens*, see www.youtube.com/watch?v=vAxFZtyFepE.

30 Miss17, email interview with author, April 2, 2002.

31 See Lennon, " 'Bombing' Brooklyn"; ClawMoney, *Claw Money Miss17 Graffiti Interview*.

32 See Majors and Billson, *Cool Pose*.

33 Jeffries, *Thug Life*, 60.

34 See hooks, *We Real Cool*; Mutua, *Progressive Black Masculinities?*

35 In "Dance in Hip Hop Culture," Katrina Hazzard-Donald traces the sociohistorical import of Hip Hop's origins and existence as an ever-growing popular culture. She states quite plainly that "hip hop dance is clearly masculine in style." She builds her argument by constructing masculinity as something performed for but "rarely" by "females." Hip Hop dance is "assertive," a "purely male expression" for female partners in heterosexual relationships: a form that "aggressively assert[s] male dominance." The equation of Hip Hop with what she notes as "aggressive," "dominant," essentially "male" behavior informs her later contention that the dance must be understood as a response to postindustrial economic conditions and changes in "traditional female roles" (mainly a result of feminism). For Hazzard-Donald, cultivating aggressive (heteropatriarchal) masculinity through Hip Hop culture is a productive means by which African American males contend with their continual alienation and marginalization. Hazzard-Donald, "Dance in Hip Hop Culture," 225–229.

The potential for empowerment in performing masculinity for minorities (racial, gendered, and sexual) is not the point I take issue with in this text—in fact, I agree with this contention. Rather, following Rose and Sharpley-Whiting, I want to advocate that we take necessary and critical precautions when celebrating empowerment generated at the expense of others by dominant performances of Hip Hop masculinity. Tricia Rose points to the utility of Hip Hop culture as a mode of resistance to social oppression and invisibility in her groundbreaking text *Black Noise: Rap Music and Black Culture in Contemporary America*. She demonstrates the pleasure and the political potential in rap music's aesthetic imperatives (flow, rupture, and layering) and then demands a more nuanced consideration of gender relations and sexism within Hip Hop culture. In *The Hip Hop Wars: What We Talk about When We Talk about Hip Hop—and Why It Matters*, she tackles the major debates about, and within, Hip Hop culture—a central theme being the proliferation of hypermasculinity and the corresponding effects on women. Rose argues that neither "side" of the debate—is Hip Hop culture or mainstream culture to "blame"?—adequately addresses the complexity of how sexism is produced and reproduced by institutionalized social structures and, reciprocally, by popular cultures like Hip Hop. In *Pimps Up, Ho's Down*, Sharpley-Whiting argues that what we are seeing in contemporary Hip Hop "is a new black gender politics completely in the service of a jack-legged black masculinity [. . . that] has been cobbled together from the stultifying remains of white supremacy, media, and the undeserved privileges accrued globally by American manhood" (51).

36 Gardiner, *Masculinity Studies and Feminist Theory*, 3; Connell, *Masculinities*, 42.

37 Bélisle-Springer, "Crossing Borders 007."

38 All quotes from Ivey are from interviews conducted over email in 2012 unless otherwise noted.

39 Gill and Scharff, *New Femininities*, 7.

40 The scare quotes around the term "Third Wave" gesture toward my discomfort in relying upon and thus reinforcing a wave model to describe feminist movement. Feminist scholars have argued that, though the widely used wave model offers an easy-to-conceptualize historical lineage of feminist activism to draw upon, the term highlights U.S.-based white hegemonic feminist movement, generalizes the shifting constitution of feminist activism, marginalizes antiracist and women of color feminist politics, and erases the critical feminist activism that took place in between waves (e.g., the labor feminists between the '20s and '60s). See Rowley, "Idea of Ancestry"; Nicholson, "Feminism in 'Waves': Useful Metaphor or Not?"; B. Thompson, "Multiracial Feminism"; and Cobble, "Lost Visions of Equality." See also Hopkins, *Girl Heroes*. The majority white "girl power" evident in these examples should be noted and understood in relation to white supremacist capitalism. For a critical perspective on the politics of race and Riot Grrrl historiography, see Nguyen, "Riot Grrrl, Race, and Revival."

41 Brushwood Rose and Camilleri, *Brazen Femme*, 13.

42 McRobbie, *Aftermath of Feminism*, 90.

43 The limitations of the postfeminist girl power that informs the Powerpuff franchise is perhaps most evident in the new character who was introduced in September 2017: Blisstina Francesca Francia Mariam Alicia Utonium, the older Black sister who is physically more voluptuous and emotionally more erratic (she ran away because she couldn't control her anger). For critiques of the new Powerpuff girl and the controversy surrounding her introduction, see Cummings, "There's Going to Be a Black Powerpuff Girl and Some Racists Are Big Mad"; and Nicole,

"Here We Go Again: Even a Black Powerpuff Girl Isn't Allowed to Be Great without Being Stereotyped."

44 All quotes from Jerk are from interviews conducted over email in 2013 unless otherwise noted.

45 See Swenson, *Jerk: Female Graffiti Legend*.

46 Ibid.

47 Ibid.

48 Lemons, "Trouble Girl."

49 Muñoz, *Disidentifications*, 193.

50 Though her direct and assertive gestures signify her identity in relation to class (and the stigmas associated with working-class Chicana subjectivity under a normative white bourgeois gaze), Jerk embodies a performative excess that is positioned firmly outside of the realm of the conventional feminine constricts for proper heterosexual Latina subjectivity produced by and in line with Latino heteropatriarchal norms. Jerk's performance of excess is not related to hypersexuality—or sexuality at all, really; it cannot be described as an "overly" perfumed and/or "overly" made-up hyperfemininity or queer hyper *femme*-ininity that is deemed "too much." And yet, in the way that her embodiment of excess simultaneously reconfigures Western notions of racialized masculinity within graffiti subculture *and* responds to the value of machismo behavior within a heteropatriarchal *latinidad* (be it benevolent paternalism or violent emotional, economic, and physical dominance), Jerk's performance of surly excess carries a similar kind of precarious liberatory potential as José Esteban Muñoz's *chusmería* (in *Disidentifications*), Jillian Hernandez's *chonga* girls, and Deborah Vargas's *suciedad*. Her surly performance of excess is an act of claiming ownership—of space, of masculinity, of artistic practice, of belonging, of power. Hers is a claim made against and in active resistance to gendered, raced, and classed conventions of her cisgender Chicana body. Her gender performance is not a simple "role" reversal of machismo; it is not the same male masculine performance that marginalizes graffiti grrlz. Hers does the work of feminism within Hip Hop graffiti; because it is a feminist masculine performance it uplifts, it builds community, it resists gendered restrictions and expectations. Hernandez, "'Miss, You Look Like a Bratz Doll'"; Derno and Washburne, "Masquerading Machismo"; Vargas, "Ruminations on Lo Sucio."

51 "Acting white," Muñoz reminds, "has everything to do with the performance of a particular affect, the specific performance of which grounds the subject performing white affect in a normative life world." He goes on: "From the vantage point of this national affect code, Latina/o affect appears over the top and excessive." Muñoz, "Feeling Brown," 68, 69.

52 All quotes from Motel7 are from our interview on January 15, 2014, in South Africa unless otherwise noted.

53 In a 2009 interview with the graffiti website whatyouwrite.com, Mrs was asked to "state your name rank and bra size." whatyouwrite, "Interview with Mrs."

54 I tried to get in touch with Nard Star when I was in South Africa, but our paths did not cross. You can follow her on Twitter (twitter.com/nard_star) and visit her website (www.thisisnardstar.com).

55 For more information on Falko, see Ellie Anzilotti, "The South African Artist Painting Elephants on Houses," *Citylab*, June 1, 2016, www.citylab.com.

56 All quotes from Queen MCTash are from our email interview in October 2009 unless otherwise noted.

57 Gill and Scharff provide four ways in which the term "postfeminism" is and can be used in contemporary feminist discourse: epistemologically (marking a break from "hegemonic Anglo-American feminism" and a relation to post-modernism and poststructuralism); temporally (working within a historical wave theorization of feminist movement and sometimes used interchangeably with "Third Wave" feminism); politically (denoting the backlash against feminist teachings); and, lastly, as a sensibility. Gill and Scharff, *New Femininities*, 3–4.

58 Ferrell, *Crimes of Style*, 85.

59 Morgan and Neal, "Brand-New Feminism," 238.

60 Macdonald, "Something for the Boys?," 191, 190.

61 Pabón, "Ways of Being Seen," 79.

62 She writes, "It would seem that boys will be boys." Macdonald, "Something for the Boys?," 192.

63 Macdonald, *Graffiti Subculture*, 149.

64 Jeffries, *Thug Life*, 5.

CHAPTER 2. DOING FEMINIST COMMUNITY WITHOUT "FEMINIST" IDENTITY

1 All quotes in this chapter are from interviews conducted during my fieldwork in August 2010 in Brazil and Chile unless otherwise noted.

2 Carrillo Rowe, *Power Lines*.

3 A "toy" is an inexperienced writer, one who is "toying" with the form, whose commitment and mastery has yet to be established.

4 On Latin America and feminist movement, see Saporta Sternbach et al., "Feminisms in Latin America"; González-Rivera and Kampwirth, *Radical Women in Latin America*; González-Rivera, *Before the Revolution*; Kampwirth, "Resisting the Feminist Threat"; and Leitinger, *Costa Rican Women's Movement*.

5 Interviews were completed in Spanish and Portuguese. Anarkia Boladona (aka Panmela Castro) translated the Portuguese interviews. The Spanish-speaking graffiteras and I found a common ground between their conversational English and my conversational Spanish. As with every other interview, anything that was unclear after transcription was clarified via email.

6 Boladona, email interview with author, October 27, 2009.

7 Pardue, *Brazilian Hip Hoppers*, 158.

8 See the 2014 annual report at www.redenami.com.

9 The success of these efforts led to their decision to focus their resources on domestic violence prevention in 2014, beginning with programming in high schools.

10 In 2015, they launched the #AfroGrafiteiras project to uplift AfroBrazilian women's voices, presence, and power. Programming under this project focuses on four themes: (1) urban art as a vehicle for communication, (2) empowerment regarding gender and race issues, (3) social entrepreneurship, cultural production and creative economy, and (4) new communication technologies, information and viral marketing. See https://www.redenami.com/afrografiteiras.

11 N30 left the group in 2011 to pursue a master's degree in art history.

12 Boal, *Theatre of the Oppressed*, 12.

13 Dolan, *Utopia in Performance*, 5.

14 All quotes from Naska are from our interview on August 19, 2010, in Santiago, Chile, unless otherwise noted.

15 The graffiteras of Crazis Crew, in addition to painting for pleasure—whether it is done illegally or legally—persistently cultivate the means to make a living from their graffiti art. When we met they expressed the hope that one day they would be able to support themselves collectively through their art for public and private monies. Little by little they have accomplished this goal. The first major milestone was in April 2011 when the Ruth Cardoso Youth Center in São Paulo, Brazil, commissioned Crazis Crew to design a production as part of the exhibition *Art Alameda da Rua* (Alameda street art). And in November 2012, the members of Crazis Crew produced Polanco Graffestival, the first Chilean festival of graffiti murals in Valparaiso.

16 Crazis Crew, "Crazis Crew Collective Statement."

17 All quotes from Shape are from our interview on August 19, 2010, in Santiago, Chile, unless otherwise noted.

18 All quotes from Dana are from an email exchange in 2011 unless otherwise noted.

19 All quotes from Eney are from an email exchange in 2011 unless otherwise noted.

20 Lorde, *Sister Outsider*, 54, 55.

21 Powers, *Art of Getting Over*, 6.

22 All quotes by Antisa come from an interview on August 19, 2010, and subsequent email and Google Chat conversations unless otherwise noted. I translated each interview and email. As of August 2011, Mona was no longer part of the crew.

23 Acb from Valparaiso, Chile, worked with young people and artists throughout her country, Brazil, France, and the United States on productions that promoted social justice and communal self-determination. Her death deeply affected the graffiti community transnationally.

24 Ferrell, *Crimes of Style*, 53.

25 Flatley, *Affective Mapping*.

26 Mohanty, *Feminism without Borders*, 226.

27 Pabón, "No Somos 'Mariposas,' Somos 'MariPUSSY.'" I blogged about "Chillin' with Few and Far in Miami" here: jessicapabon.com. For more on LDC, see Pabón, "Daring to Be 'Mujeres Libres, Lindas, Locas.'"

28 Butler, *Gender Trouble*, 163, 185.

29 Zeisler, *We Were Feminists Once*, 137.

CHAPTER 3. CULTIVATING AFFECTIVE DIGITAL NETWORKS

1 danah boyd explains that networked publics are a kind of mediated public, differentiated from unmediated publics (face-to-face interactions) by four properties having to do with the structure of social interaction: persistence (digital happenings are recorded and thus challenge the ephemerality of speech acts), searchability (with a few keywords one can "find like minds"), replicability (posts can be saved and copied so there is "no way to distinguish the 'original' from the 'copy' "), and invisible audiences (there is no way to gauge "who might run across our expressions"). boyd, "Why Youth (Heart) Social Network Sites."

2 Hemmings, "Affective Solidarity," 150.

3 Ibid., 158.

4 Sinae, instant message with author, June 1, 2016. There is one "member" of SUG not listed here: Bunny Kitty (USA), a female character painted by Persue, a male writer.

5 Sax, email interview with author, February 14, 2012.

6 Fluro, email interview with author, October 28, 2009.

7 Forman, '*Hood Comes First*; Schloss, *Foundation*.

8 In 1971, the *New York Times* made his tagging efforts well known and cited some of the "pen pals" he was inspiring (e.g., Barbara 62) as he wrote his name across the surfaces of any and every stop along his route. " 'Taki 183' Spawns Pen Pals."

9 Castleman, *Getting Up*, 105.

10 Ferrell, *Crimes of Style*, 51.

11 Ibid., 68.

12 Bourland, "Graffiti's Discursive Spaces," 78.

13 Sinae, email interview with author, February 1, 2012.

14 There is another Tumblr blog, "Gurls Love Vandal," tied to a Facebook page of the same name. Aside from the slogan—"Vandal gurls just wanna have fun!"—there is not much information to consider. See gurlslovevandal.tumblr.com.

15 Pabón, "Ways of Being Seen," 79.

16 "I want to insist that it is this question of affect—misery, rage, passion, pleasure— that gives feminism its life." Hemmings, "Affective Solidarity," 150.

17 Jee-Nice, "F.LADY | Anattitude Is Fresh!"

18 All quotes from Foxy Lady are from our email interview on October 10, 2010, unless otherwise noted.

19 Cvetkovich, "Public Feelings." Cvetkovich explains her role in the Public Feelings Group, which sought "to explore the role of feelings in public life, the project emerged from collective meetings on the future of gender and sexuality and the question of how to give feminism greater impact in the public sphere" (459). See also Jee-Nice, "F.LADY | Anattitude Is Fresh!"

20 Cvetkovich, "Public Feelings," 461.

21 My survey included Mailer and Naar, *Faith of Graffiti*; Castleman, *Getting Up*; Ferrell, *Crimes of Style*; Walsh, *Graffito*; Powers, *Art of Getting Over*; Austin, *Taking the Train*; Macdonald, *Graffiti Subculture*; and Miller, *Aerosol Kingdom*.

22 In 2003, I was leafing through the Hip Hop magazine *XLR8R: Accelerating Music and Culture* and noticed an article on graffiti. As I expected, out of eleven artists there was one woman mentioned: Fafi (a French street artist famous for her "Fafinettes"; see www.tumblr.com/tagged/fafinette). In this magazine, Fafi's picture is all about being a "girl." She is depicted sitting on her bed, bare leg outstretched, teddy bear right next to her, looking straight at the viewer with deep brown eyes. The imagery is joined by the question "Do you encounter difficulty in the male-dominated graffiti world?" The images included for the other writers in this article are taken outside or in a studio atmosphere, and the questions always revolve around the *action of graffiti*. Hill, "Urban Blight," 47, 57.

23 Kennedy names blogs "virtual consciousness raising" platforms, but I refer to them as digital consciousness raising. Kennedy, "Personal Is Political," 2.

24 Ibid.

25 Foxy Lady, "CatFight: Female Graff Update Issue 00."

26 Jee-Nice, "F.LADY | Anattitude Is Fresh!"

27 Foxy Lady, "CatFight: Female Graff Update Issue 3," 3.

28 Foxy Lady, "CatFight: Female Graff Update Issue 9," 3.

29 I. A. and E. J., "Words of Passion," 5.

30 Ibid.

31 I. A. and E. J., "Issue 3," 3.

32 The editors asked me to use the pseudonyms I. A. and E. J.

33 I. A. and E. J., "Words of Passion," 5.

34 I. A. and E. J., "Special Mini-Issue: The Stick Up Girlz," 5.

35 Meltzer, "'Binders Full of Women'"; Rentschler and Thrift, "Doing Feminism in the Network," 351–352, emphasis mine.

36 There are various "how to's" on this very topic in forums and on websites. For example, the *London Vandal* blog post "Don't Get Caught-On the Net," February 12, 2012, www.thelondonvandal.com.

37 The phrase "writer's bench" stems from the first generation of subway writer culture in New York City; it refers to a literal bench in a subway station where writers would meet, exchange blackbooks, and talk "shop" while watching graffiti-covered trains roll by. According to the website @149st, which launched in 1998 to preserve the history of New York graffiti's development, "The last active location was the 149th Street Grand Concourse subway station in The Bronx, on the 2 and 5 IRT lines. It was active from the 1970s until the decline of subway painting in the late 1980s." See www.at149st.com.

38 Facebook has three kinds of groups: public, closed, and secret. Secret groups are the most private: you have to be added by a current member; only current and former members can see that the group exists, the description, and find the group in a search; only current members can see the member list and posts. In 2015,

Gigi of Turronas Crew created the public group International Female Graffiti and Street Art Crew, which has 283 members. There is overlap in membership between the two pages, but FIG is the most active. On March 10, 2015, Gigi posted the following: "I made this group in memory of my lovely friend Acb, thanks Andrea for believing in me and support my work when anybody did. Hice este grupo en memoria de mi amada amiga Acb, gracias Andrea por creer en mi y apoyar mi trabajo cuando nadie lo hizo." The "About" page reads, "This is a [*sic*] international female network to promote street art, graffiti and all kind of art made by women. Each one of them can show their work in this page, publish meetings, exhibitions and every important thing you are doing, Girls we have to be closer, let's make projects to change the world!"

39 All quotes from Kif are from our November 4, 2009, email interview unless otherwise noted.

40 Rentschler and Thrift, "Doing Feminism in the Network," 331.

41 See Pabón, "Ways of Being Seen," for information about Women on Walls.

42 Created in 2007, Tumblr is a microblogging social media platform, available in sixteen languages, that was designed for frequent short posts and easy cross-platform sharing. See www.tumblr.com/about.

43 On Instagram, a social media platform suited to visual artists and popular with graffiti grrlz, the search term #graffgirl has over 7,000 posts; #graffgirls has over 5,000 posts; and #graffitiwomen has over 5,000. There are also #graffgirlproblems, #graffgirlsdoitbetter, and #womeningraffiti.

44 Mrs, "Dear Women Who Are into Graffiti."

45 I. A. and E. J., "Special Mini-Issue: The Stick Up Girlz," 37.

46 In *TechnoFeminism*, Judy Wajcman affirms that "feminism [can] steer a path between technophobia and technophilia." Feminist critique can, and should, simultaneously account for the "seductive" nature of "bodily transcendence," equality, and participation offered by the digital world, while attending to the undeniable "material resources and power" structures that will always affect women's ability to participate fully as producers and consumers. Wajcman, *TechnoFeminism*, 3, 6, 62.

47 Peggy Phelan levels her skepticism of this equation in *Unmarked*, 2.

48 See Spivak, *Outside in the Teaching Machine*; Haraway, *Simians, Cyborgs, and Women*; and Sandoval, "U.S. Third World Feminism."

49 Rentschler and Thrift, "Doing Feminism," 240.

50 Scott, "Feminist Reverberations," 11–12.

51 Flatley, *Affective Mapping*, 7.

CHAPTER 4. RE-MEMBERING HERSTORY AND THE
TRANSEPHEMERAL PERFORMATIVE

1 Z, GraffGirlz interview with Z.

2 Derrida, "Signature, Event, Context," 311.

3 *Oxford English Dictionary*, " 'Ephemera, N.2'," *Oxford English Dictionary* online, Oxford University Press, www.oed.com (accessed July 14, 2012).

4 Here I refer to the "broken windows" theory that was initially proposed in a *Public Interest* article by Nathan Glazer ("On Subway Graffiti"), and later expanded by the criminologist George L. Kelling and the political scientist James Q. Wilson writing in the *Atlantic Monthly* ("Broken Windows"). What came to be known as the "broken windows" theory relies on aesthetic and ideological presuppositions about the conditions necessary to create a visually pleasing and safe urban environment for citizens and uses those ideologies to dictate how bodies should exist within, relate to, and utilize urban space (in effect, policing the body materially and perceptually within an urban context).

5 " 'Ephemeral, Adj. and N.'," *Oxford English Dictionary* online, Oxford University Press, www.oed.com (accessed July 14, 2012).

6 In the *Performance Research* special issue "On Trans/Performance," Christopher Engdahl argues, "Because performances are enacted within or supported by digitally mediated networks, and this is crucial, they incessantly expand temporally. . . . Online performance is never fully present but immanently distended through remediation." He deems the "unsettled and incomplete temporality" of online performance "transtemporality." Engdahl, "Transtemporality of Online Performance," 107–108.

7 MUTO, painted and filmed in Buenos Aires by Blu, is a work of animated street art that provoked my thinking on the transephemeral. See notblu, *MUTO a Wall-Painted Animation by BLU*.

8 See Merchant, *Death of Nature*; Griffin, *Woman and Nature*; and Rich, *Of Woman Born*.

9 All quotes from Prima Donna are from our interview on August 16, 2010, in Rio de Janeiro, Brazil, unless otherwise noted.

10 "Brazil's Quilombola People."

11 Ahmed, *Promise of Happiness*, 213.

12 Stryker, Currah, and Moore, "Introduction," 13.

13 Ibid., 12.

14 Hayward, "More Lessons from a Starfish."

15 Though he was not referring to graffiti writing, but rather what happens to the aura of fine art in the age of mechanical reproduction, Benjamin aptly describes the development of the graffiti tag name: "the work of art reproduced becomes the work of art *designed for reproducibility.*" Benjamin, "The Work of Art in the Age of Mechanical Reproduction," in *Illuminations*, 224, emphasis mine.

16 Bourland, "Graffiti's Discursive Spaces," 67.

17 Butler, *Excitable Speech*, 161.

18 Pardue, *Brazilian Hip Hoppers*, 137–138.

19 Derrida, *Archive Fever*, 4, footnote 1.

20 Ibid., 313.

21 Auslander, *Liveness*. See also Jones and Heathfield, *Perform, Repeat, Record*.

22 Phelan, *Unmarked*, 146.

23 Derrida, "Signature, Event, Context," 316.

24 Schneider, "Archives," 100.

25 Ibid.

26 All quotes from Om are from our interview on August 9, 2010, in Rio de Janeiro, Brazil, unless otherwise noted.

27 Miller, *Aerosol Kingdom*, 189.

28 Muñoz, "Ephemera as Evidence," 6.

29 Ibid., 10–11.

30 Halberstam, *In a Queer Time and Place*, 161.

31 Connerton, *How Societies Remember*, 13.

32 Ibid., 8.

33 Anderson, *Imagined Communities*, 6.

34 Bourland, "Graffiti's Discursive Spaces," 67.

35 Ignacio, "E-scaping Boundaries," 182.

36 Benjamin, *Illuminations*, 98.

37 Taylor, *Archive and the Repertoire*, 2–3.

38 The interview originally appeared in English; I edited for spelling and grammar, but the content is unchanged. Z, GraffGirlz.com interview with Z.

39 Nora, "Between Memory and History," 7.

40 If not on active pages then in dead code somewhere (a cache, a digital-if-obscure trace) like on www.archive.org/web, which can search back to 1996.

41 Nora, "Between Memory and History," 8.

42 Butler, *Excitable Speech*, 10.

43 Ibid., 22.

44 Chang, "American Graffiti."

45 Stavsky, "Her Story."

46 See the flyer for the May 2016 event here: www.instagram.com/p/BFW_YWyLODC/.

CHAPTER 5. TRANSFORMING PRECARITY AT INTERNATIONAL ALL-GRRL JAMS

1 All quotes from JesOne come from our October 18, 2010, interview at the Tisch School of the Arts, New York University, unless otherwise noted. Unfortunately, her t-shirt line was a short-lived endeavor.

2 In "Writin', Breakin', Beatboxin'," I explored the creation of similar events across breakdancing (b-boying), beatboxing, and graffiti subculture. The ideas developed in that article seeded this chapter.

3 *Versus Hip Hop on Trial Debate*. hampton makes her claim at the 18:40 mark.

4 For Butler, there is a distinction between precariousness, "a function of our social vulnerability and exposure that is always given some political form"; precarity, which is "differentially distributed"; and precaritization, which she sees as "an ongoing process, so that we do not reduce the power of precarious to single acts or single events." Puar et al., "Precarity Talk," 169.

5 Ibid., 168.

6   All quotes from Joske are from our email exchange on August 12, 2014.

7   Joske Films, *PROM PARTY—LADIE KILLERZ.*

8   Bae and Ivashkevich, *Girls, Cultural Productions, and Resistance*, 5.

9   Halberstam, *Female Masculinity*, 28.

10 "Women's Day" was created in the early 1900s to celebrate women (usually through the giving of small gifts and flowers) in the states and shortly thereafter become "International Women's Day." IWD is now a day of global protests, marches, rallies, and events seeking to not only celebrate women but also recognize the need for social justice on behalf of women. See www.internationalwomensday.com for a brief history of the day, which is March 8th every year. See *Girls on Top—Movie about Femme Fierce: Leake Street*, www.youtube.com/watch?v=N25vQMSHwc0. At a workshop on the history of Leake Street, held the Saturday before Femme Fierce 2015, I learned that the tunnel was transformed from a decrepit, forgotten space to an unmonitored, free-for-all haven for street artists because Banksy hosted the "Cans Festival" there in 2008. See www.atlasobscura.com.

11 Unless otherwise noted, all quotes from Chock in this chapter are from our email exchange on June 23, 2015.

12 "Girls on Top" also brings to mind the "girls to the front" directive made by the Riot Grrrl band Bikini Kill. See www.youtube.com/watch?v=LU1bEeKsHs8.

13 Chock, email interview with author, May 8, 2012.

14 Plan UK's website states that "the Because I am a Girl campaign supports millions of girls in getting the education, skills and support they need to move from poverty to a future of opportunity" (plan-uk.org). The campaign motif is blue and pink, so in an effort to pick a color that fit the theme but stood in contrast to the choice of pink for breast cancer the year before, the tunnel went blue.

15 McAuliffe, "Graffiti or Street Art?," 203.

16 Ibid.

17 In the United States, two such areas come to mind: the Wynwood District in Miami, Florida (that hosts Art Basel every year), and 5Pointz in Long Island City, New York. The latter was whitewashed overnight, razed, and became high-rise apartments with a "design [that] attempts to capitalize on 5 Pointz's legacy as a graffiti mecca by incorporating artwork into its common spaces." See Walker, "First Look inside the 5 Pointz-Replacing Rentals in Long Island City." I blogged about the whitewashing, "Notes on 5Pointz: Feelings, Responses, and the Desire to 'Save,'" at jessicapabon.com.

18 "Neoliberal rhetoric promotes 'creativity' as the front of economic promise." See Ridout and Schneider, "Precarity and Performance," 7.

19 Butler, "Performativity, Precarity and Sexual Politics," xiii.

20 "Precarious life characterizes such lives who do not qualify as recognizable, readable, or grievable. And in this way, precarity is a rubric that brings together women, queers, transgender people, the poor, and the stateless." Ibid., xii–xiii.

21 All quotes from Mons are from our interview in the Leake Street tunnel during Femme Fierce on March 8, 2015, unless otherwise noted.

22 Ahmed, *Promise of Happiness*, 521.

23 All quotes from Itsa are from our interview in the Leake Street tunnel during Femme Fierce on March 8, 2015, unless otherwise noted.

24 I posted the image on Instagram. You can view it here: www.instagram.com /p/oFSodYDlT4/.

25 All quotes from Evay are from our interview in the Leake Street tunnel during Femme Fierce on March 8, 2015, unless otherwise noted.

26 The hashtag promoted by the event organizers was #femmefierce, but as hashtags are not "property," searching that term on Instagram will populate wildly different results (you also cannot do an advanced search by date). However, if you search for #femmefierce2015, 288 images populate. As just one person who was posting under various hashtags I know there are hundreds of other posts under different tags. Using Twitter's advanced search function, you can look for the hashtag #femmefierce and enter specific dates to limit your results to the most relevant posts (i.e., March 1, 2015, to March 15, 2015). To organize the seemingly endless feed that Twitter generates, you can select what kind of result you desire: Top, Live, Accounts, Photos, or Videos.

27 Throne79 and I spoke briefly, but through our interaction I learned about Tits 'n' Tampons, "an all girl graffiti crew from up norf" (www.facebook.com/pages /TT/678941628854087). Tits 'n' Tampons includes Aylo, CBloxx, Ruby, Oner, and Throne. You can view a video of their first painting jam here: www.youtube.com /watch?v=91OXYusBeAk. All quotes from Throne are from our interview in the Leake Street tunnel during Femme Fierce on March 8, 2015.

28 Itsa, interview with author, March 6, 2015.

29 Forman, 'Hood Comes First.

30 McRobbie, *Aftermath of Feminism*, 1; Forman, 'Hood Comes First, 12, 60.

31 hooks, *Feminist Theory*, 44.

CONCLUSION

1 You can see a (very small) panoramic of the entire finished wall here: "My Thuggy Pony" at www.girlsontopcrew.co.uk.

2 Patricia Hill Collins defines the matrix as the "overall social organization [education, housing, employment] within which intersecting oppressions [gender, race, sexuality, class] originate, develop, and are contained." Collins, *Black Feminist Thought*, 227–228.

3 Lorde, *Sister Outsider*; Massumi, *Parables for the Virtual*, 8.

4 For more on "dead" or "impossible" subjects, see Viego, *Dead Subjects*; and Chuh, *Imagine Otherwise*, respectively.

5 Massumi, *Parables for the Virtual*, 9.

6 See Miss Reds's Instagram account at www.instagram.com/missreds_/.

7 Knight, "To Catch a Graffiti Artist."

BIBLIOGRAPHY

A. I. and E. J. "Issue 3." *C.O.P.: Meet the New Guard*, 2010.
——. "Issue 4." *C.O.P.: Meet the New Guard*, 2011.
——. "Special Mini-Issue: The Stick Up Girlz." *C.O.P.: Meet the New Guard*, 2011.
——. "Words of Passion." *Crimes of Passion*, 2008.
AbbyTC5. Email interview with author. November 4, 2011.
——. Email interview with author. October 18, 2012.
——. Email interview with author. August 31, 2013.
——. Public interview with author. Transcribed by Eileen Quaranto. Hip Hop Scholar Artist Series, Davidson College, North Carolina, October 18, 2012.
Ahearn, Charlie. *Wild Style*. Documentary, 1983.
Ahmed, Sara. *The Promise of Happiness*. Durham, NC: Duke University Press, 2010.
Alim, H. Samy, and Hi-Tek. "'The Natti Ain't No Punk City': Emic Views of Hip Hop Cultures." *Callaloo* 29, no. 3 (2006): 969–990.
Anarkia Boladona. Email interview with author. October 27, 2009.
——. Interview with author. Rio de Janeiro, Brazil, August 8, 2010.
Anderson, Benedict. *Imagined Communities: Reflections on the Origin and Spread of Nationalism*. New York: Verso, 2006.
Antisa. Interview with author. Santiago, Chile, August 19, 2010.
Anzaldúa, Gloria, ed. *Making Face, Making Soul / Haciendo Caras: Creative and Critical Perspectives by Feminists of Color*. San Francisco: Aunt Lute Books, 1990.
Are2. Email interview with author. August 6, 2009.
——. Email interview with author. November 5, 2009.
——. Email interview with author. February 18, 2013.
——. Email response to GraffGirlz call for participation. July 23, 2009.
Auslander, Philip. *Liveness: Performance in a Mediatized Culture*. London: Routledge, 1999.
Austin, Joe. *Taking the Train: How Graffiti Art Became an Urban Crisis in New York City*. New York: Columbia University Press, 2001.
Bae, Michelle S., and Olga Ivashkevich. *Girls, Cultural Productions, and Resistance*. New York: Peter Lang, 2012.
Baldwin, Davarian L. "Black Empires, White Desires: The Spatial Politics of Identity in the Age of Hip-Hop." In *That's the Joint! The Hip-Hop Studies Reader*, edited by Mark Anthony Neal and Murray Forman, 159–178. New York: Routledge, 2004.
Banes, Sally. "Physical Graffiti: Breaking Is Hard to Do." In *And It Don't Stop: The Best American Hip-Hop Journalism of the Last 25 Years*, edited by Raquel Cepeda, 7–11. New York: Faber and Faber, 2004.

Banks, Daniel. *Say Word! Voices from Hip Hop Theater*. Ann Arbor: University of Michigan Press, 2011.

Basu, Dipannita, and Sidney J. Lemelle, eds. *The Vinyl Ain't Final: Hip-Hop and the Globalisation of Black Popular Culture*. London: Pluto, 2006.

"Because I Am a Girl." *Plan International*. Accessed November 4, 2015. plan-international.org.

Bélisle-Springer, Zoé. "Crossing Borders 007: EGR—Freshpaint Gallery." *Fresh Paint*. May 29, 2015. www.freshpaintgallery.ca.

Benjamin, Walter. *Illuminations*. New York: Harcourt, Brace and World, 1968.

Boal, Augusto. *Theatre of the Oppressed*. Translated by Charles A. McBride and Maria-Odilia Leal McBride. New York: Theatre Communications Group, 1985.

Bogner, Verena. "Let Us Spray: The All-Woman Graffiti Documentary Celebrating Illegal Art." *Broadly*. Accessed June 8, 2016. broadly.vice.com.

Boowhan, Lim, and Lim Kyounghee. "Bad Girls, Bad Girls, Whatcha Gonna Do." *King of the Hill*. Fox. November 17, 2002.

Bourland, Ian. "Graffiti's Discursive Spaces." *Chicago Art Journal* 17 (2007): 56–83. ianbourland.typepad.com.

Bowen, Tracey E. "Graffiti Art: A Contemporary Study of Toronto Artists." *Studies in Art Education* 41, no. 1 (Autumn 1999): 22–39.

boyd, danah. "Why Youth (Heart) Social Network Sites: The Role of Networked Publics in Teenage Social Life." SSRN Scholarly Paper. Rochester, NY: Social Science Research Network. December 3, 2007. papers.ssrn.com.

"Brazil's Quilombola People Count Cost of Land Rights Battle—in Pictures." *Guardian*, June 24, 2013. Sec. Global Development. www.theguardian.com.

Briggs, Laura, Gladys McCormick, and J. T. Way. "Transnationalism: A Category of Analysis." *American Quarterly* 60, no. 3 (2008): 625–648. doi:10.1353/aq.0.0038.

Brushwood Rose, Chloë, and Anna Camilleri. *Brazen Femme: Queering Femininity*. Vancouver, BC: Arsenal Pulp Press, 2002.

Butler, Judith. *Bodies That Matter: On the Discursive Limits of Sex*. New York: Routledge, 1993.

———. *Excitable Speech: A Politics of the Performative*. New York: Routledge, 1997.

———. *Gender Trouble: Feminism and the Subversion of Identity*. Routledge Classics. New York: Routledge, 1999.

———. "Imitation and Gender Insubordination." In *The Lesbian and Gay Studies Reader*, edited by Henry Abelove, Michele Aina Barale, and David M. Halperin, 307–320. New York: Routledge, 1993.

———. "Performativity, Precarity and Sexual Politics." *AIBR: Revista de Antropología Iberoamericana* 4, no. 3 (2009): i–xiii.

Cantwo. "Introduction." *C.O.P. Special Mini-Issue: The Stick Up Girlz*, 2011.

Carrillo Rowe, Aimee. *Power Lines: On the Subject of Feminist Alliances*. Durham, NC: Duke University Press, 2008.

Cassandra, Rachel, and Lauren Gucik. *Women Street Artists of Latin America: Art without Fear*. San Francisco: Manic D Press, 2015.

Castleman, Craig. *Getting Up: Subway Graffiti in New York.* Cambridge, MA: MIT Press, 1982.

Cepeda, Raquel, ed. *And It Don't Stop: The Best American Hip-Hop Journalism of the Last 25 Years.* New York: Faber and Faber, 2004.

Chalfant, Henry, and Sacha Jenkins. *Training Days: The Subway Artists Then and Now.* New York: Thames and Hudson, 2014.

Chalfant, Henry, and James Prigoff. *Spraycan Art.* New York: Thames and Hudson, 1987.

Chalfant, Henry, and Tony Silver. *Style Wars.* DVD, Documentary, 1984.

Chang, Jeff. "American Graffiti." *Village Voice.* September 2002.

———. *Can't Stop Won't Stop: A History of the Hip-Hop Generation.* New York: Picador, 2005.

———. *Total Chaos: The Art and Aesthetics of Hip-Hop.* New York: Basic Civitas Books, 2006.

Chesney-Lind, Meda, and John M. Hagedorn. *Female Gangs in America: Essays on Girls, Gangs and Gender.* Chicago: Lake View Press, 1999.

Chock. Email interview with author. May 8, 2012.

———. Email interview with author. April 2014.

———. Email interview with author. June 23, 2015.

Chuh, Kandice. *Imagine Otherwise: On Asian Americanist Critique.* Durham, NC: Duke University Press, 2003.

ClawMoney. *Bombshell: The Life and Crimes of Claw Money.* New York: Power House, 2007.

———. *Claw Money Miss17 Graffiti Interview.* Accessed September 7, 2015. www.you tube.com/watch?v=4G77apHP3VY.

———. Interview with author. ClawMoney Studios, New York, January 20, 2011.

ClawMoney, Miss17, Lady Pink, and Dona. Interview with author. Tucson, AZ, January 2004.

Clay, Andreana. " 'I Used to Be Scared of the Dick': Queer Women of Color, Hip Hop, and Black Masculinity." In *Home Girls Make Some Noise! Hip-Hop Feminism Anthology*, edited by Gwendolyn D. Pough, Aisha Durham, Elaine Richardson, and Rachel Raimist, 149–165. Mira Loma, CA: Parker, 2007.

Cobble, Dorothy Sue. "Lost Visions of Equality: The Labor Origins of the Next Women's Movement." *New Politics* 10, no. 3 (2005). Accessed November 7, 2017. http://nova.wpunj.edu/newpolitics/issue39/Cobble39.htm.

Collins, Patricia Hill. *Black Feminist Thought: Knowledge, Consciousness, and the Politics of Empowerment.* 2nd edition. New York: Routledge, 2009.

———. *Black Sexual Politics: African Americans, Gender, and the New Racism.* New York: Routledge, 2004.

———. *From Black Power to Hip Hop: Racism, Nationalism, and Feminism.* Philadelphia: Temple University Press, 2006.

Combahee River Collective. "Black Feminist Statement." In *Feminist Theory Reader: Local and Global Perspectives*, edited by Carole McCann and Seung-kyung Kim, 3rd edition, 116–122. New York: Routledge, 1977.

Condry, Ian. *Hip-Hop Japan: Rap and the Paths of Cultural Globalization*. Durham, NC: Duke University Press, 2006.

Connell, R. W. *Masculinities*. 2nd edition. Berkeley: University of California Press, 2005.

Connerton, Paul. *How Societies Remember*. Cambridge: Cambridge University Press, 1989.

Cooper, Martha, and Henry Chalfant. *Subway Art*. New York: Holt, Rinehart and Winston, 1984.

Crazis Crew. Crazis Crew Collective Statement emailed to author. August 18, 2011.

Cummings, Moriba. "There's Going to Be a Black Powerpuff Girl and Some Racists Are Big Mad." *BET.com*, September 8, 2017. Accessed November 7, 2017. http://www.bet.com/celebrities/news/2017/09/08/powerpuff-girl-reactions.html.

Currie, Dawn H., Deirdre M. Kelly, and Shauna Pomerantz. *"Girl Power": Girls Reinventing Girlhood*. New York: Peter Lang, 2009.

———. "Skater Girlhood: Resignifying Femininity, Resignifying Feminism." In *New Femininities: Postfeminism, Neoliberalism and Subjectivity*, edited by Rosalind Gill and Christina Scharff, 293–305. London: Palgrave Macmillan, 2011.

Cvetkovich, Ann. "Public Feelings." *SAQ: South Atlantic Quarterly* 106, no. 3 (Summer 2007): 459–468.

DanaPink. Email interview with author. August 28, 2011.

darthlady. *The Punk Singer—Bikini Kill, Girls to the Front*. Accessed May 27, 2017. www.youtube.com/watch?v=LU1bEeKsHs8.

Derno, Maiken, and Christopher Washburne. "Masquerading Machismo: La India and the Staging of Chusmería on the Salsa Scene." *Women and Performance: A Journal of Feminist Theory* 12, no. 2 (January 1, 2002): 139–156. doi:10.1080/07407700208571375.

Derrida, Jacques. *Archive Fever: A Freudian Impression*. Chicago: University of Chicago Press, 1998.

———. "Signature, Event, Context." In *Margins of Philosophy*, 307–330. Chicago: University of Chicago Press, 1985.

Dimitriadis, Greg. *Performing Identity/Performing Culture: Hip Hop as Text, Pedagogy, and Lived Practice*. New York: Peter Lang, 2009.

Dolan, Jill. *Utopia in Performance: Finding Hope at the Theater*. Ann Arbor: University of Michigan Press, 2005.

Dona. Instant message with author. January 4, 2016.

Douglas, Cedric. Personal Facebook message with author. February 5, 2013.

Durham, Aisha. *Home with Hip Hop Feminism: Performances in Communication and Culture*. New York: Peter Lang, 2014.

Durham, Aisha, Brittney C. Cooper, and Susana M. Morris. "The Stage Hip-Hop Feminism Built: A New Directions Essay." *Signs* 38, no. 3 (March 2013): 721–737. doi:10.1086/668843.

Egr. Email interview with author. October 29, 2009.

Eliz. Email interview with author. May 7, 2014.

Eney. Interview with author. September 2, 2011.

Engdahl, Christopher. "The Transtemporality of Online Performance." *Performance Research* 21, no. 5 (September 2, 2016): 107–110. doi:10.1080/13528165.2016.1224339.

Eure, Joseph D. *Nation Conscious Rap: The Hip Hop Vision.* Edited by James G. Spady. New York: PC International Press, 1991.

Evay. Interview with author. Leake Street Tunnel, London, March 8, 2015.

"Exclusive Interview with Utah and Ether, Graffiti's Bonnie and Clyde | The Hundreds." Accessed January 11, 2017. thehundreds.com.

Felisbret, Eric, and Luke Felisbret. *Graffiti New York.* New York: Harry N. Abrams, 2009.

Fernandes, Sujatha. *Close to the Edge: In Search of the Global Hip Hop Generation.* New York: Verso, 2011.

Ferrell, Jeff. *Crimes of Style: Urban Graffiti and the Politics of Criminality.* Boston: Northeastern University Press, 1996.

Fielding, Nigel G., Raymond M. Lee, and Grant Blank. *The SAGE Handbook of Online Research Methods.* Thousand Oaks, CA: SAGE, 2008.

Fisher, Alice. "How the Tate Got Streetwise." *Guardian.* May 10, 2008, Art and Design. www.theguardian.com.

Fluro. Email interview with author. October 28, 2009.

Forman, Murray. *The 'Hood Comes First: Race, Space, and Place in Rap and Hip-Hop.* Middletown, CT: Wesleyan University Press, 2002.

Foxy Lady. "Blog Archive: About Catfight." Accessed April 17, 2014. www.catfightmagazine.com.

———. "CatFight: Female Graff Update Issue 00." April 2005. www.catfightmagazine.com.

———. "CatFight: Female Graff Update Issue 1." July 2005. www.catfightmagazine.com.

———. "CatFight: Female Graff Update Issue 2." October 2005. www.catfightmagazine.com.

———. "CatFight: Female Graff Update Issue 3." April 2006. www.catfightmagazine.com.

———. "CatFight: Female Graff Update Issue 4." August 2006. www.catfightmagazine.com.

———. "CatFight: Female Graff Update Issue 5." December 2006. www.catfightmagazine.com.

———. "CatFight: Female Graff Update Issue 7." August 2007. www.catfightmagazine.com.

———. "CatFight: Female Graff Update Issue 8." October 2008. www.catfightmagazine.com.

———. "CatFight: Female Graff Update Issue 9." August 2009. www.catfightmagazine.com.

———. "CatFight Magazine." 2007. www.catfightmagazine.com.

———. Email interview with author. October 10, 2010.

Ganz, Nicholas. *Graffiti Women: Street Art from Five Continents.* New York: Abrams, 2006.

———. *Graffiti World: Street Art from Five Continents*. New York: Abrams, 2004.

Gardiner, Judith Kegan. *Masculinity Studies and Feminist Theory*. New York: Columbia University Press, 2002.

Gastman, Roger, and Caleb Neelon. *The History of American Graffiti*. New York: Harper Design, 2011.

Gaunt, Kyra D. *The Games Black Girls Play: Learning the Ropes from Double-Dutch to Hip-Hop*. New York: NYU Press, 2006.

Gigi. Email interview with author. August 22, 2011.

Gill, Rosalind. "Culture and Subjectivity in Neoliberal and Postfeminist Times." *Subjectivity* 25, no. 1 (December 2008): 432–445. doi: dx.doi.org/10.1057/sub.2008.28.

Gill, Rosalind, and Christina Scharff. *New Femininities: Postfeminism, Neoliberalism and Subjectivity*. London: Palgrave Macmillan, 2011.

Gilroy, Paul. *The Black Atlantic: Modernity and Double Consciousness*. Cambridge, MA: Harvard University Press, 1993.

"Girl Graffiti." Accessed January 13, 2017. bust.com.

Glazer, Nathan. "On Subway Graffiti in New York." *Public Interest* 54 (Winter 1979): 3–11.

González-Rivera, Victoria. *Before the Revolution: Women's Rights and Right-Wing Politics in Nicaragua, 1821–1979*. University Park: Pennsylvania State University Press, 2012.

González-Rivera, Victoria, and Karen Kampwirth, eds. *Radical Women in Latin America: Left and Right*. University Park: Pennsylvania State University Press, 2001.

Grewal, Inderpal, and Caren Kaplan, eds. *Scattered Hegemonies: Postmodernity and Transnational Feminist Practices*. Minneapolis: University of Minnesota Press, 1994.

Griffin, Susan. *Woman and Nature: The Roaring inside Her*. New York: Harper and Row, 1978.

Grody, Steve. *Graffiti L.A.: Street Styles and Art*. New York: Abrams, 2006.

Guevara, Nancy. "Women Writin' Rappin' Breakin'." In *Droppin' Science: Critical Essays on Rap Music and Hip Hop Culture*, edited by William Perkins, 49–62. Philadelphia: Temple University Press, 1987.

Halberstam, [Judith] Jack. *Female Masculinity*. Durham: Duke University Press, 1998.

———. "The Good, the Bad, and the Ugly: Men, Women, and Masculinity." In *Masculinity Studies and Feminist Theory*, edited by Judith Kegan Gardiner, 344–367. New York: Columbia University Press, 2002.

———. *In a Queer Time and Place: Transgender Bodies, Subcultural Lives*. New York: NYU Press, 2005.

Hall, Stuart. "What Is This 'Black' in Black Popular Culture?" *Social Justice* 20, no. 1–2 (1993): 104–111.

Hall, Stuart, and Tony Jefferson, eds. *Resistance through Rituals: Youth Subcultures in Post-War Britain*. London: Hutchinson, 1976.

Haraway, Donna. *Simians, Cyborgs, and Women: The Reinvention of Nature*. New York: Routledge, 1990.

———. "Situated Knowledges: The Science Question in Feminism and the Privilege of Partial Perspective." *Feminist Studies* 14, no. 3 (1988): 575–599. doi:10.2307/3178066.

Harrison, Anthony Kwame. *Hip Hop Underground: The Integrity and Ethics of Racial Identification*. Philadelphia: Temple University Press, 2009.

Hayward, Eva. "More Lessons from a Starfish: Prefixial Flesh and Transspeciated Selves." *WSQ: Women's Studies Quarterly* 36, no. 3–4 (2008): 64–84.

Hazzard-Donald, Katrina. "Dance in Hip Hop Culture." In *Droppin' Science: Critical Essays on Rap Music and Hip Hop Culture*, edited by William Perkins, 220–235. Philadelphia: Temple University Press, 1996.

Hemmings, Clare. "Affective Solidarity: Feminist Reflexivity and Political Transformation." *Feminist Theory* 13, no. 2 (August 1, 2012): 147–161. doi:10.1177/1464700112442643.

Hernandez, Jillian. "'Miss, You Look Like a Bratz Doll': On Chonga Girls and Sexual-Aesthetic Excess." *NWSA Journal* 21, no. 3 (2009): 63–90.

Hill, Lennox. "Urban Blight." *XLR8R: Accelerating Music and Culture*. January 2003.

Hine, Christine M. *Virtual Ethnography*. Thousand Oaks, CA: SAGE, 2000.

Hoch, Danny. "Toward a Hip-Hop Aesthetic: A Manifesto for the Hip-Hop Arts Movement." In *Total Chaos: The Art and Aesthetics of Hip-Hop*, edited by Jeff Chang, 349–363. New York: Basic Civitas Books, 2007.

Hodges-Persley, Nicole. "Sampling Blackness: Performing African Americanness in Hip-Hop Theater and Performance." Dissertation, University of Southern California, 2009.

hooks, bell. *Feminism Is for Everybody: Passionate Politics*. Cambridge, MA: South End Press, 2000.

———. *Feminist Theory: From Margin to Center*. 2nd edition. Cambridge, MA: South End Press, 2000.

———. *Talking Back: Thinking Feminist, Thinking Black*. Cambridge, MA: South End Press, 1989.

———. *We Real Cool: Black Men and Masculinity*. New York: Routledge, 2003.

Hopkins, Susan. *Girl Heroes: The New Force in Popular Culture*. London: Pluto, 2002.

Hops. Email interview with author. February 6, 2013.

Ignacio, Emily Noelle. "E-Scaping Boundaries: Bridging Cyberspace and Diaspora Studies through Nethnography." In *Critical Cyberculture Studies*, edited by David Silver, Adrienne Massanari, and Steve Jones, 181–193. New York: NYU Press, 2006.

Injah. Instant message with author. April 6, 2009.

———. Interview with author. Rio de Janeiro, Brazil, August 12, 2010.

Itsa. Interview with author. March 6, 2015.

———. Interview with author. Leake Street Tunnel, London, March 8, 2015.

Ivey. Email interview with author. August 5, 2012.

Jackson Jr., John L. *Real Black: Adventures in Racial Sincerity*. Chicago: University of Chicago Press, 2005.

Jee-Nice. "F.LADY | Anattitude Is Fresh!" *Anattitude* magazine. June 18, 2009. www.anattitude.net.

Jeffries, Michael P. "Re: Definitions: The Name and the Game of Hip-Hop Feminism." In *Home Girls Make Some Noise! Hip-Hop Feminism Anthology*, edited by

Gwendolyn D. Pough, Elaine Richardson, Rachel Raimist, and Aisha Durham, 208–227. Mira Loma, CA: Parker, 2007.

———. *Thug Life: Race, Gender, and the Meaning of Hip-Hop*. Chicago: University of Chicago Press, 2011.

Jerk. Email interview with author. January 30, 2013.

JesOne. Interview with author. Tisch School of the Arts, New York University, October 18, 2010.

Johnson, E. Patrick. *Appropriating Blackness: Performance and the Politics of Authenticity*. Durham, NC: Duke University Press, 2003.

Johnson, Imani Kai. Email interview with author. November 5, 2013.

———. "From Blues Women to B-Girls: Performing Badass Femininity." *Women and Performance: A Journal of Feminist Theory*, All Hail the Queenz: A Queer Feminist Recalibration of Hip Hop, 24, no. 1 (2014): 15–28.

Jones, Amelia, and Adrian Heathfield. *Perform, Repeat, Record: Live Art in History*. Bristol, UK: Intellect Books, 2012.

Jones, Russell M. *Inside the Graffiti Subculture: Why Graffiti Is Not Art*. Saarbrücken: AV Akademikerverlag, 2007.

Joseph, Miranda. *Against the Romance of Community*. Minneapolis: University of Minnesota Press, 2002.

Joske. Email exchange with author. August 12, 2014.

Joske Films. *PROM PARTY—LADIE KILLERZ*. Accessed September 17, 2015. vimeo.com/57127094.

Jups. Interview with author. Translated by Panmela Castro. Rio das Pedras, Brazil, August 15, 2010.

Kampwirth, Karen. "Resisting the Feminist Threat: Antifeminist Politics in Post-Sandinista Nicaragua." *NWSA Journal* 18, no. 2 (2006): 73–100.

Kandiyoti, Deniz. "Bargaining with Patriarchy." *Gender and Society* 2, no. 3 (September 1, 1988): 274–290. doi:10.1177/089124388002003004.

Kaplan, Caren, Norma Alarcon, and Minoo Moallem, eds. *Between Woman and Nation: Nationalisms, Transnational Feminisms, and the State*. Durham, NC: Duke University Press, 1999.

Kelley, Robin D. G. "Foreword." In *The Vinyl Ain't Final: Hip-Hop and the Globalisation of Black Popular Culture*, edited by Dipannita Basu and Sidney J. Lemelle, xi–xvii. London: Pluto, 2006.

———. *Yo' Mama's Disfunktional! Fighting the Culture Wars in Urban America*. Boston: Beacon, 1997.

Kelling, George L., and James Q. Wilson. "Broken Windows." *Atlantic*. 1982. www.theatlantic.com.

Kennedy, Tracy L. M. "The Personal Is Political: Feminist Blogging and Virtual Consciousness-Raising." *Scholar and Feminist Online* 5, no. 2 (2007): 1–11.

Keyes, Cheryl L. *Rap Music and Street Consciousness*. Urbana: University of Illinois Press, 2004.

Kif. Email interview with author. November 4, 2009.

———. Instant message with author. October 29, 2015.

Kitty. Interview with author. Rio de Janeiro, Brazil, August 9, 2010.

Kitwana, Bakari. *Why White Kids Love Hip Hop: Wankstas, Wiggers, Wannabes, and the New Reality of Race in America*. New York: Basic Civitas Books, 2005.

Knight, Meribah. "To Catch a Graffiti Artist." *New Yorker*. July 9, 2016. www.new yorker.com.

Kozinets, Robert. *Netnography: Doing Ethnographic Research Online*. Thousand Oaks, CA: SAGE, 2010.

Kr. Interview with author. Translated by Panmela Castro. Rio de Janeiro, Brazil, August 14, 2010.

Kwakye, Chamara Jewel, and Ruth Nicole Brown, eds. *Wish to Live: The Hip-Hop Feminism Pedagogy Reader*. New York: Peter Lang, 2012.

La Fountain-Stokes, Lawrence. "Trans/Bolero/Drag/Migration: Music, Cultural Translation, and Diasporic Puerto Rican Theatricalities." *WSQ: Women's Studies Quarterly* 36, no. 3–4 (2008): 190–209.

La Kyd. Email interview with author. May 3, 2014.

Land of Chrome. "Earsnot Interview—Graffiti Artist." Accessed May 18, 2017. www .youtube.com/watch?v=h3LoGUlig-I.

Lapovsky Kennedy, Elizabeth, and Madeline Davis. "Constructing an Ethnohistory of the Buffalo Lesbian Community: Reflexivity, Dialogue, and Politics." In *Out in the Field: Reflections of Lesbian and Gay Anthropologists*, edited by Ellen Lewin and William L. Leap, 171–199. Urbana: University of Illinois Press, 1996.

Leblanc, Lauraine. *Pretty in Punk: Girls' Gender Resistance in a Boys' Subculture*. New Brunswick, NJ: Rutgers University Press, 1999.

Leitinger, Ilse Abshagen, ed. *The Costa Rican Women's Movement: A Reader*. Pittsburgh, PA: University of Pittsburgh Press, 1997.

Lemons, Stephen. "Trouble Girl." *L.A. Weekly*. Accessed July 27, 2015. www.laweekly.com.

Lennon, John. "'Bombing' Brooklyn: Graffiti, Language and Gentrification." *Rhizomes*, no. 19 (2009). rhizomes.net.

Lewin, Ellen, and William L. Leap. *Out in the Field: Reflections of Lesbian and Gay Anthropologists*. Urbana: University of Illinois Press, 1996.

Lorde, Audre. "I Am Your Sister: Black Women Organizing across Sexualities." In *Feminist Theory Reader: Local and Global Perspectives*, edited by Carole Mccann and Seung-kyung Kim, 3rd edition, 292–295. New York: Routledge, 1988.

———. "The Master's Tools Will Never Dismantle the Master's House." In *Sister Outsider: Essays and Speeches*, Reprint. Crossing Press Feminist Series. Trumansburg, NY: Crossing Press, 2007.

———. *Zami, Sister Outsider, Undersong*. New York: Book-of-the-Month Club, 1993.

Love, H. *Miami Graffiti Art*. Atglen, PA: Schiffer, 2014.

Macdonald, Nancy. *The Graffiti Subculture: Youth, Masculinity and Identity in London and New York*. New York: Palgrave Macmillan, 2001.

———. "Something for the Boys? Exploring the Changing Gender Dynamics of the Graffiti Subculture." In *Routledge Handbook of Graffiti and Street Art*, edited by

Jeffrey Ian Ross, 183–193. Routledge International Handbooks. New York: Routledge, 2016. www.routledge.com.

Mailer, Norman, and Jon Naar. *The Faith of Graffiti*. New York: It Books, 1974.

Majors, Richard, and Janet Mancini Billson. *Cool Pose: The Dilemmas of Black Manhood in America*. Reprint edition. New York: Touchstone, 1993.

"Martin Wong: Exploration in Race and Masculinity in Graffiti Culture—Asian/Pacific/American Institute at NYU." Accessed January 12, 2017. apa.nyu.edu.

Martinez, Hugo, and Nato. *Graffiti NYC*. Munich: Prestel, 2007.

Masi308. *Corn Bread. Worlds First Graffiti Writer*. Accessed January 10, 2017. www .youtube.com/watch?v=WvDlGGSsof8.

Massumi, Brian. *Parables for the Virtual: Movement, Affect, Sensation*. Durham, NC: Duke University Press, 2002.

Mazzarella, Sharon R. *Girl Wide Web 2.0: Revisiting Girls, the Internet, and the Negotiation of Identity*. New York: Peter Lang, 2010.

McAuliffe, Cameron. "Graffiti or Street Art? Negotiating the Moral Geographies of the Creative City." *Journal of Urban Affairs* 34, no. 2 (May 1, 2012): 189–206. doi:10.1111/j.1467–9906.2012.00610.x.

McCormick, Carlo, Sean Corcoran, Lee Quinones, Sacha Jenkins, and Christopher Daze Ellis. *City as Canvas: New York City Graffiti from the Martin Wong Collection*. New York: Skira Rizzoli, 2013.

McCune, Jeffrey Q. "'Out' in the Club: The Down Low, Hip-Hop, and the Architexture of Black Masculinity." *Text and Performance Quarterly* 28, no. 3 (July 1, 2008): 298–314. doi:10.1080/10462930802107415.

McFarland, Pancho. *The Chican@ Hip Hop Nation: Politics of a New Millennial Mestizaje*. East Lansing: Michigan State University Press, 2013.

McRobbie, Angela. *The Aftermath of Feminism: Gender, Culture and Social Change*. Los Angeles: SAGE, 2009.

———. "Top Girls? Young Women and the Post-Feminist Sexual Contract." *Cultural Studies* 21, no. 4/5 (2007): 718–737. doi:10.1080/09502380701279044.

McRobbie, Angela, and Jenny Garber. "Girls and Subcultures." In *Feminism and Youth Culture*, 2nd edition, 12–23. London: Macmillan, 1976.

Meltzer, Tom. "'Binders Full of Women': Romney's Four Words That Alienated Women Voters." *Guardian*. n.d. www.theguardian.com.

Meme. Email interview with author. February 18, 2013.

Merchant, Carolyn. *The Death of Nature: Women, Ecology, and the Scientific Revolution*. New York: HarperOne, 1990.

Miky. Email interview with author. May 8, 2014.

Miller, Ivor L. *Aerosol Kingdom: Subway Painters of New York City*. Jackson: University Press of Mississippi, 2002.

Miss163. Email interview with author. November 19, 2012.

———. Interview with author. Manhattan, May 20, 2013.

Miss17. Email interview with author. April 2, 2002.

——. Email interview with author. October 26, 2009.

——. Instant message with author. April 6, 2009.

Mitchell, Tony, ed. *Global Noise: Rap and Hip Hop outside the USA*. Middletown, CT: Wesleyan University Press, 2002.

Moghadam, Valentine M. *Globalizing Women: Transnational Feminist Networks*. Baltimore, MD: Johns Hopkins University Press, 2005.

Mohanty, Chandra. *Feminism without Borders: Decolonizing Theory, Practicing Solidarity*. Durham, NC: Duke University Press, 2003.

Mons. Interview with author. Leake Street Tunnel, London, March 8, 2015.

Morgan, Joan. "Hip-Hop Feminist." In *That's the Joint! The Hip-Hop Studies Reader*, edited by Murray Forman and Mark Anthony Neal, 277–281. New York: Routledge, 2004.

——. *When Chickenheads Come Home to Roost: A Hip-Hop Feminist Breaks It Down*. New York: Simon and Schuster, 2000.

Morgan, Joan, and Mark Anthony Neal. "A Brand-New Feminism: A Conversation between Joan Morgan and Mark Anthony Neal." In *Total Chaos: The Art and Aesthetics of Hip-Hop*, edited by Jeff Chang, 233–244. New York: Basic Civitas Books, 2006.

Motel7. Interview with author. Cape Town, South Africa, January 15, 2014.

Moxxa. Email interview with author. May 9, 2014.

Mrs. "Dear Women Who Are into Graffiti." *MRS.Bigstuff*. Accessed January 14, 2017. mrsbigstuff.tumblr.com/post/118914035181/dear-women-who-are-into-graffiti.

——. Interview with author. New York, June 12, 2012.

Muñoz, José Esteban. *Cruising Utopia: The Then and There of Queer Futurity*. New York: NYU Press, 2009.

——. *Disidentifications: Queers of Color and the Performance of Politics*. Minneapolis: University of Minnesota Press, 1999.

——. "Ephemera as Evidence: Introductory Notes to Queer Acts." *Women and Performance* 8, no. 16 (1996): 5–15.

——. "Feeling Brown: Ethnicity and Affect in Ricardo Bracho's 'The Sweetest Hangover (and Other STDs).'" *Theatre Journal*, no. 1 (2000): 67–79.

Murray, James T., and Karla L. Murray. *Broken Windows: Graffiti NYC*. Corte Madera, CA: Gingko, 2002.

Mutua, Athena D. *Progressive Black Masculinities?* New York: Routledge, 2006.

Naar, Jon. *The Birth of Grafitti*. New York: Prestel, 2007.

Nalu and Gisella. Interview with author. Translated by Panmela Castro. Rio de Janeiro, Brazil, August 14, 2010.

Naska. Interview with author. Santiago, Chile, August 19, 2010.

Neal, Mark Anthony, and Murray Forman, eds. *That's the Joint! The Hip-Hop Studies Reader*. New York: Routledge, 2004.

Newton, Esther. "My Best Informants Dress: The Erotic Equation in Fieldwork." In *Feminist Anthropology: A Reader*, edited by Ellen Lewin, 170–185. Urbana: University of Illinois Press, 2006.

Nguyen, Mimi Thi. "Riot Grrrl, Race, and Revival." *Women and Performance: A Journal of Feminist Theory* 22, no. 2–3 (July 1, 2012): 173–196. doi:10.1080/07407 70X.2012.721082.

Nicholson, Linda. "Feminism in 'Waves': Useful Metaphor or Not?" *New Politics* 12, no. 4 (2010).

Nicole, Izetta. "Here We Go Again: Even a Black Powerpuff Girl Isn't Allowed to Be Great without Being Stereotyped." *Black Nerd Problems*, September 19, 2017. Accessed November 7, 2017. http://blacknerdproblems.com/here-we-go-aga in-even-a-black-powerpuff-girl-isnt-allowed-to-be-great-without-being-stereoty ped/.

NishCash. Email interview with author. October 8, 2012.

Nochlin, Linda. "Why Have There Been No Great Women Artists?" In *Women, Art, and Power*, 145–78. New York: Harper and Row, 1988.

Nora, Pierre. "Between Memory and History: Les Lieux de Mémoire." *Representations*, no. 26 (Spring 1989): 7–24.

notblu. *MUTO a Wall-Painted Animation by BLU*. Accessed May 28, 2017. www.you tube.com/watch?v=uuGaqLT-gO4.

Noz, Andrew. "The 50 Greatest Rap Commercials—#28. Kurtis Blow for Sprite." *Complex*. February 24, 2011. www.complex.com.

N30. Interview with author. Rio de Janeiro, Brazil, August 10, 2010.

Om. Interview with author. Rio de Janeiro, Brazil, August 9, 2010.

Osumare, Halifu. *The Africanist Aesthetic in Global Hip-Hop: Power Moves*. New York: Palgrave Macmillan, 2008.

Pabón, Jessica N. "Be about It: Graffiteras Performing Feminist Community." *TDR: The Journal of Performance Studies* 59, no. 219 (2013): 88–116.

———. "Daring to Be 'Mujeres Libres, Lindas, Locas': An Interview with the Ladies Destroying Crew of Nicaragua and Costa Rica." In *La Verdad: An International Dialogue on Hip Hop Latinidades*, edited by Melissa Castillo-Garsow, 203–213. Columbus: Ohio State University Press, 2016.

———. "Following Carmen Sandiego . . . er Miss17 around Athens." *BUSTOLEUM*. October 24, 2013. jessicapabon.com.

———. "Interview: Claw." In *All City Queens*, edited by Syrup and Cyris, 37–40. London: CFC Books, 2015. www.facebook.com/allcityqueens/.

———. "Interview with AbbyTC5: A Pioneering 'HomeGirl' in Hip Hop Herstory." *Women and Performance: A Journal of Feminist Theory*, All Hail the Queenz: A Queer Feminist Recalibration of Hip Hop, 24, no. 1 (2014): 8–14.

———. "No Somos 'Mariposas,' Somos 'MariPUSSY': An Interview with Graffiti Art Activist Miss163 aka Sharon Lee De La Cruz." In *Identity and Anonymity—An Art-ful Anthology*, edited by Jonathan Talbot, Leslie Fandrich, and Steven M. Specht, 112–119. N.p.: Mizzentop, 2016.

———. "Shifting Aesthetics: The Stick Up Girlz Perform Crew in a Virtual World." Edited by John Lennon and Matthew Burns. *Rhizomes*, no. 25 (2013). rhizomes.net.

————. "Ways of Being Seen: Gender and the Writing on the Wall." In *Routledge Handbook of Graffiti and Street Art*, edited by Jeffrey Ian Ross, 78–91. Routledge International Handbooks. London: Routledge, 2016.

Pabón, Jessica N., and Shanté Paradigm Smalls. "Critical Intimacies: Hip Hop as Queer Feminist Pedagogy." *Women and Performance: A Journal of Feminist Theory* 24, no. 1 (January 2, 2014): 1–7. doi:10.1080/0740770X.2014.902650.

Pabón, Jorge "PopMaster Fabel." "Physical Graffiti: The History of Hip-Hop Dance." In *Total Chaos: The Art and Aesthetics of Hip-Hop*, edited by Jeff Chang, 18–26. New York: Basic Civitas Books, 2006.

Pabón-Colón, Jessica N. "Writin', Breakin', Beatboxin': Strategically Performing 'Women' in Hip Hop." *Signs: Journal of Women in Culture and Society* 43, no. 1 (2017): 175–200.

Pardue, Derek. *Brazilian Hip Hoppers Speak from the Margins: We's on Tape.* New York: Palgrave Macmillan, 2011.

Peoples, Whitney A. "'Under Construction': Identifying Foundations of Hip-Hop Feminism and Exploring Bridges between Black Second-Wave and Hip-Hop Feminisms." *Meridians: Feminism, Race, Transnationalism* 8, no. 1 (2008): 19–52.

Perkins, William. *Droppin' Science: Critical Essays on Rap Music and Hip Hop Culture.* Philadelphia: Temple University Press, 1996.

Perry, Imani. *Prophets of the Hood: Politics and Poetics in Hip Hop.* Durham, NC: Duke University Press, 2004.

Phelan, Peggy. *Unmarked: The Politics of Performance.* New York: Routledge, 1993.

Phillips, Susan A. *Wallbangin': Graffiti and Gangs in L.A.* Chicago: University of Chicago Press, 1999.

Pile, Steve, and Michael Keith. *Place and the Politics of Identity.* New York: Routledge, 1993.

Pinto, Samantha. *Difficult Diasporas: The Transnational Feminist Aesthetic of the Black Atlantic.* New York: NYU Press, 2013.

Pough, Gwendolyn D. *Check It While I Wreck It: Black Womanhood, Hip-Hop Culture, and the Public Sphere.* Boston: Northeastern University Press, 2004.

Pough, Gwendolyn D., Elaine Richardson, Rachel Raimist, and Aisha Durham. *Home Girls Make Some Noise! Hip-Hop Feminism Anthology.* Mira Loma, CA: Parker, 2007.

Powers, Stephen. *The Art of Getting Over.* New York: St. Martin's, 1999.

Prima Donna. Interview with author. Rio de Janeiro, August 16, 2010.

Puar, Jasbir. *Terrorist Assemblages: Homonationalism in Queer Times.* Durham, NC: Duke University Press, 2007.

Puar, Jasbir, Lauren Berlant, Judith Butler, Bojana Cvejic, Isabell Lorey, and Ana Vujanovic. "Precarity Talk: A Virtual Roundtable with Lauren Berlant, Judith Butler, Bojana Cvejić, Isabell Lorey, Jasbir Puar, and Ana Vujanović." *TDR: The Drama Review* 56, no. 4 (2012): 163–177.

Queen Andrea. Interview with author. Queens, New York, June 15, 2012.

Rahn, Janice. *Painting without Permission: Hip-Hop Graffiti Subculture.* Westport, CT: Bergin and Garvey, 2002.

Reilly, Maura, and Linda Nochlin, eds. *Global Feminisms: New Directions in Contemporary Art*. New York: Merrell, Brooklyn Museum, 2007.

Reinharz, Shulamit. *Feminist Methods in Social Research*. 1st edition. New York: Oxford University Press, 1992.

RenOne. Email interview with author. February 10, 2013.

——. Email interview with author. February 11, 2013.

——. Email interview with author. February 15, 2013.

——. Instant message with author. May 15, 2017.

Rentschler, Carrie A., and Samantha C. Thrift. "Doing Feminism: Event, Archive, Techné." *Feminist Theory* 16, no. 3 (2015): 239–249. doi:10.1177/1464700115604138.

——. "Doing Feminism in the Network: Networked Laughter and the 'Binders Full of Women' Meme." *Feminist Theory* 16, no. 3 (2015): 329–359. doi:10.1177/1464700115604136.

Rich, Adrienne. *Of Woman Born: Motherhood as Experience and Institution*. New York: W. W. Norton, 1995.

Ridout, Nicholas, and Rebecca Schneider. "Precarity and Performance: An Introduction." *TDR: The Drama Review* 56, no. 4 (November 19, 2012): 5–9. doi:10.1162/DRAM_a_00210.

Rivera, Raquel Z. *New York Ricans from the Hip Hop Zone*. New York: Palgrave Macmillan, 2003.

Rivera, Raquel Z., Wayne Marshall, and Deborah Pacini Hernandez, eds. *Reggaeton*. Durham, NC: Duke University Press, 2009.

Rivera-Rideau, Petra R. *Remixing Reggaetón: The Cultural Politics of Race in Puerto Rico*. Durham, NC: Duke University Press, 2015.

Rodríguez, Juana Maria. *Queer Latinidad: Identity Practices, Discursive Spaces*. New York: NYU Press, 2003.

Rose, Tricia. *Black Noise: Rap Music and Black Culture in Contemporary America*. Middletown, CT: Wesleyan University Press, 1994.

——. *The Hip Hop Wars: What We Talk about When We Talk about Hip Hop—and Why It Matters*. New York: Basic Civitas Books, 2008.

Rowley, Michelle V. "The Idea of Ancestry: Of Feminist Genealogies and Many Other Things." In *Feminist Theory Reader: Local and Global Perspectives*, edited by Carole R. McCann and Seung-kyung Kim, 80–85. New York: Routledge, 2017.

Russ, Joanna. *How to Suppress Women's Writing*. Austin: University of Texas Press, 1989.

Samer, Roxanne. "Revising 'Re-Vision': Documenting 1970s Feminisms and the Queer Potentiality of Digital Feminist Archives." *Ada: A Journal of Gender, New Media, and Technology*, no. 5 (July 7, 2014). adanewmedia.org.

Sandoval, Chela. "U.S. Third World Feminism: The Theory and Method of Oppositional Consciousness in the Postmodern World." *Genders: Journal of Social Theory, Representation, Race, Gender, Sex*, Theorizing Nation, Sex, and Race (1991): 1–24.

Sany. *Girl Power Movie*, 2016. www.girlpowermovie.com.

——. Instant message with author. October 29, 2015.

——. Interview with author. Manhattan, November 2, 2012.

Saporta Sternbach, Nancy, Marysa Navarro-Aranguren, Patricia Chuchryk, and Sonia E. Alvarez. "Feminisms in Latin America: From Bogotá to San Bernardo." *Signs* 17, no. 2 (1992): 393–434.

Sax. Email interview with author. February 14, 2012.

Schloss, Joseph G. *Foundation: B-Boys, B-Girls and Hip-Hop Culture in New York.* Oxford: Oxford University Press, 2009.

——. *Making Beats: The Art of Sample-Based Hip-Hop.* Middletown, CT: Wesleyan University Press, 2014.

Schneider, Rebecca. "Archives: Performance Remains." *Performance Research* 6, no. 1 (2001): 100–108.

Scott, Joan Wallach. "The Evidence of Experience." *Critical Inquiry* 17, no. 4 (Summer 1991): 773–797.

——. "Feminist Reverberations." *Differences* 13, no. 3 (2002): 1–23. doi:10.1215/10407391-13-3-1.

Shape. Interview with author. Galindo Restaurant, Santiago, Chile, August 19, 2010.

Sharma, Nitasha Tamar. *Hip Hop Desis: South Asian Americans, Blackness, and a Global Race Consciousness.* Durham, NC: Duke University Press, 2010.

Sharpley-Whiting, T. Denean. *Pimps Up, Ho's Down: Hip Hop's Hold on Young Black Women.* New York: NYU Press, 2008.

Sherman, Maria. "A Brief History of Rappers in Soda Commercials." *BuzzFeed.* Accessed December 2, 2015. www.buzzfeed.com.

Shiro. Email interview with author. October 25, 2009.

Si. Interview with author. Translated by Panmela Castro. Rio de Janeiro, Brazil, August 14, 2010.

Sinae. Email interview with author. February 1, 2012.

——. Instant message with author. June 1, 2016.

Smalls, Shanté Paradigm. "'The Rain Comes Down': Jean Grae and Hip Hop Heteronormativity." *American Behavioral Scientist* 55, no. 1 (January 1, 2011): 86–95. doi:10.1177/0002764210381730.

Snorton, C. Riley. "As Queer as Hip Hop." *Palimpsest: A Journal on Women, Gender, and the Black International* 2, no. 2 (2013): vi–x.

Snyder, Gregory J. *Graffiti Lives: Beyond the Tag in New York's Urban Underground.* New York: NYU Press, 2011.

Spady, James G. "Grandmaster Caz and the HipHopography of the Bronx." In *Nation Conscious Rap: The Hip Hop Vision.* New York: PC International Press, 1991.

Spivak, Gayatri Chakravorty. *Outside in the Teaching Machine.* New York: Routledge, 1993.

Stavsky, Lois. "Her Story, the First Annual Female Graffiti Series, Launches Uptown with Lady K Fever, Meli, Rocky 184, Charmin 65, Miss Boombox, Gem13 and Neks." *Street Art NYC.* May 16, 2016. streetartnyc.org.

"STICK UP GIRLZ." Accessed November 25, 2009. www.stickupgirlz.com.

Stryker, Susan, Paisley Currah, and Lisa Jean Moore. "Introduction: Trans-, Trans, or Transgender?" *WSQ: Women's Studies Quarterly* 36, no. 3–4 (2008): 12–22.

Swenson, Eric Minh. *Jerk: Female Graffiti Legend.* 2013. www.youtube.com/watch?v=5w WEGGrPARA&feature=youtube_gdata_player.

Syrup, and Cyris, eds. *All City Queens.* London: CFC Books, 2015.

Taft, Jessica K. *Rebel Girls: Youth Activism and Social Change across the Americas.* New York: NYU Press, 2011.

"'Taki 183' Spawns Pen Pals." *New York Times.* July 21, 1971.

Taylor, Diana. *The Archive and the Repertoire: Performing Cultural Memory in the Americas.* Durham, NC: Duke University Press, 2003.

TEDx Talks. *Feminism on the Wall: Jessica Pabón at TEDxWomen 2012.* 2012. www .youtube.com/watch?v=z_4JOexUjoM&feature=youtube_gdata_player.

Teeling, Jane. *Kiss It Goodbye: Lady Pink Paints New York City.* 2012. vimeo. com/52989678.

Thompson, Becky. "Multiracial Feminism: Recasting the Chronology of Second Wave Feminism." *Feminist Studies* 28, no. 2 (2002): 337–360. doi:10.2307/3178747.

Thompson, Margo. *American Graffiti.* Singapore: Parkstone International, 2009.

Thompson, Robert Farris, ed. "Hip Hop 101." In *Droppin' Science: Critical Essays on Rap Music and Hip Hop Culture,* 211–218. Philadelphia: Temple University Press, 1987.

Throne. Interview with author. Leake Street Tunnel, London, March 8, 2015.

Tiongson Jr., Antonio T. *Filipinos Represent: DJs, Racial Authenticity, and the Hip-Hop Nation.* Minneapolis: University of Minnesota Press, 2013.

Valentine, Gill. "Globalizing Intimacy: The Role of Information and Communication Technologies in Maintaining and Creating Relationships." *Women's Studies Quarterly* 34, no. 1/2 (Spring–Summer 2006): 365–393.

Vargas, Deborah R. "Ruminations on Lo Sucio as a Latino Queer Analytic." *American Quarterly* 66, no. 3 (September 2014): 715–726.

Versus Hip Hop on Trial Debate. 2012. www.youtube.com/watch?v=r3–7YoxG89Q& feature=youtube_gdata_player.

Viego, Antonio. *Dead Subjects: Toward a Politics of Loss in Latino Studies.* Durham, NC: Duke University Press, 2007.

Vincent, Rickey. *Funk: The Music, the People, and the Rhythm of the One.* New York: St. Martin's, 1996.

Wacławek, Anna. *Graffiti and Street Art.* New York: Thames and Hudson, 2011.

Wajcman, Judy. *TechnoFeminism.* Malden, MA: Polity Press, 2004.

Walker, Ameena. "First Look inside the 5 Pointz-Replacing Rentals in Long Island City." *Curbed NY.* May 25, 2017. ny.curbed.com.

Walsh, Michael. *Graffito.* Berkeley, CA: North Atlantic, 1996.

Warner, Michael. "Publics and Counterpublics." *Public Culture* 14, no. 1 (2002): 49–90.

West, Tim'm, and Juba Kalamka. "'It's All One:' A Conversation between Juba Kalamka and Tim'm West." In *Total Chaos: The Art and Aesthetics of Hip-Hop,* edited by Jeff Chang, 198–208. New York: Basic Civitas Books, 2007.

whatyouwrite. "Interview with Mrs." *what you write.com.* April 26, 2009. whatyou write.wordpress.com.

Youngs, Gillian. "Making the Virtual Real: Feminist Challenges in the Twenty-First Century." *Scholar and Feminist Online* 5, no. 2 (2007): 1–14.

Z. Interview with Z. Interview by GraffGirlz.com. 2009. www.graffgirlz.com.

Zeisler, Andi. *We Were Feminists Once: From Riot Grrrl to CoverGirl®, the Buying and Selling of a Political Movement.* New York: PublicAffairs, 2016.

Ziff, Bruce H., and P. V. Rao, *Borrowed Power: Essays on Cultural Appropriation.* New Brunswick, NJ: Rutgers University Press, 1997.

INDEX

AbbyTC5 (Abby), 1–2, 115, 191, 211

Acb, 101, 230n23, 233

aesthetics: acts of negation, 138, 142; Afro-Caribbean diasporic, 13, 32; Black Atlantic feminist, 33; DIY, 118; ephemeral, 143; feminist, 33; Hip Hop, 19, 33–34, 52, 70, 118; masculinist, 223n5; performance, 32, 38; proliferation, 138, 143; regional differences, 91

affect, 34–36, 87: affective digital network, 113, 123; affective environment space, 170–172; affective investment of crews, 112; affective mapping, 103, 105; affective solidarity, 108, 119, 123, 128, 130, 183; collective, 183; feminist, 97, 104; how painting feels, 101; pleasure, 97; racialized, 228n51. *See also* Flatley, Jonathan

Afro-Caribbean diaspora: aesthetics, 1, 7, 31–32; visual call and response, 2, 53

"@GraffitiHerstory" Instagram project, 157

Ahmed, Sara, *Promise of Happiness*, 172

Aila, 83, 191

Ale, 86

all city, 8, 52

all-grrl crews, 38, 75: Altona Female Crew, ix, 114; Crazis Crew, ix, 88–98; Few and Far, ix, 55, 76, 104, 225n24, 230n27; Girls on Top, ix, 167, 209; Helen Keller Crew, ix, 163; lack of in the U.S., 75; Ladies Destroying Crew, ix, 104; Ladies of the Arts (L.O.T.A.), ix, 5; Maripussy, ix, 230n27; new politics of relation, 76; PMS, ix, xii, 55; Rede Nami, ix, 77–88,

102–107; Stick Up Girlz, ix, 110–113; Tits 'n' Tampons, ix, x; Transgressão Para Mulheres, ix, 79, 137–156; Turronas Crew, ix, 76

all-grrl paint jams, 158, 159–183, 185

Alma, 73, 191

Ana, 192

Anarkia Boladona, 55, 77–78, 156, 202

Annatomix, 173

anticapitalist, 48

Antisa, 98–100, 192

apprenticeship, 177–178; finding mentors, 128, 177

archive, 7, 119, 148–158: digital self-archiving, 112, 139; patrilineal white-cultural logic, 146

Are2, 48–51, 192

ArtCrimes.org (Graffiti.org), xi, 20, 25, 124

"art of getting ovaries," 36–37

Australia, 59, 61, 70, 120, 162–169

authenticity, 15, 43, 91, 134. *See also* "real writer"

backlash, 165, 173, 229

"balls," 43–45, 51, 69–72

Banksy Leake Street Tunnel, 167, 170, 236n10

Barbara 62, 9, 192; forefather of graffiti, 46

be about it, 75, 76

beef (hostility between writers), 13–15, 56, 127, 191

belonging, 15, 43, 161

b-girl, 92, 141, 225n21. *See also* breakdancing

Bisy, 90, 92, 192

blackbook: archive, 202; blogs, 116, 232n23; definition, 201; space for digital ups, 26; style exchange, 112

bomber, 44, 52, 54

bombing science, 3

Boston, Massachusetts, 11–15

boys: "boys will be boys," 4, 65; boys club, 6, 45; "boys will be toys," 165

Brazil, 75, 142, 144: Rio de Janeiro, 78, 82–83

breakdancing, 92, 235n2

broken windows theory (policing urban space), 7, 138, 234n4

Butler, Judith, *Bodies that Matter*, 226

Canada: Montreal, 129; Toronto, 56–59

Castleman, Craig, *Getting Up*, 9, 19

Catfight: Female Graff Update, ix, 113–119

Chalfant, Henry: "Graffiti Rock" show, 216n43; *Spraycan Art* (with Prigoff), 214n12; *Style Wars* (with Silver), 214n11; *Subway Art* (with Cooper), 9; *Training Days* (with Jenkins), 214n18

characters, 3, 213n7: associated with street art, 170, 175, 178; Frankensteinian, 84; ghosts, 82; goddess, 83, 140; indigenous, 140; Mapuche, 96; Mimi, 34–36; muñecas, 94; pre-Columbian, 101; Queen of Spades, 57–58; returning the gaze, 78

Charmin 65, 9, 157; forefather of graffiti, 46

Chicana, 63–66, 228n50

Chicks on Powertrips (magazine), ix, 119–125

Chile, 139, 230n15; Santiago, 73–102

Chock, 167–168

chosen family, 101, 113; sisters, 112, 118

circulation, 115, 132–133, 147, 188; feminist sensibilities, 130–131

cisgender, 10, 41, 161: cismale masculinity and Hip Hop, 27, 43, 223n3, 224n7; grrlz' gender nonconformity, 164

claiming: (taking) place, 88, 143; (taking) space, 91, 165, 181

ClawMoney, 28–29, 41, 43–45, 192, 211, 219n73; being about it, 75; Claw&Co, 44; PMS, 55

collective performance, 170

Colombia, 137

community: building, 36; digital, 25, 47; feminist, 73–107, 87, 181; graffiti as aesthetic community, 31, 70, 80, 102, 105, 145, 178; hetero/sexism in graffiti community, xii, 102, 117, 134, 141, 142, 148, 158; producing e-zines in, 114, 116; sense of community, 25, 127, 179, 181; subcultural, 26, 28, 98, 111–112, 117, 134, 142; transnational, 20, 25, 28, 36, 125. *See also* feminism: performance of

consciousness raising, 116–117, 187; blogs as sites for, 116, 232n23

Cooper, Martha: Hip Hop as a package, 216n47; *Subway Art* (with Chalfant), 9

Costa Rica, 104, 229n4

crazy girls, 81, 84; sick bitches, 121

creative city, 169, 182

crews, 1, 111; distinct from gangs, 221n75; Ex-Vandals, 111; formation and purpose, 90. *See also* all-grrl crews

cultural appropriation, 30–32

Czech Republic, 26

DanaPink, 94–96, 192; partner in crime with Naska, 89

diaspora, 27; digital, 129, 155; as discourse and ideology, 33–36

digital: disappearance, 138–156; ethnography, 22–23; network, 113, 125, 130, 136, 158; revolution; 24, 109, 113, 132; ups, 24, 25, 125, 135, 142, 144, 152

"digital ups," defined, 25

Dona, 36, 41, 192, 211

Egr (Canada), 56–59, 192

Eney, 96–97, 192

ephemeral, 138–139, 142: aesthetic, 147, 155; erasure, 16; strategy, 162, 180, 183; queered, 150; vanishment, 146

Erotica67, 185, 192, 210

ethnography: "hiphopography," 215n38; queer feminist, 216n38. *See also* digital: ethnography

Eva 62, 9, 192; forefather of graffiti, 46

Evay, 172–179, 192, 210

Faith47, 67–68

"FEMALE CAPS," ix, 129–132

Female International Graffiti Facebook page, ix, 119, 125–129

femininity, 43, 54, 68: as a demand put on female bodies, 62; strategic performance, 89, 161; and street art, 71; symbolizing femininity, 12, 35–37, 84; in tandem with feminist masculinity, 47, 60, 67, 164, 186. *See also* performance: of femininity

feminism: identifying with versus identifying as, 123; as a noun becomes a static knowable entity), 97; performance of, 38; rejecting identification of, 75–76; undoing, 180; as a verb (doing), 38, 98, 127

feminist killjoy, 18, 141–142

feminist masculinity: defined, 46–47; performed en masse, 161

feminist movement, 38, 72; burnout, 136; as a tool, 75; failure of feminist movement, 48, 103–106; limitations of wave metaphor, 227n40;

feminist sensibility, 39, 113, 123, 166; intentions, 127

femme fatales, 159, 180

Femme Fierce, 167–179

Ferrell, Jeff, *Crimes of Style*, 70, 102

5 Pointz, 236n17

Flatley, Jonathan, *Affective Mapping*, 103

Fluro, 108, 110, 221n76

forefathers of graffiti, 46

Foxy Lady, 24, 113

four elements of Hip Hop, 18, 27

Free, 192

friendship, 89, 93, 112; feminism rooted in friendship, 102

gaze: returning and initiating, 78, 94; white bourgeois gaze, 228n50

gender: construction and cost of conventions, 45, 59, 161, 165, 187; difference, 5–6, 8–9, 36, 39, 50, 59, 80, 96, 124, 160, 165, 181, 219n68; politics, 6, 45

getting over, 8, 144

getting up, 2, 7, 47, 76. *See also* "digital ups," defined

Gigi, 100–101, 193, 233n38

girl: lessons, 41–42; questions, 67; global girl, 51, 222n95; phallic girl, 51

girl power, 47: postfeminist, 60; "Powerpuff girl power," 60, 62

Girl Power, 26, 218n62

globalization, 51; of Hip Hop, 219n67, 221n80

GraffGirlz.com, 24–27, 109, 110; origins, ix, 218n60

GraffiterasBR, ix, 142

graffiti art writing, 1: aerosol art, 1; art activism, 79; compared to street art, 2, 70–71, 91, 99; legal versus illegal, 130; married to Hip Hop, 216n43; ontology, 145–148; spray-can art, 1; studies, 9

graffiti writer, xii, 213n4; archetype, 26, 188, 220n75; female writer, 5; graffitera, 3, 141; graffiti artist, 1; graffiti grrlz, 3, 5; vandals, 130 Greece, 53

guerrera, 74

Halberstam, Jack: *Female Masculinity*, 164; *In a Queer Time and Place*, 217n53

hazards for female writers, 122–124

Helen Keller Crew, 163

herstory, 3, 39, 136

hetero/sexism (defined), 10

heteronormativity, 21, 28, 62, 186, 224n11

heteropatriarchy, 16, 51

heterosexuality, 10; and cisgender male masculinity, 224n7, 226n35

High School of Art and Design, 3

Hip Hop: culture, 5; diaspora, 16; feminism, 47; generation, 47; graffiti subculture, 1, 7; male-dominated xii; Hip Hop head, 6; nation, 28; spelling, 213n1

Hip Hop body, 22, 58, 224n11; archetype, 27, 32

Hip Hop graffiti, 1–2: blocks, 54; bubble letters, 2; burners, 124; chromie, 164; dead letter, 11; family, 52; fill in, 2; handstyle, 11, 215n31; New York public, 28, 60, 162; piece, 2; production (graffiti mural), 2; "shout-out," 111; tag name, xi, 2; tag, 1; throw-up (throwies), 2, 3; vertical, 52; wildstyle, 1, 213n5

Hip Hop studies, 17–20

hiphopography, 215n38

history of difference, 17

Hops, 193, 208

identity, 2, 32; construction, 121; feminist, 104–107; identity-based communities, 104; tag name as secret identity, 67

Injah, 80–81, 193

International Women's Day, 167, 175, 236n10

Internet Archive Wayback Machine, 25, 109, 125

Itsa, 167, 172, 175–176, 179, 193, 208

Ivey, 59–63, 193

Jeffries, Michael, *Thug Life*, 57–59. *See also* masculinity: complex coolness

Jerk LA, 63–66, 193, 228n50

JesOne, 159, 207

Joske, 162, 193

Jups, 82

Kif, 125–127, 193

king, 19, 115, 201; defined, 52

Kitty, 81

LadieKillerz, 162–166

Lady Heart, 5

Lady Pink, 211; on ephemerality, 147; on femininity, 41; "first lady" of graffiti, 5; tokenization, 5–6

LadysGraff.blogspot.com, ix, 127

La Kyd, 193

Latina, 65–66, 228n50, 228n51

liberal feminist, 50, 105

live painting, 178

Los Angeles, California, 63; LAGraffiti-Girls blogumentary, 130

Macdonald, Nancy, *Graffiti Subculture*, 24, 42, 70–71

Mailer, Norman, *The Faith of Graffiti*, 7

male privilege, 173

masculinity, 11; complex coolness, 57; female masculinity, 47; hard, 72; Hip Hop masculinity, 45–71; hypermasculinity, 173; toxic masculinity, 46, 165. *See also* feminist masculinity

mashup methodology, 17

McRobbie, Angela, *Aftermath of Feminism*, 50, 180

Meme, 193, 201

memory, 144–156

mentorship, 89. *See also* apprenticeship

Merlot, 207

Mickey, 193, 218n60

militarism, 59; militant, 69, 70

Miller, Ivor, *Aerosol Kingdom*, 19, 220n75

Miss163, 185, 194, 206

Miss17 (17), xi–xii, 22, 52–56, 189, 193, 211; on masculinity, 41–42

Mons, 171, 172, 178, 194

Motel7, 66–69, 194, 205

motherhood, 73, 83, 94; childcare, 93; maternity leave, 162; parenting, 93; pregnancy, 93

Mrs, 36–37, 54, 131, 194

Mugre, 137, 194

Murray and Murray, *Broken Windows*, 115

"My Thuggy Pony" jam, 185

Nalu, 85

Naska, 89–92, 194, 205

nation building, 152

neoliberal, 47, 170, 222n95, 225n16

"new guard," 119–125

New York City: as birthplace of Hip Hop culture, 1; graffiti scene's "founding fathers," 5

NishCash, 194

N30, 81–82

Nungi, 16, 22, 194

Om, 147–148, 194

oral history, 151, 156–158

orgasm, 97

"Others," 50; otherness, 45

Pardue, Derek, *Brazilian Hip Hoppers*, 78, 144

patriarchal bargain, 51

Pau, 101, 194

performance, 32; of belonging, 111; of collective, 170; of community, 38, 75, 111; consequences of, for trans and cis women, 166; of excess, 64–66; of femininity, 47; of feminism, 25, 33, 38; of gender, 21, 159–183; of masculinity, 38; of place, 111; of presence, 145

Phelan, Peggy, *Unmarked: The Politics of Performance*, 145

pixação (form of writing), 78, 137

Pixie, 182, 195

politics: of difference, 7; of gender, 45; of identification, 75; of race and ethnicity, 28; of respectability, 5; of sexuality, 15

Poo-Ni 167, 46. *See also* forefathers of graffiti

postfeminism, 47, 165, 182–183; defined, 229n57

Powers, Stephen, *The Art of Getting Over*, 9

precarity, 39, 159–183

Prima Donna, 79, 140–142, 204

public performance, 161

Queen Andrea, 195, 204

Queen MCTash (TashRock), 70, 196, 217n52

queen (queenz), 52

queer: acts, 152; archive, 150; ephemera, 149–150; graffiti subculture as queer, 22; as insult, 15; time and space, 217n53; writers, 21–22

racking, 224n12

"real writer," 10; realness, 215n28. *See also* authenticity

rebellion, 46, 183

remains, 146–149

RenOne, 10–15, 195, 215n30

representation, 34, 116; effects of digital, 134–135; of stereotypical writer, 220n75

resistance, 21, 164; symbol, 137, 147

Riot Grrrl, 3, 30, 60, 227n40, 236n12

rumor mill, 10, 15, 90, 128

safe spaces, 127, 178

Santiago, Chile, 88

Sany, 26, 195

Sax, 100, 195

Scotland (Edinburgh), 175

sex/gender binary, 43, 45; distinguishing graffiti and street art, 71

sexism, 10, 45–46, 227n35; masculinity as scapegoat, 58

sexuality, 81; bisexual, 21; lesbian, 21; queer, 21; sexualization, 16; slut-shaming, 50
Shape, 92–94, 195, 203
Shiro, 34, 195, 203
Si Caramujo, 83, 196
Sinae, 196
sisterhood, 127, 191; bell hooks, 180
skateboarding, 162, 167
social justice, 38, 47, 79
social media, 3: networking, 129; positive implications, 134; for self-archiving, 112
solidarity, 38, 109; affective solidarity, 108, 119, 123, 128, 130, 183. *See also* affect
Solitas, 73–75, 196
something out of nothing, 62
South Africa, 66–69
standpoint epistemology, 39, 187–188
Stick Up Girlz, 110–113
strategic essentialism, 161, 181
subcultural economy, 161: capital, 14, 170; value, 39, 149, 153
subculture, 213n4: lack of girls, 8; youth-led, 3
Summer BBQ Jam, 55

take back the night, 54; reclaim the night, 162
techné, 132–136
TEDxWomen, 10
Throne79, 174
Tits n' Tampons, 237n27
token, 5, 168; tokenization, 5

tomboy, 43, 44, 121
ToughLove NYC, 159
toy, 76, 85; defined, 229n3
transephemera, 139–156; transephem-erality, 39; transephemeral objects, 152; transephemeral performative, 144; Transgressão Para Mulheres, 137–156
transnational: feminist movement, 72, 75, 222n95; network, 26, 186; subculture, 7, 19, 160
Tucson, Arizona, 41–42, 190
Tuff City, 54

United Kingdom, 168
United States, 28, 48, 189; legal painting, 236n17
Universal Zulu Nation, 36
Utah, 189

visual gender violence, 173

wall ownership, 165–166
We B*Girlz Festival, 25, 34, 36
white: white Hip Hop heads, 31, 220n75; white womanhood, 61
whitewashing, 30, 65. *See also* cultural appropriation
Women on Walls, 127
writer's bench, 232n37; digital, 125
Wynwood District, 236n17

Yo Geisha, 125

ABOUT THE AUTHOR

Jessica Nydia Pabón-Colón is Assistant Professor of Women's, Gender, and Sexuality Studies at the State University of New York at New Paltz. She is an interdisciplinary Latina feminist performance studies scholar from Boston, MA.